Women Opera Composers

Women Opera Composers

Biographies from the 1500s to the 21st Century

Mary F. McVicker

McFarland & Company, Inc., Publishers

Jefferson, North Carolina

LIBRARY OF CONGRESS CATALOGUING-IN-PUBLICATION DATA

Names: McVicker, Mary Frech, author.
Title: Women opera composers : biographies from the 1500s to the 21st
century / Mary F. McVicker.
Description: Jefferson, North Carolina : McFarland & Company, Inc.,
Publishers, 2016. | Includes bibliographical references and index.
Identifiers: LCCN 2016014917 | ISBN 9780786495139 (softcover : acid free
paper) ∞
Subjects: LCSH: Women composers. | Opera. | Women librettists.
Classification: LCC ML82 .M4 2016 | DDC 782.1092/52 [B]—dc23
LC record available at https://lccn.loc.gov/2016014917

BRITISH LIBRARY CATALOGUING DATA ARE AVAILABLE

ISBN (print) 978-0-7864-9513-9
ISBN (ebook) 978-1-4766-2361-0

Cover image of Masquerade Mask at the Opera © 2016 wragg/iStock

Printed in the United States of America

McFarland & Company, Inc., Publishers
Box 611, Jefferson, North Carolina 28640
www.mcfarlandpub.com

To the unrecognized, the under-recognized,
the lost, and the forgotten composers
and to Don

Acknowledgments

Writing might be an isolated occupation, but I suspect few books are written without the help and support of others. In my case these are most notably my family and friends, in particular my husband, Don. The Newberry Library in Chicago was an essential resource. I appreciate very much the patience of the various librarians there who answered my questions and sought out material. Thank you all.

Table of Contents

Introduction

When I was working on *Women Composers of Classical Music* I became increasingly aware of how many women had composed operas and had them performed, and I had the idea of compiling a similar book on women opera composers—if there were enough of them.

After *Women Composers* was published and I got over my "I'll never write another book" phase, I began to consider the idea seriously. Eventually, the process that led to this book was in place. As I worked on the book I was intrigued by how many of the women composers' operas were produced, some quite successfully. The women were recognized for their works, and their works were sought after. Of course, for many women composers this wasn't true; but the women persevered, they composed, and often their operas were produced.

The emphasis in the book is on historical composers and librettists, with some material relating to the last part of the 20th century to the present. The discography of operas by women composers is meager, hence there is no "Discography" as there was in *Women Composers of Classical Music*. May that eventually change!

A word on nationalities: As borders and nationalities changed, questions arose about the best designation of nationality. I used the nationalities as given in my principle sources. This makes for some seeming inconsistencies, particularly with respect to the USSR—the Soviet Union—and various other areas.

Books about opera often have to confront or sidestep questions—"Is this an opera? A musical? A play with music?"—and so on. Authors just have to give it their best judgment call. And while there are more than five hundred composers in this book, there are inevitably omissions.

Of course, gender issues underlie *Women Opera Composers*, but they aren't the focus of the book. This book is about creating, persevering, often achieving, and sometimes not succeeding; it's about people having the initiative to participate in the rich world of opera. It's a story about the importance of what happened—the operas and the composers—and not about what didn't happen.

1

1590–1636

Opera began in Renaissance Italy in the late sixteenth century. During the Middle Ages pageants, masques, and religious dramas had been popular throughout Europe. In retrospect opera seems the logical next step. *Dafne*, performed in the mid–1590s, is widely considered to be the first opera. The music was by Jacopo Peri. In 1600 *Euridice*, with music by Giulio Caccini, was published, and this convenient date is often cited as the beginning of opera. Caccini's daughter Francesca is considered to be the first woman to compose opera, and she was the first composer whose opera was performed outside of Italy.

Italy

Most of what little we know of **Maddalena Casulana** (c1544–fl. 1566–1583) are the dates of publications and performances of her music—and those dates often vary. We know she spent time in Florence, where she received at least part of her education and gave her earliest performances.

She published a book of four madrigals in 1566, which is considered to be the first book of European music by a woman to be printed. By that time she already was well known as a composer. In 1588 she published a second book of madrigals, which she dedicated to Isabella de Medici Orsini, "not only to give witness to my devotion to Your Excellency, but also to show to the world (to the degree that it is granted to me in this profession of music) the foolish error of men, who so greatly believe themselves to be the masters of high intellectual gifts that [these gifts] cannot, it seems to them, be equally common among women" (Sadie and Samuel 110). Maddalena also was a poet and often used her poetry for her texts. Her last known book was published in 1583, although it's likely she wrote more poetry. In addition, she was a talented singer and played the lute. *Women of Notes* states, "An opera by her was presented at the wedding of Duke William of Bavaria" (77).

Music and opera were the family business for many composers, particularly in Renaissance Italy, and the Caccini family was the most notable of these families. **Francesca Caccini** (September 18, 1587, Florence–after June 1638) was the daughter, sister, wife and mother of singers. Her father, Giulio Caccini, was of the generation who created the "new music" that marked the beginning of the Baroque era. This period was one of those all-too-few "golden times" for women in the arts, a time when the sun shone for them. As with many such women of that time, Francesca was very well educated, particularly—but not solely—in music. This was also the time when Jacopo Peri composed what is considered by most to be the first opera.

In 1604 the Caccini family travelled to France to sing for that country's king and queen. While she was there Francesca had her first independent job offer. Marie de Medici offered her a position as a salaried court singer in exchange for a dowry of 1000 Scudi. However, Francesca elected to return to Italy with her family. In 1607 she composed her first music for the stage which was described as having "una musica stupenda." That same year she married the court singer Giovanni Battista Signorini.

Francesca had an active career composing, singing, and teaching. She had a post at the Florentine court, and by the 1620s she was the highest-paid musician at the court. Her husband died in 1626. The following year Francesca married Tomaso Raffaelli, an aristocrat and patron. At the same time, she left the Medici payroll. In 1628 she had a son. Her husband died in 1630, leaving Francesca as a wealthy landowner. Quarantined for almost three years in Lucca during the plague, once released she returned to the Medici payroll, remaining there until at least late in 1637.

Works

1614 *Il ballo delle Zingare*, opera, Librettist: Ferdinando Saracinelli
1622 *Il martirio di Sant'Agata*, sacred drama with G. Gagliano
1625 *La liberazione di Ruggiero dall'isola d'Alcina*, opera, libretto from Ariosto's
    Orlando Furioso by Saracinelli, Florence

(Sources: Glickman and Schleifer; Cohen; Laurence)

1637–1700

Opera caught on quickly, particularly in France and in Germany. The early performances were in private residences. Then, in 1637, the first opera house opened, marking the "transfer of the patronage of opera from the nobles to the people" (Sadie and Samuel 693). The "transfer" was gradual and slow, as royal courts and nobility continued to be the venues for operas in most areas for a long time. Demand for new operas was incessant, and having the "latest" in opera quickly became the new status symbol in royal courts.

French opera evolved from the troubadours and trouvères, the old religious plays, and the song plays and dances at fairs. The increasing attention paid to opera in Italy enhanced the allure of opera in France, ever competitive with Italy and things Italian.

Enter Jean-Baptiste Lully (1632–1687), who was brought to France by the Duke de Guise. Lully entered the household of Mademoiselle Montpensier, the cousin of King Louis XIV, and Lully eventually became her orchestra leader and established himself as one of the best violinists in France. When King Louis was fourteen he decided that Lully should be part of *his* court instead of his cousin's—and so Lully's brilliant career was launched.

Louis XIV, with his insatiable appetite for entertainment, provided the perfect opportunity and Versailles the perfect setting for new forms of opera and dance. Lully and opera also fit beautifully with King Louis' strategy for keeping the nobles in line: isolate them in stupendous luxury at Versailles where the path to "success" was Louis' favor. His strategy was to entertain them to the point of exhaustion yet wanting still more.

Not only was Lully a superb musician and conductor, he was an outstanding manager and organizer. Politically, Lully and Louis were made for each other. Lully was savvy as well. He knew that transplanting Italian opera forms and style to Versailles wasn't the solution to creating French opera. No, French opera needed to be built on traditions of French music and style: it needed to be recitative, and especially it needed ballet. It also needed to reflect the French language, which has different rhythms and sounds than Italian.

Lully dominated or controlled opera in France for much of the seventeenth century. Elisabeth Claude Jacquet de la Guerre's opera, *Céphale et Procris*, the first opera by a woman to be performed at the Paris Opéra, couldn't be performed until after Lully's death.

The first operas in Germany were Italian imports, but once "singspiel"— in German—began to be performed, the door opened for German opera. In 1697 Reinhard Keiser began the series of 116 operas he composed for Hamburg.

France

Elisabeth-Claude Jacquet de la Guerre (baptized March 17, 1665, d. June 27, 1729, Paris) began performing on the harpsichord in Paris about the time of Lully's first opera, in 1672.

The Jacquet family had been harpsichord builders for several generations, the father a noted organist and the mother from a musical family herself. Elisabeth-Claude became known for her virtuosity at the harpsichord early on. When she was eight she was invited to play at Versailles, and her playing greatly impressed Louis XIV and Madame de Maintenon, his mistress. They offered her the opportunity to live at Versailles, where she could be educated and study music. Louis always encouraged Elisabeth-Claude's playing and composing, and he allowed her to dedicate her publications to him.

After Elisabeth-Claude's marriage to Marin de la Guerre, an organist and harpsichord teacher, she moved to Paris. However, she always kept her ties to the French court, and she continued to compose and perform. She was a prolific composer, open to new musical styles and ideas; she introduced the new Italian style to France and was one of the early composers of the French cantata. Everything she did musically was a success.

Eventually she wrote an opera, *Céphale et Procris*—and there she ran afoul of Jean-Baptiste Lully, the dictator of most of the music at the court and of opera. *Céphale et Procris* wasn't performed until 1692, seven years after Lully's death.

Works

1694 *Céphale et Procris*, Trajédie-lyrique, Librettist: Duché de Vancy, Paris Opera
(Sources: Sadie and Samuel; Glickman and Schleifer; Giroud)

Italy

Barbara Strozzi (1619, Venice–after 1664, Venice?) is one of the better-known women composers of her time. She was the adopted daughter of Giulio Strozzi, a librettist, and is considered to have been his natural daughter. He made Barbara his sole heir. She studied with the composer Francesco Cavalli, who was prominent in those early years of opera in Venice. Barbara's first publication of music, a volume of madrigals, was in 1644. The texts were by Giulio Strozzi. Altogether she had eight publications, almost all were published after Giulio's death in 1652. The fact they are dedicated to important patrons suggests she depending on her composing. Barbara is thought to be one of the first women to compose in cantata form.

Barbara never married. She had four children. The painting *Female Musician with Viola da Gama* in the Gemäldegalerie Dresden painted by Bernardo Strozzi may be her portrait.

Works

1659 *Diporti di Euterpe*, opera
(Source: Sadie and Samuel)

Germany

Sophie Elisabeth, Duchess of Brunswick-Lüneburg (August 20, 1613, Güstrow–July 12, 1676, Luchow) grew up in an excellent musical setting—the court of her father, Duke Johann Albrecht of Mecklenburg-Güstrow. The court orchestra was well known for its English instrumentalists. The Thirty Years War disrupted her childhood—and the court—and Sophie had to flee. She then lived at the Kassel court, which was also known for its music. She married Duke August the Younger of Brunswick-Lüneburg, known for his founding of the Wolfenbüttel library. Sophie Elisabeth composed from an early age. Many of her works are sacred songs.

Works

New Grove Dictionary of Opera states only the music of two operettas remain:

1642 *Friedens Sieg*
1652 *Glückwünschende Freudensdarstellung*
   Her librettos include:
1654 *Der Natur Banquet*
1655 *Ballet der Zeit*
1656 *Glückwünschende Wahrsagung und Ankunft der Königin Nicaulae*
1655 *Ballet der Zeit*, operetta
1655 *Minerva Banquett*, operetta

(Sources: Cohen; Sadie and Samuel)

1700–1800

At the beginning of the 18th century opera was a hybrid of theater and musical performance, a combination of music and speech. By the end of the century it had become a form of its own, a new species, as it were. Just what comprised "opera," that new species, was open to debate. How much music should there be? How much talking? Or singing? What was the "right" form? What was the proper subject?

Elaborate spectacles, always a crowd pleaser, were very popular, and opera producers often tried to outdo each other in extravagance, especially in Italy. By the mid–1760s operas tended to be collections of arias and elaborate spectacles, more a pastiche than a unified whole. Then along came Gluck with his radical idea that there should be a clear connection between music and drama, and music should support the drama. His opera *Orfeo* in 1762 showed how enormously effective this could be.

Few women composed operas in the first half of the eighteenth century. Perhaps the most notable was the Frenchwoman Antonia Bembo. In England, George Frideric Handel so dominated the world of opera and oratorio that few other composers, male or female, had a chance. After 1750, the gates seemed to open, and on the Continent there was a steady stream of performances of operas by women. Entertainments with music and word developed in all sorts of formats; in many areas these formats became the roots of opera. They originated in Italy and France and quickly became popular in England, developing eventually into an elaborate combination of poetry, singing, scenery, dancing, and music. Some were quite splendid, with elaborate costumes and machinery. They were performed at royal courts or the houses of great nobles, and with such grand settings they must have been stunning.

Henry Purcell's *Dido and Aeneas*, a landmark of opera in England, was a departure from all the contrivances of the masque, with its dominance of music and story. This opera's first documented performance was in 1689–1690, but it may have been composed earlier. There were two performances in 1700 and 1704, then it wasn't revived until 1895. Purcell was a "victim" of the masque and never wrote another opera, but he always regretted the submissive role of music in the masques.

Ballad operas originally used English, Irish or Scottish ballads and folk tunes, but at times used familiar tunes by composers like Purcell. As time went on composers had more of a role (there were only so many folk tunes), and increasingly ballad operas more closely resembled early operas. John Gay's *The Beggar's Opera* in 1728 firmly established the popularity of ballad operas. (John Gay wasn't the composer. He was a poet and playwright and wrote the words. He also wrote the libretto for Handel's *Acis and Galatea*, and the music was arranged and partially composed by John Pepusch.) Opera was in danger of becoming so rigid it had little life to it—and *The Beggar's Opera* was a sharp contrast, with its life, energy, and characters who resembled real people rather than archetypes and solemn people from the past.

Opera continued to thrive in Italy. Maria Teresa Agnesi, who came from one of those remarkable Italian families where everyone was extraordinarily talented, had an opera performed in 1753. Maria Antonia Walpurgis, Electress of Saxony, had two operas performed in 1754. Momentum grew, and by the 1780s more women were having their operas produced, particularly in France.

In France, the upheaval of the French Revolution complicated matters enormously for anyone in the arts—the arts being the province of royalty and nobility. What did composers do during the revolution? Many fled. Some went to the provinces and lived as unobtrusively as they could. Others left

France. In some instances a noble person was hidden by a servant. Yet—and this may seem curious given the context—between 1780 and 1820, women composers in general flourished in France, particularly composers of opera.

The disruptions of the revolution forced many well-born women to earn money to support their families. For some women this had a liberating aspect. And, although opera had been the purview of the aristocracy, it quickly became a medium of political propaganda. The subject matter of operas was becoming broader and less confined to classical stories and themes. Audiences were seeing current subject matter, with singers in current dress. Classical themes gave way to emphasis on the common man and resonances of the social and political aspects of that time.

One significant change was the abolition of the power and privileges of the royal theaters—the declaration of the freedom of the theaters in 1791—which meant that anyone could open a theater—and they did. These theaters provided many opportunities for playwrights and composers to have their work performed. Such constant change was exceedingly difficult to navigate: some women did it better than others—or were luckier. Yet, despite the upheaval and atmosphere of constant change and threat, operas continued to be written and performed.

Austria

Throughout music history there have been several blind composers, including several women. **Maria Theresa von Paradis** (May 15, 1759, Vienna–February 1, 1824, Vienna) was blind from the age of three. She was named after the Empress Maria Theresa. Maria Theresa von Paradis's father was the empress's Imperial Secretary and Court Councillor.

From an early age it was obvious Maria had remarkable musical ability. In recognition of that the empress gave her a stipend for her education, and she was performing in the Viennese salons as a pianist and singer by the time she was fifteen. She had a prodigious memory for music and a large repertoire. Mozart, Salieri and Haydn were among the composers who wrote for her.

The librettist Johann Riedinger invented a composition board for her, a peg-board system with variously shaped pegs for different note values. A copyist then transcribed the music into standard notation. Riedinger accompanied Maria and her mother on Maria's concert tour, which lasted two-and-a-half years, and it was while she was on the tour (with long hours in the carriage) that she began composing. Her tour was wide-ranging—including Switzerland and France, particularly Paris, then England, Brussels, Amsterdam, Hamburg, Berlin and Prague. After her return, plans were made to tour Russia and Italy, but this tour never materialized.

Maria turned her focus more to composition, and between 1789 and 1797 she wrote at least five operas and three cantatas. Her opera *Rinaldo und Alcina* was a failure. Subsequently she turned her attention to teaching and founded her own music school in 1808.

Works

1791 *Ariadne auf Naxos*, opera, Librettist: Riedinger(?), work is lost
1792 *Der Schulkandidat*, Vienna, operetta or mourning cantata, Librettist: Riedinger(?)
1797 *Rinaldo und Alcina*, opera, Librettist: von Baczko, Prague
1805(?) *Grosse militarische*, opera, Librettist: F. von Niederstradon, work is lost
            Zwei ländliche Opern, opera, work is lost

(Sources: Cohen; Sadie and Samuel)

Denmark

Countess Maria Theresia Ahlefeldt (February 28, 1755, Regensburg– December 10, 1810) was the daughter of Count Alexander of Thurn and Taxis; his court was a center for musicians and writers. After Maria Theresia's marriage in 1780 to Count Ferdinand Ahlefeldt, a Danish count, she lived at the court of Anspach. At that time Anspach was a center for music and opera and Maria Theresia was active in operatic circles. She composed a symphony during that time and wrote the libretto and possibly the music for *La Folie*. Count Ahlefeldt was made *Hofmarskal* and director of the Kongelige Teater in Copenhagen. While he held that position Maria Theresia composed *Telemak*, an opera ballet, which was frequently performed, with 27 performances by 1812. In 1798 the Ahlefeldts moved to Dresden, and two years later to Prague.

Works

1789 *La Folie, ou Quel conte!*, opera, Librettist: Ahlefeldt, Anspach, music is lost
1792 *Telemak paa Calypsos Øe* or *Telemachus and Calypso*, opera, librettist: C. Pram
c1795 *S. Sonnischen*, opera

(Source: Sadie and Samuel)

England

Elizabeth Craven (December 17, 1750, London–January 13, 1828, Naples), who is sometimes listed as Elizabeth Anspach or Ansbach, had many dimensions. Her father was the fourth Earl of Berkeley. Elizabeth was well educated, and she particularly loved music and amateur theatricals.

When she was sixteen she married Lord Craven, with whom she had seven children. Eventually Lord Craven fell in love with someone else. After

Elizabeth, who was not one to mince matters, confronted him about this he went to the Continent, apparently to consider the situation. When he returned he informed her he had decided to leave her, after thirteen years of marriage.

Elizabeth then decided to travel. After spending some time in Italy she went to Vienna, Cracow and Warsaw, where she was presented to the king of Poland. She also met the margrave and margravine at Anspach, where she was welcomed into their household and treated like a member of the family. Elizabeth was close to both the margrave and the margravine, but she and the margrave eventually fell in love. Elizabeth left Anspach and resumed her travels. Sometime later, the margravine died. Soon after that, Lord Craven died. (Elizabeth wasn't in the area at the time, lest anyone should wonder at the convenience of this death.) The margrave and Elizabeth then married.

Anspach was incorporated into Prussia in 1792. The court at Anspach was dissolved, and Elizabeth and the margrave went to live in England. Elizabeth became involved with singing, acting, writing and composing, often composing music for her plays. She is also known as a traveler. Her accounts of her travels in *A Journey Through the Crimea to Constantinople, in a Series of Letters* (Dublin: H. Chamberlain, 1789) are lively and entertaining.

Her earlier opera (for which Samuel Arnold composed some of the music) was *The Silver Tankard*, which is sometimes described as a farce, and was performed at Haymarket Theatre. Elizabeth composed music, or part of the music, for *The Princess of Georgia*, which was performed at Covent Garden.

Works

1780 *The Silver Tankard*, opera; some of the music by Samuel Arnold
1794 *The Princess of Georgia*, opera, Covent Garden, London

Books by or about Elizabeth Craven:

Margravine of Anspach. *Memoirs of the Margravine of Anspach*. London: H. Colburn, 1826.

(Source: Sadie and Samuel)

It wasn't unusual for a woman composer to have other careers and occupations as well, and many, like Elizabeth Craven, were known for both. **Mary Linwood** (1755 or 1756, Birmingham–March 2, 1845, Leicester) had a remarkable talent as an artist in needlework.

When her father, a wine merchant, went bankrupt and died, her mother opened a school for young ladies. Upon her mother's death Mary took over the school. Artists in needlework would reproduce pictures or paintings, in Mary's case using embroidery. She became very successful and had many exhibits. She specialized in full-size reproductions of old masters, many of them quite large, all extraordinarily detailed with variations in stitches that gave them texture. It's rather staggering to contemplate the work involved in doing all that—and she also composed! In addition to some vocal music, much of which was published in London, she composed an oratorio, *David's First Victory*, which was performed at the Queen's Concert Rooms in Hanover Square. She is less known as a composer. Her two known operas (there may have been others), *The Kellerin* and *The White Wreath*, were never published.

(Source: Sadie and Samuel)

France

When Louis XIV died, Philippe d'Orléans served as regent, as Louis XV was only five years old at the time. Louis XIV had lost some of his enthusiasm for opera the last twenty years of his life, preferring "small operas," which tended to last an hour or so. Philippe must have been a welcome contrast for opera composers. Not only had he studied with Charpentier, but he had also collaborated with him on writing an opera and had written two other operas with Gervais, his music master.

The business of operas and opera houses gave rise to much competition, and an intense rivalry grew up between the Comédie Italienne and the Comédie Française. A veritable "Battle of the Houses" ensued. The Comédie Française succeeded in restricting the operations of the Comédie Italienne from 1718 to 1720 and 1721 to 1724. Other theaters became involved, Opéra and Opéra-Comique, and much was at stake: audiences, money, and power. In 1725 a truce of sorts allowed for the four theaters—Opéra, Comédie Française, Comédie Italienne, and Opéra-Comique to operate. This lasted until 1745, when the Comédie Française used its muscle to force the Opéra-Comique to close for seven years.

That rather golden era ended when Louis XV came of age; he had little interest in music or culture or in keeping up an extensive—and expensive—court at Versailles. Eventually the cultural focus shifted to Paris. Although court connections continued to be significant, music and opera took on their own momentum and flourished. The second half of the century was a time of opportunity for many composers, including women. It's not entirely coincidental that nearly a dozen women were successful composers of operas.

The life spans of these women overlap—and in some cases almost match. They undoubtedly knew and interacted with each other; they lived through much—including the French Revolution and its aftermath—and saw and experienced many changes. Although this period is one of the most richly documented, with respect to these women one wishes for more:

Isabelle de Charrière (1740–1805)
Marie-Emmanuelle Bayon (1746–1825)
Henriette Adélaïde Villard de Beaumesnil (1748–1813)
Jeanne-Hippolyte Devismes (1765–1834?)
Josephine-Rosalie-Pauline de Walckiers (1765–1837)
Caroline Wuiet (1766–1835)
Florine Dezède (1766–c1792)
(Amélie) Julie Candeille (1767–1834)
Lucile Grétry (1772–1790)
Sophie de Bawr (1773–1860)
Sophie Gail (1775–1819)

Marquise de la Mizangere (February 10, 1693, Bourret–c1779) was an accomplished harpsichordist—she was taught by Couperin—and established a career giving concert tours and private concerts. She composed a string quartet, pieces for harp, and pieces for harpsichord, and may have been the first Frenchwoman to compose piano music. Little is known of her life. After her daughter died she held an administrative post in a parish for thirty years.

Works

Der Heimliche Bund, opera
(Source: Cohen)

The second opera by a woman to be performed at the Paris Opéra was *Les Génies*, 1736, by **Mlle. Duval** (1718?–after 1775, Paris). The review in the *Mercure de France*, November 1736, said the opera was "varied and extremely well developed in many regards." She dedicated the opera to her protector, the prince of Carignan. She was a dancer, singer and harpsichordist, and it's sometimes suggested that she may have sung with the Paris Opéra. That certainly is plausible, but there is likely more than one woman named "Mlle. Duval" who was active in music composition and performance in and around Paris at that time (and there were perhaps several more).

Works

1736 *Les Génies*, Librettist: Fleury [de Lyon], Paris Opera
(Sources: Sadie and Samuel; Letzer and Adelson)

Helene Guerin (c1739, Amiens–fl. 1755) composed the opera *Daphnis et d'Amalthée* when she was sixteen. It was performed in Amiens, where Guerin probably lived. A letter in the *Mercure de France* on August 8, 1755, tells of the performance and admires the composer's musical and intellectual abilities.

Works

1755 *Daphnis et d'Amalthée*, Amiens
(Sources: Sadie and Samuel; Letzer and Adelson)

Mlle. Duhamel (18th century)

Works

1763 *Agnes*, opera
(Source: Cohen)

Marie-Emmanuelle Bayon (Bayon-Louis) (August 30/31, 1746–March 19, 1825, Paris) lived through a significant number of changes in music and in France. From an early age she was recognized as an accomplished musician, and she was one of the early advocates of the pianoforte in France. Her friends included Stéphanie-Félicité de Genlis, known for her salons and many friendships with people in the arts, and Denis Diderot, whose daughter she taught. Her first opera (title unknown) was performed at Madame de Genlis' salon. According to *Women Writing Opera* Marie probably wrote three operas, two of which may have been performed in her own salon.

The librettist for *Fleur-d'épine* was Claude-Henri Fusée, Abbé de Voisenon. Getting the libretto was a coup for Bayon. She was asked by the Comtesse Turpin to write the music for *Fleur-d'épine*. The libretto had been found in the estate of the Abbé de Voisenon, who had died in 1775. The abbé had been a well-known dramatist, and his writing often was a factor in an opera's success. This was an opportunity not to miss. Bayon wrote the opera house, and thanks to Voisenon's reputation the work was soon performed at the Comédie Italienne, jumping the queue of other works that had been received before hers.

In 1770 Bayon married Victor Louis, who already was a famous theater architect known for his design of the Grand Théâtre in Bordeaux. The couple lived in Bordeaux for about a decade, moving back to Paris in 1780. Although her husband was influential in theater circles, Bayon apparently did not utilize his influence for getting her own works performed. The family was in Paris during the French Revolution, and Victor Louis continued his success throughout that time. By the 1790s the couple were estranged. After her husband's death in 1800, Marie Bayon lived with Angélique Diderot, her former student, who was at that time Madame de Vandeul.

Works

1767 Title unknown, Opéra-comique, Librettist: Sauvigny, Salon of Mme. De Genlis
1781 *Fleur d'épine*, operetta, Comédie Italienne, Paris, Librettist: Claude-Henri Fusée Abbé de Voisenon, adapted from a popular fairy tale by Antoine Hamilton
An unidentified third opera
(Sources: Sadie and Samuel; Letzer and Adelson)

From an early age **Henriette Adélaïde Villard de Beaumesnil** (August 30, 1748, Paris–1813, Paris) was active in the theater, having begun singing in comedies when she was seven. She made her debut at the Paris Opéra when she was eighteen. Unfortunately, poor health compelled her to retire when she was thirty-three, at which point she promptly began to write operas. The result was *Anacreon*, a one-act opera, which was privately performed. About that time she married Phillipi Cauvy, an actor at the Comédie Italienne. Her next opera, *Les Fêtes grecques et romaines*, premiered at court, then was performed a month later at the Paris Opéra. This was the third work composed by a woman performed at the Paris Opéra. What she did during the French Revolution isn't known, nor is much known about her later life.

Works

1781 *Anacreon*, opera, Paris Opéra
1784 *Les Fêtes grecques et romaines*, opera, Paris Opéra
1784 *Tibulle et Délie, ou les Saturnales*, opera, Librettist: Fuzelier
1792 *Les Législatrices*, opera
1792 *Plaire, c'est commander!* opera, Librettist: Marquis de La Salle
(Sources: Sadie and Samuel; Letzer and Adelson)

Family connections had a strong impact on **Florine Dezède** and **Louise Grétry**, each the daughter of a celebrated Parisian opera composer. André Grétry is still well known today; Nicolas Dezède is not. André Grétry, the father of **Lucile (Angélique Dorothée Louise) Grétry** (July 15, 1772, Paris–March 1790, Paris), strongly believed in educating women, particularly in music. Three of his four composition students were women, and each had a successful career as a composer. André was prominent as a court composer, and Lucile's exceptional talent in music caught the attention of Marie Antoinette. Lucile's first opera, *Le Mariage d'Antoine*, written when she was fourteen, had forty-seven performances over five years at the Comédie Italienne. Her father influenced her composing and likely did the orchestration for *Le Mariage d'Antoine*.

Unfortunately, her other opera, *Toinette et Louis*, was a dismal failure. At that time Lucile was in the midst of a very unhappy marriage, and her family maintained that the situation was a substantial reason for the failure of the opera. And yet, *Women Writing Opera* quotes Arsène Houssaye, a noted critic and author of *Portraits du dix-huitième siècle*, strongly commending Lucile's music: "If not for death, which took her at the age of sixteen [*sic*] … the greatest musician of the eighteenth century would perhaps have been a woman" (WWO 27). Lucile died of tuberculosis at age eighteen.

Works

1786 *Le Mariage d'Antoine*, opera, Librettist: Mme. de Beaunoir (Alexandre Bertrand Robinson), Comédie Italienne, Paris
1787 *Toinette et Louis*, Librettist: Joseph Patrat

(Sources: Letzer and Adelson; Sadie and Samuel)

Nicolas Dezède, the father of **Florine Dezède** (1766–c1792), also was a prominent opera composer. His connections at the Comédie Italienne were useful. Florine's opera *Lucette et Lucas* had forty-three performances between 1781 and 1792. At least one performance was at Versailles. *Lucette et Lucas* was often paired with one of her father's operas. Yet, for all his prominence, today very little is known of Nicolas Dezède. Grove's 1927 edition states he was born at Turin in 1744 and died in Paris about 1792. What little is known of his life could form the basis for a libretto. He was illegitimate but received a generous allowance. Curious about his parentage, he began making inquiries, at which point he was warned that if he continued with his inquiries his allowance would cease. He continued—and the allowance didn't. At that point he decided to compose opera, and his first opera, *Julie*, was performed in Paris in 1772. He composed at least thirteen additional operas, the most famous of which was *Blaise et Babet*. He died about 1792. Even less is known of his daughter Florine, who is said also to have died about 1792, age twenty-seven.

Works

1781 *Lucette et Lucas*, opera, Librettist: Forgeot, Paris

(Sources: Letzer and Adelson; *Grove Dictionary of Music and Musicians*, 1927 edition)

Caroline Wuiet (1766–1835) was one of the three women who were André Grétry's composition students (the others were Sophie de Bawr and his daughter Lucile). Caroline, like his other two students, was a child prodigy, with perhaps the broadest abilities of these three extraordinary women.

Caroline's father, Clément, an organist, taught her piano. Her musical abilities were obvious at a very early age. At five she was presented to Marie Antoinette, who immediately took her studies in hand: music with Grétry, painting with Jean-Baptiste Greuze (Greuze's teacher was Grétry's father-in-law), and drama with Beaumarchais and Charles Desmoustier. At age eleven Caroline made her debut performing on the harpsichord at the Concert Spirituel; some of the works she played were by Grétry. Five years later her first play, *Angélina*, was performed at the Théâtre des Beaujolais. A second play was published five years later. Her professional life seemed to be off to a good start. But when she tried to have her operas performed, she ran afoul of opera politics and the convoluted process of having an opera produced. And convoluted it was, with various committees passing judgment on the desirability of perhaps eventually producing a particular opera.

The first aspect to be considered was the libretto. If the committee, having considered the libretto, thought it worthy, they might ask the author of the libretto to read aloud to the committee. Since most of the libretti were rejected, the music usually hadn't been composed. In fact, the matter of selecting the composer was up to either the librettist or the committee. Once the music (finally!) was written it was submitted to a committee of musicians. If the opera was still in the running, it would next be performed before the entire committee, which required having parts copied and singers and a small orchestra selected and rehearsed. Even if the opera made it through that stage, there were no guarantees of performance. Operas weren't performed in order of acceptance, and an opera that had been accepted might languish for years. Worse, the opera could still be rejected even after having made it through the process. That process must have been frustrating in the extreme. Obviously clout was a big factor, but, even so, there were no guarantees. With so many factions involved, there was always the chance that an attempt to influence could alienate the wrong people and backfire.

Caroline was in her teens when she submitted her libretto for *Le Trompeur trompé*. The committee rejected it, citing several criticisms: too little substance for three acts, verses badly written, and an unrealistic and bizarre plot. Then she submitted the libretto for *L'Heureuse erreur*, which was a sequel to Grétry's 1784 opera, *L'Épreuve villageoise*. In that instance the libretto was accepted. Caroline had been ordered by the court to perform the work for the queen. Caroline was only sixteen, and naturally she was elated. But eight days before the premiere the music was refused after eight rehearsals. She was tempted to protest, but even though she was young, she knew the realities of the politics. Her enemies were too powerful.

Discouraged, Caroline considered giving up her career as an opera composer and librettist. Instead, she turned to the Théâtre des Beaujolais, where *Angelina* had been performed. They selected her to write the music for Guilliame Saulnier's libretto "L'heureux stratagème, ou le vol supposé." It was successfully given in 1786, but its success did little to compensate for Caroline's experience with the Comédie Italienne. Since the Théâtre des Beaujolais wasn't one of the privileged theaters, it was not permitted to perform opéra-comique.

Utterly discouraged by this time, Caroline decided to go on a concert tour to Germany and France—where her piano playing was well received. Her future looked more promising. However, when she returned, the French Revolution was underway. She was arrested as a royalist but went into exile in England and then in Holland. For some reason she returned during the Terror, hiding out in Versailles. (This may sound improbable, but by that time Versailles was likely well deserted, everything having shifted to Paris.)

Caroline was intrepid. She founded a women's charitable club, which the government abolished. She then turned to publishing sonatas and romances, an endeavor that was quite successful. The Directory was in place by then, and Caroline was getting wealthy with her publishing and gaining access to important women. She then began a fashionable daily newspaper, writing and editing for it. The paper had a series of titles and changes, but in part it served to publish her poetry and editorials. She grew tired of running a newspaper and instead wrote for at least one other publication.

We don't know much about her private life through those years. The first we hear of it is her marriage to Colonel Joseph Auffdiener, with whom she moved to Lisbon. However, Portugal was having its own political upheavals, so Caroline returned to France. Auffdiener stayed in Portugal to see to his business matters but ran afoul of the politics, was imprisoned and died there. Caroline then turned to writing fiction and teaching piano to support herself. The changes under the Restoration seem to have disoriented her, and she died homeless, destitute, and, eventually, mad.

Works

1783 *L'Heureux stratagème*, opera bouffon, Librettist: G. Saulnier, Paris
1786 *L'Heureuse erreur*, Paris, 1786, Librettist: Wuiet, opera rehearsed with orchestra at the Comédie Italienne but not voted for public performance

(Sources: Sadie and Samuel; Letzer and Adelson)

Andre Grétry's third female pupil was **Sophie de Bawr** (October 8, 1773, Paris–December 31, 1860). Like so many of the women of this time, she was a prolific and successful writer, penning novels, histories, stories, and one-act plays, plays for which she composed the music. Her plays in particular were widely performed.

Sophie was illegitimate. Her parents were the marquis Charles-Jean de Champgrand and Madeleine-Virginie Vian, an opera singer. When Sophie was two her mother left for Russia, apparently in search of a husband. Her father gave Sophie an excellent education, arranging for her to study with significant teachers such as Grétry. Her father was well connected and had a notable salon, where Sophie often sang her compositions. He was, however, an aristocrat; he was imprisoned during the revolution and his possessions were confiscated. Friends turned their backs on him. Grétry refused to have anything to do with Sophie during the revolution. However, after her father died Sophie lived in the Grétry household.

She married Count Claude-Henri de Saint-Simon, the social theorist, in 1801. The marriage lasted only a year but she ran a salon for him that attracted prominent musicians and writers, both valuable to Sophie. She conveniently, but wrongly, kept the title "Comtesse" after his death.

Sophie next married Baron de Bawr, a Russian. Very soon after their marriage he went bankrupt, and soon after that he was killed, hit by a cart. Finally, in 1816, Sophie received a pension from Louis XVIII, which relieved her of financial pressures. With that independence she moved away from the theater and wrote in other genres, particularly historical novels and children's literature. She was the first woman to write on the history of music, and one of her books, *Soirées des jeunes personnes*, received a prize from the Académie Française. In her memoirs, *Mes Souvenirs*, published when she was eighty, she recalls many of the people, particularly the women, she had known throughout her life.

Works

1804 *Les Chevaliers du lion*, opera, Librettist: Bawr
1811 *Léon, ou Le château de Montaldi*, opera, Librettist: Bawr, Paris
1813 *Un Quart d'heure de dépit*, opera comique, Librettist: Bawr, never performed

Books by or about Sophie Bawr:

Bawr, Alexandrine. *Mes Souvenirs*. Paris: Passard, 1863.
(Source: Sadie and Samuel)

The creative energy of **Isabelle de Charrière** (October 20, 1740, Zuylen, near Utrecht–December 27, 1805, Neufchatel) seemingly had no limits. Her greatest fame lies in her stories, essays, comedies and novels, particularly epistolary novels. She was a prolific letter writer herself—the epistolary form must have come naturally to her—and she was an accomplished pianist, composer and librettist. She was also subject to the criticism—almost always ill-natured—that "if she does so many things she can't be doing any of them well." Yet she did. She was a Dutch woman who wrote French operas, and that, too, probably made her suspect to certain personages.

Accounts of her and her work often list her as Belle van Zuylen, the name by which she was known in the Netherlands. When she was ten she spent a year travelling through Switzerland and France. During that time she spoke only French, absorbing it to the extent that she had to relearn Dutch when she went back home. Her parents gave her an unusually good education.

She was twenty-six when her first novel was published, and she went on to write poetry, plays and more novels, but she eventually realized that what she really wanted to write was opera librettos. After her marriage to Charles-Emmanuel de Charrière de Penthaz in 1771, she and her husband settled in Switzerland. They were famous for their hospitality, and many of her guests were musicians who helped her with her composing.

Isabelle began seriously composing opera in the early 1780s, and she decided to further her education by going where she could hear contemporary opera. She was strongly drawn to Italy, but instead she spent eighteen months in Paris, where she studied and went to the opera. We don't know if she met any other women composers and librettists, but she likely was exposed to their music. *Le Mariage d'Antonio* by Lucile Grétry—a sensation, with a sixteen-year-old author—was being performed, as was *Lucette et Lucas* with music by Florine Dezède, who was also very young. It seems likely Isabelle would have seen those operas. And Caroline Wuiet's opera *L'Heureux stratagème* premiered as well at that time.

When Isabelle returned to Neuchâtel she was even more convinced she wanted to write operas, and she thought perhaps she might compose with a collaborator. From 1788 to 1793 she wrote eight operas. None were ever performed. Undeniably there were barriers for women composers, particularly in opera, and there were barriers in general in the ludicrously complicated and cumbersome process of getting an opera performed. Some of her critics disparage the quality of her music—an issue hard to address now since none of her operatic music survives.

The authors of *Women Writing Opera* suggest there were other factors that affected Isabelle's unsuccessful attempts to get her operas performed. While she was growing up in Holland there were Italian musicians at the court of The Hague, and she grew up hearing Italian music and opera. She appreciated the differences between French and Italian opera, with some preference for Italian because of their composers' skill in working with songs. Also, she liked the plots in the Italian *opera seria* as opposed to the French *opéra-comique*, with its sentimentality. There was no middle ground in France. Isabelle's view that there was worth and merit in Italian opera (never mind that there might be room for improvement in French opera) was the kiss of death.

Works

1788 *Les Phéniciennes*, Librettist: Charrière, never performed
1788 *Pénélope*, Librettist: Charrière, never performed

1790 *Polyphème ou le Cyclope*, Librettist: Charrière, never performed
1790 *Junon*, Librettist: Charrière, never performed
1790 *Les Femmes*, Librettist: Charrière, never performed
1790 *L'Olimpiade*, Librettist: Charrière, never performed
1791 *Zadig*, Librettist: Charrière, never performed
1792 Title unknown, Librettist: Charrière, never performed

Books by or about Isabella Charrière:

Charrière, Isabella. *Caliste, ou, Lettres écrites de Lausanne.* Madame de Charrière; présentée par Claudine Herrmann. Paris: Des Femmes, c1979.
_____. *Œuvres completes.* Isabelle de Charrière (Belle de Zuylen). Éd. critique par Jean-Daniel Candaux et al. Amsterdam: G.A. van Oorschot, 1979.
_____. *Four tales by Zélide* (pseud.). Translated by Sybil Marjorie Scott. New York: C. Scribner's Sons, 1926.
_____. *Lettres neuchâteloises: suivi de Trois femmes.* Lausanne: Bibliothèque Romande, 1971.

Charrière is included in:

Boswell in Holland, 1763–1764: Including the Correspondence with Belle de Zuylen (Zélide). Edited by Frederick A. Pottle. Melbourne: Heinemann, 1952.

(Sources: Cohen; Letzer and Adelson)

Josephine-Rosalie-Pauline de Walckiers (1765–1837)

Works

1784 *Borée et Flore*, opera comique, Brussels
1788 Title unknown, divertissement, Théâtre de Schaerbeek
1792 *La Répétition villageoise*, opera, Théâtre de Schaerbeek

(Source: Letzer and Adelson)

Contacts and insider access—always critical at this time—were often a family matter for opera composers. The fact that the father of **(Amélie) Julie Candeille** (July 31, 1767, Paris–February 4, 1834, Paris) was a composer and a singer opened doors for his daughter. Julie was first known as a child prodigy at the harp and piano. When she was fourteen she began singing at the Opéra.

Acting interested her, and she began acting in plays at the Comédie Francaise. She soon discovered that comedy suited her better, both in terms of her writing and acting. *Catherine or la belle fermière*—for which she wrote both words and music, singing and accompanying herself on the piano and harp—was an immense success and ran for 154 performances. Her next two operas, *Bathilde, ou le duc* and *La Bayadère, ou Le Français à surate*, did poorly, likely because of political influences.

Julie married Louis-Nicholas Delaroche in 1794, but within three years they divorced. In 1798 she married Jean Simons, a Belgian coach builder, and moved with him to Brussels. Unfortunately, four years later he went bankrupt and soon afterward showed aspects of mental instability. Julie moved back to Paris to earn money for his support. She wrote plays, essays, and historical novels, and gave private lessons. In 1815 during Napoleon's Hundred Days, she sought political asylum in England. While there she gave concerts and continued her writing and teaching to keep herself afloat. The next year she returned to Paris, having been given a generous pension by Louis XVIII.

Jean Simons died in 1821; a year later Julie married Hilaire-Henri Périé, a painter. They moved to Nîmes, where Julie had found a position for her husband. Julie supported her father for many years, and after his death in 1827 she provided for his second wife. After the death of her third husband, Hilaire-Henri Périé, in 1834, Julie returned to Paris. She died there the next year, indigent.

Works

1792 *Catherine or la belle fermière*, opera, Librettist: Candeille
1793 *Bathilde, ou le duc*, opera, Librettist: Candeille
1795 *La Bayadère, ou Le Français à surate*, opera, Librettist: Candeille
1807 *Ida, ou L'Orpheline de Berlin*, opera, Librettist: Candeille, based on the life of Madame de Genlis

(Sources: Sadie and Samuel; Letzer and Adelson)

Germany

Anna Amalia, Duchess of Saxe-Weimar (October 24, 1739, Wolfenbüttel–April 10, 1807, Weimar), niece of Frederick the Great, was the daughter of Duke Karl I of Brunswick. Music was important at his court, and Anna Amalia had a good musical education. She married when she was sixteen; her husband, the Duke of Saxe Weimar, was two years older than she was. He died two years after the marriage, and Anna Amalia became regent for her eldest son, Duke Karl August. Her court was a center for learning and culture as Anna Amalia opened her court to scholars, poets and musicians. Throughout this time she took lessons in composition and keyboard playing and immersed herself in the cultural activities at the court. She collected a significant library of about 2,000 volumes.

Works

1776 *Erwin und Elmire*, operetta, libretto: based on Goethe, or from Goethe

(Source: Sadie and Samuel)

Sophie (de) Charrière is often confused with Isabelle de Charrière; however the authors Letzer and Adelson make a strong case for there being two people having the same last name and who likely were not related. Furthermore it seems likely that Sophie is not French.

In part this is based on the language of *Julien et Juliette*, which is not in the fluid French that Isabelle de Charriere would have used. Also, the opera is dedicated to Maria Walpurgis, electress of Saxony, and it's logical to conclude that Sophie was likely a native German speaker. The French surname may have been through marriage.

Works

c1771 *Julien et Juliette*, opera
(Sources: Letzer and Adelson; Cohen)

Maria Antonia Walpurgis, Electress of Saxony (July 18, 1724, Munich–April 25, 1780, Dresden), was the daughter of the Elector Karl Albert of Bavaria, who later was Emperor Karl VII, and the Archduchess Maria Amalia of Austria. As was characteristic of many, if not most, of the German courts at that time, she had excellent education in the arts, particularly music, and in painting and poetry as well. In 1747 she married Friedrich Christian, who became the Elector of Saxony. They had seven surviving children. Maria took an active role in the cultural life of the court, often as a singer in her own operas, or as a keyboard player in concerts.

In addition to composing, she was a painter and a poet; she was a member of the Arcadian Academy in Rome.

During the Seven Years' War she lived in Prague in Munich. When her husband acceded to the throne she returned to the court. Within weeks of her return he died, and their son, then ten years old, succeeded. For five years Maria was joint Regent with Franz Xaver, her brother-in-law, and political manners—and controversies, were paramount in her life. Economic matters were also a consideration. During the Regency she founded a brewery and a textile factory.

After the Regency, her life at the Dresden court changed substantially, and she felt increasingly isolated from changes in the music and art. Nonetheless she continued her participation as a patron and continued to perform as a singer or keyboard player.

Works

1754 *Il trionfo della fedeltà*, opera, Librettist: Maria Walpurgis
1754 *Frederick II*, opera
1760 *Talestri, regina delle amazon*, opera, Librettist: Maria Walpurgis
      Lavinia e turno, opera
(Source: Sadie and Samuel)

Wilhelmina, Princess of Prussia, Margravine of Bayreuth (July 3, 1709, Berlin–October 14, 1758, Bayreuth), shared the musical interests of her brother, Frederick the Great, and the two were close. She married Prince Frederick of Bayreuth when she was twenty-two; in large part through her interests and personality the court at Bayreuth became a center for music and culture, particularly music. She and her husband bought the Baroque opera house that would later attract Wagner to Bayreuth.

Works

1740 *Argenore*, opera
(Source: Sadie and Samuel)

Italy

Antonia Bembo (Venice, c1643–before 1715) studied with Francesco Cavalli. She and Barbara Strozzi undoubtedly knew of each other and perhaps were acquainted. Antonio was a contemporary of Élisabeth Jacquet de La Guerre. In 1659 she married a nobleman, but at some time before 1676 she left her husband and three children and went to Paris with someone who is not identified. She stayed in Paris the rest of her life. Louis XIV was so impressed with her singing that he gave her a pension, which enabled her to enter a religious community.

Antonio wrote vocal music in a variety of forms. As with other Italian composers who lived in France, her music reflects both Italian and French influences. She dedicated her music to Louis XIV and other members of the royal family. Much of her music was published. Antonia Bembo "disappeared" from view and was rediscovered when her manuscripts came to light in 1937 in the French National Library.

Works

1707 *L'Ercole amante*, opera, Librettist: Cavalli, Italian verses by Abbe Buti
(Source: Sadie and Samuel)

Dionisia Zamparelli (18th century; born Naples)

Works

1731 *Artaserse*, opera, Librettist: Pietro Metastasio (Pietro Trapassi)
1746 *La Zoe*, opera, Librettist: F. Silvestri
1753 *Il Teuzzone*, opera, Librettist: A. Zeno
1760 *Roma liberate dalla Signoria dei Re*, opera, Librettist: G.B. Montecatini
(Source: Cohen)

The family of **Maria Teresa Agnesi** (October 17, 1720 [dates vary], Milan–January 19, 1795) was remarkable in a time and place of remarkable people and families. Her sister, Maria Gaetana, was a brilliant mathematician. The family home was a gathering place for the cultured and intellectual, and Maria Gaetana would more than hold her own in a debate in Latin. Maria Theresa, who was a skilled harpsichordist and singer, would play and sing and her "concerts" often included her own compositions. Her first work for the stage, a cantata, was presented at the Ducal Palace in 1747. Maria produced several collections of arias and instrumental pieces, and she often dedicated them to the rulers of Saxony and Austria. In 1752 she married Pier Antonio Pinottini; the couple had no children. The following year her opera *Ciro in Armenia* with her libretto was produced at the Regio Ducal Teatro. Subsequently she wrote at least three more. Her portrait is at the theater museum of La Scala.

Works

1753 *Ciro in Armenia*, opera, Librettist Agnesi
1765 *La sofonisba*, Naples, opera, Librettist G. F. Zanetti
1766 *L'insubria consolata*, opera, Librettist: Agnesi, Milan (possibly lost)
1771 *Nitocri*, opera, Librettist: A. Zeno, Venice

(Source: Sadie and Samuel)

Maria Rosa Coccia (1759, Rome–November 1833) showed musical talent from a very early age. When she was fifteen she composed a canonic exercise for four examiners from the Roman Accademia di S. Cecilia, later the Rome Conservatory of Saint Cecilia. The next year the canon was published along with her portrait. Around this time she was made a member of the Accademia Filarmonica of Bologna. Unfortunately, little is known of her adult life, and it is not clear whether she continued in music.

Works

1772 *L'isola disabitata*, opera, Librettist: Pietro Metastasio (Pietro Trapassi)

Books by or about Maria Rose Coccia:

Coccia, Maria Rosa. *Elogio storico della Signora Maria Rosa Coccia, Romana, maestro publica di capella, Accademia Filarmonicca di Bologna, etc.*

(Source: Sadie and Samuel)

Teresa Guidi Lionetti (b. ca. 1769) was a conductor as well as a composer. Her brother was the poet Achille Guidi.

Works

Don Cesare di Bazan, opera

Le Nozze di Florina, opera
Rosa di Perona, opera
Susinette, opera
(Sources: Cohen; http://operadata.stanford.edu/)

1800–1849

Opera exploded in the 19th century. Suddenly, instead of only a few areas having an opera life, opera was seemingly everywhere in Europe. The arts tend to flourish when the economics are good, and now the emerging middle class had the interest and money to spend on opera. Nationalism was also a factor. Why should opera be the monopoly of a few countries or courts? Why don't "we" have opera?

Private "residences" often had performance halls that could accommodate an audience of 100 or more people. Operas for smaller audiences, often called chamber operas, were increasingly popular. Seemingly every prince or princeling had an opera company. Public opera flourished. "Everyone" wanted to go to the opera—and many composers wanted to write opera. As a result, opera gained a certain amount of independence.

Opera was in flux, with stylistic changes in singing, in the music itself, and especially in the combining of the two. Composers often wrote—or needed to write—for specific singers, which could affect a particular opera. The appropriate subject matter for operas shifted radically. Romantic-historical and "rescue" operas were popular, and novels and plays were often the sources for librettos.

Some operas reflected regional traditions in music and stories and the vernacular language. Composers didn't just incorporate already existing national musical material into their operas. Rather they used elements of traditional rhythm and harmonies, so that their music was evocative of traditional music but not a copy or imitation. Seemingly every composer became caught up in the opera world. (There were times when the question of the day could have been "who wasn't composing opera?") Certainly women composers were composing!

In the early part of the century Marie Friederike Auguste Amalie, Princess of Saxony, who composed a least fourteen operas, was prominent. Louise Bertin in France composed four operas and likely would have written more, but her family's connection with a prominent newspaper made her—and her operas—a political target. In Italy, Adelaide Orsola Appignani, who was also known as a conductor, had several of her stage works/operas performed. And there were more, many more.

Opera—along with the composing of opera—was flourishing, and women were part of it.

Austria

Marie Leopoldine Blahetka (November 15, 1811, Guntramsdorf, Baden, Austria–January 12, 1887, Boulogne) first studied music with her mother, then was a student with Carl Czerny, Friedrich Kalkbrenner and Ignaz Moscheles. When Leopoldine Marie was eight she appeared in a concert as a special attraction. Her appearance placed her firmly in the Viennese Biedermeier musical world, and she became a member of Schubert's circle of friends.

In 1824, at age thirteen, she performed a work by Schubert in a concert. When she was eighteen, she was performing widely. Her father requested Josef Doppler to write and ask Schubert if he would kindly compose a piece for piano and orchestra for Leopoldine, which he did. Leopoldine had a successful career as a concert pianist, performing in Germany, The Netherlands, Bohemia, England and France.

When Chopin visited Vienna, he wrote a friend about the beautiful young pianist. When Chopin left Vienna, Leopoldine gave him a composition of her own that she had dedicated to him.

In 1840 she left Vienna and settled in Boulogne. Increasingly she was concentrating on her teaching and composing. In addition to her opera she composed works for orchestra, chamber ensembles, piano, and vocal music.

Works
1830 *Die Rauber und der Sanger*, opera
(Source: Sadie and Samuel)

Anna Benfey-Schuppe (1831, Landeck–May 27, 1903, Weimar)

Works
1836 *Adelheid, Gemahlin Ottos des Grossen*, opera
(Source: Cohen)

Josepha Müellner-Gollenhofer (b. ca. 1769, Vienna) studied harp in Italy on a scholarship. When she was nineteen she made a successful tour of Europe. She was a harpist in the court orchestra in Vienna from 1811 to 1823.

Beethoven's only piece for the harp, *Die Geschöpfe des Prometheus* was written for her. Her first known compositions appeared in 1805. She wrote a string quartet and music for harp, as well as songs.

Works

Der heimliche Bund, opera
(Source: Cohen)

Bohemia

Bernhardine Prohaska (b. ca. 1803)

Works

1846 *Der Blick des Basilisken*, opera, performed in Leipzig
(Source: Cohen)

England

The one opera we know of that **Marie Fauche** (19th century) composed was performed at the London Lyceum in 1823:

Works

1823 *The Shepherd King, or The Conquest of Sidon*, opera
(Sources: Cohen; http://operadata.stanford.edu/)

Theater and opera was the family business for **Mary Anne A'Beckett** (1817, London–December 11, 1863, London). One of her brothers was an actor and theater producer, another was an impresario. Her father, Joseph Glossop, was a producer, and her mother, who had fled the French Revolution, was a professional singer. Her husband, Gilbert Abbott A'Beckett, in addition to being a magistrate, was a writer; he wrote Mary Anne's libretti.

She was invited to conduct her operas but declined as she didn't want to make public appearances. In addition to operas she wrote songs and some piano music.

Works

The Young Pretender, opera, three songs were published
1835 *Agnes Sorel*, opera, librettist: Gilbert A'Beckett, London
1842 *Little Red Riding Hood*, opera, librettist: Gilbert A'Beckett, London
(Source: Sadie and Samuel)

Kate Loder (August 21, 1825 [date varies], Bath–August 30, 1904, Headley, Surrey) was well known as a pianist, composer and teacher. Her mother was a piano teacher.

Kate entered the Royal Academy of Music (RAM) when she was twelve. Among her teachers was her aunt Lucy Anderson, who was pianist to the queen. Kate later was a professor of harmony at the RAM. In 1851 she married Henry Thompson, a surgeon, who died in 1904. Kate died two months later. In the last decades of her life she had become increasing paralyzed.

In her time she was well known as a composer, and was particularly noted for her piano music.

Works

c1850 *L'Élisir d'amore*, opera
(Source: Sadie and Samuel)

As a composer **Mary Ann Virginia Gabriel** (February 7, 1825, Banstead–August 7, 1877, London) was known for her songs—over 300—and her piano works. She also composed at least two cantatas: *Evangeline*, based on the Longfellow poem, and *Dreamland*. She also became known for her operettas, many of which toured extensively. Some of her librettos were written by George E. March, her husband.

Works

1860 *Lost and Found*, operetta, librettist: G. March
1860 *The Follies of a Night*, operetta
1864 *The Shepherd of Cournouailles*, operetta, librettist: T.G. Lacy
1865 *Widows Bewitched*, operetta, librettist: H. Aidé
1870 *Who's the Heir?* operetta, librettist: G. March
1873 *The Grass Widows*, operetta, librettist: G. March
1875 *Graziella*, operetta, librettist: J.J. Londsdale
The Love Tests, operetta, librettist: V. Amcotts
(Sources: Sadie and Samuel; Cohen)

Elizabeth Stirling (February 26, 1819, Greenwich–March 25, 1895, London), an organist and pianist, studied at the Royal Academy of Music. She was appointed organist of All Saints' Poplar, retaining the position for almost twenty years. She then competed for the position of organist at St. Andrew's Undershaft and held that position for about twenty years.

In 1856 women weren't eligible for a degree at Oxford; nonetheless she submitted an exercise (Psalm 110 for five voices and orchestra) for the BMus. Although her submission was accepted it wasn't performed, as she wasn't eligible for a degree.

She and her husband, organist F.A. Bridge, had a chamber opera company which produced her opera *Bleakmoor for Copsleigh*.

Works

Bleakmoor for Copsleigh, opera, unpublished

(Sources: Cohen; Sadie and Samuel)

France

Jeanne-Hippolyte Devismes (1765, Lyon–1834? Paris) was the only woman to have an opera performed at the Opéra between 1784 and 1836. While women were having some successes and making inroads at the other houses, the Opéra held firm in staging operas only by men. And, of course they could protect themselves with the cumbersome committee system of selecting operas. Jeanne's "case" was likely helped by the fact her husband, Anne-Pierre-Jacques Devismes du Valgay, was director of the Opéra for two brief periods of time. Her opera was performed during one of the periods when he was director. *Praxtèle* had sixteen performances, and the music was used for three parodies.

Jeanne was an excellent pianist, but beyond that little is known of her life. Nor is it known if she wrote any other operas or composed other music. *La Double Recompense*, 1805, is often attributed to Jeanne but was composed by her husband.

Works

1800 *Praxitèle, ou la Ceinture*, opera, Paris

(Source: Letzer and Adelson)

Mlle. Bellet (Early 19th century)

Her operetta was performed in Hamburg in 1901.

Works

Les Tribulations d'un réserviste, operetta, librettist: Croissot

(Source: Cohen)

Mlle. Le Sénéchal de Kerkado (c1786–1805 or later) was another of the women whose first operas were written and performed when she was in her teens.

Works

1805 *La Méprise volontaire ou La double leçon*, operetta, librettist: Alexander Duval,
   Opéra-Comique, Paris

(Source: Sadie and Samuel)

Sophie Gail (August 28, 1775, Paris–July 24, 1819) began her career in
the 1790s by publishing musical romances in popular music periodicals. She
married Jean-Baptiste Gail when she was eighteen, but they separated several
years later. She made a successful tour as a singer in southern France and
Spain. Impoverished by the revolution, she earned money as a professional
musician, working with the musicians and authors she knew, and often collaborating with them. She composed airs for a play by Alexander Duval.

Sophie's first opera, *Les Deux Jaloux*, was very successful, but her second
opera, *Mademoiselle de Launay à la Bastille*, was not (the heroine is based on
Marguerite-Jeanne Cordier Delaunay, Comtesse de Staal.) Sophie's next two
operas, performed the following year, were also unsuccessful. Critics cited
the weak libretti as the problem and not the composing.

Her last opera was a different story, in several respects. Sophie carefully
considered her choice of librettist, finally deciding on Sophie Gay, an Italian
woman who had lived in Paris for several years. Gay knew the artistic, literary
and social world of Paris at that time. She was a pianist, harpist and composer
of romances; her novels were very popular. Apparently she was ready to turn
her attention to writing dramatic works, and Sophie Gail's inquiries about
her writing a libretto came along at the right time. The result, *La Sérénade*,
was a strong success.

Sophie Gail's two most popular operas form bookends for her composing. By 1827 *Les Deux Jaloux* had been performed 196 times and *La Sérénade*
66 times. Pieces from both operas were published separately and performed.

Sophie continued her singing career, performing in London in 1816 and
touring Germany and Austria in 1818. She died in 1819 of a chest ailment. She
was the last of the noted women opera composers who had lived through the
revolution.

Works

1813 *Les Deux Jaloux*, opera, librettists: C.R. Dufresny and Jean Baptiste Charles
   Vial

1813 *Mademoiselle de Launay à la Bastille*, opera, librettists: C. de Lesser, R. Villiers
   and Mme. Villiers.

1814 *Angela, ou L'atelier de Jean Cousin*, opera, librettist: C. Montcloux d'Epinay,
   in collaboration with A. Boieldieu

1814 *La Méprise*, opera, librettist: De Lesser

1818 *La Sérénade*, opera, librettist: S. Gay, after J.F. Regnard

(Sources: Sadie and Samuel; Letzer and Adelson)

Family position and influence was a significant factor for many women composers (and men as well), but the effect of position could cut both ways. The career of **Louise Angélique Bertin** (February 15, 1805, Les Roches–April 26, 1877, Paris) certainly exemplifies the problems that can arise.

Her father, Louis Bertin, and her brother, Armand Bertin, were proprietors and editors of the influential paper *Journal des débats*. The Bertins moved in literary and artistic circles, and Louise loved painting and music and wrote poetry from an early age. Her first opera, *Guy Mannering*, reflects the enormous popularity of Sir Walter Scott's novels. Louise wrote the libretto.

Two years later *Le Loup-garou*, a one-act opera with a libretto by Eugene Scribe, a noted librettist, and E. Mazeres was produced. Louise's ambitions for larger, more complex operas resulted in *Fausto*, in 1831. It had only three performances.

Her next opera, *La Esmeralda*, from *The Hunchback of Notre Dame*, was even more ambitious. Victor Hugo apparently had considered the story's potential for an opera, as he had sketched out an operatic version of the book. Louise had become friends with Victor Hugo, and the two decided to collaborate, Louise writing the music and Hugo the libretto, the only known instance where Hugo collaborated directly with a composer on an opera. The opera opened in 1836, and problems arose immediately. There were accusations of special privilege through the connections of Louise's brother and claims of influence brought to bear on the opera administration. Tensions mounted to the point that there was a riot during the seventh performance, which ended the opera's run. Hector Berlioz had helped Louise with the staging and production, and accusations were made that he'd written the better music in the opera, which he denied.

Louise refused to write any more operas. She did continue to compose— cantatas, chamber symphonies, string quartets, and vocal music. She also wrote and published two volumes of poetry, *Les Glanes* in 1842, which won a prize from the Académie Française, and *Nouvelles glanes* in 1876. Louise died the following year.

Works

1825 *Guy Mannering*, opera, librettist: L. Bertin after Sir Walter Scott, Bievres
1827 *Le Loup-garou*, opera, librettists: Eugene Scribe and E.J. Mazeres
1831 *Fausto*, opera, from Goethe
1836 *La Esmeralda*, opera, librettist: Victor Hugo, after his novel *Notre-Dame de Paris*
(Source: Sadie and Samuel)

Louise Geneviève La Hye (March 8, 1810, Charenton–November 17, 1838, Paris), a child prodigy, studied first with her father, then at age eleven was admitted to the Paris Conservatoire. She was a pianist and organist. It is said that when she was twenty she was invited to teach harmony to a class of young women at the conservatoire; also, her fantasy for organ and orchestra (she was the organ soloist) was performed in a conservatoire performance that next year, in 1831.

After her marriage Louise gave up her conservatoire position to move to Cambrai, but she soon returned to Paris and resumed teaching. Subsequently her opera/dramatic choral work *Le Songe de la religieuse* was performed. Never in good health, she died at the age of twenty-eight, leaving two young children.

Works

1835 *Le Songe de la religieuse*, opera
(Source: Sadie and Samuel)

Romances continued to be very popular, particularly those by **Louise [Loïsa] Puget** (February 11, 1810, Paris–November 27, 1889, Pau). Louise frequently performed in the romances. She composed more than three hundred, many of them translated into English and German, and they appeared in piano arrangements and illustrated volumes.

The texts were written by Gustave Lemoine, an actor, whom Louise married in 1842. The success she had with her romances encouraged her to write opera, and she began studying with Adolphe Adam. Her first operetta, *Le Mauvais Oeil*, with libretto by Eugene Scribe and Gustave Lemoine, was performed at the Opéra-Comique in 1836. Many years later, in 1869, her second operetta, *La Veilleuse, ou Les nuits de milady*, with text by Lemoine, was performed in Paris. Little else is known about her life.

Works

1836 *Le Mauvais Oeil*, operetta, librettists: Eugene Scribe and Gustave Lemoine, Paris
1869 *La Veilleuse, ou Les nuits de milady*, operetta, librettist: Lemoine, Paris
(Source: Sadie and Samuel)

Mme. Tarbe des Sablons (fl. Mid–19th century)

Works

I Balavi, opera, based on the book *Le Siège de Leyde*, 1850s?
(Source: Cohen)

E. Françoise Péan de la Roche-Jagu (ca. 1820, Brest–1871) began composing when she was young but only later did she study music in Paris.

Works

1844 *Nell*
1845 *Gil Diaze*
1846 *La Jeunesse de Lully*
1846 *Le Jeune Militaire*
1851 *Paul et Julie*
1853 *La Retour de tasse*
1856 *Simple et coquette*
1862 *La Reine de l'onde*

Books by or about Françoise Péan de la Roche-Jagu:

de la Roche-Jagu, Françoise Péan. *Mémoires Artistique de Mlle. Péan de Roche écrit par elle meme.* Paris, 1861.

(Sources: Cohen; http://operadata.stanford.edu/)

Mme. Peigné (pseudonym, Max Silny) (b. ca. 1827)

Works

1867 *Enfermez-la!*
(Sources: Cohen; http://operadata.stanford.edu/)

Germany

Amalie, Prinzessin von Sachsen (August 10, 1794–September 18, 1870), often used the pen name A. Serena for her compositions and Amalie Heiter as a dramatist. She was very well educated; she sang, composed sacred music and chamber music, wrote, and played the harpsichord. She lived in Pillnitz Castle near Dresden all her life. During the Napoleonic wars she and her family had to flee several times, taking shelter wherever they could.

Many of her dramatic works were comedies; some were adapted to the French stage, and some were translated into English. Her composing began in 1811, and she continued to compose for many years. Her comedic operas were particularly popular.

Sources vary on the number of operas she wrote.

Works

1816 *Una donna*, opera, librettist or source: Max Prinz von Sachsen
1816 *Le nozze funeste*, opera, librettist or literary source: Friedrich August Prinz von Sachsen
1816 *Le tre cinture*, opera, librettist/literary source: Max Prinz von Sachsen
1817 *Il prigioniero*, opera
1819 *A l'honneur de Nancy*, opera librettist /literary source: Friedrich August Prinz von Sachsen

1820 *L'Americana*, opera
1821 *Elvira*, opera librettist or literary source: Max Prinz von Sachsen
1823 *Elisa ed Ernesto*, opera, librettist: Amalie, Princesse von Sachsen
1826 *La fedeltà alla prova*, opera, librettist: Amalie, Princesse von Sachsen
1828 *Vecchiezza e gioventù*, opera, librettist: Amalie, Princesse von Sachsen
1831 *Il figlio pentito* or *Il figlio perduto*, opera
1833 *Il marchesino*, opera, librettist: Amalie, Princesse von Sachsen
1835 *La casa disabitata*, opera, librettist: Amalie, Princesse von Sachsen
(Sources: Wikipedia; http://operadata.stanford.edu/)

Bettina von Arnim (1785–1859) was one of those women who seems larger than life: writer, publisher, singer, composer, illustrator ... and the friend of many of the notables of her time. Her brother was the poet Clemens Brentano; she married a poet, Achim von Arnim; and her grandmother Sophie von La Roche was a novelist.

Bettina was close friends with Goethe (for whom she had a warm attachment) and the two corresponded for years. Beethoven was also her close friend. She wrote several books and publications having to do with Goethe and with Beethoven.

Her composing was consistent with her life: unconventional. She utilized folk melodies and traditional themes but her harmonies and phrasing gave them a new sound. She wrote three operas, now lost.

Books by or about Bettina von Arnim (translated into English):

Goethe, Johann Wolfgang, von, and Bettina von Arnim. *Goethe's Correspondence with a Child*. Boston: Ticknor and Fields, 1861.
von Arnim, Bettina. *Diary of a Child*. Boston: Ticknor and Fields, 1861.
von Arnim, Bettina, et al. *Correspondence of Fräulein Günderode and Bettine von Arnim*. Boston: T.O.H.P. Burnham, 1861, c1860.
(Sources: Cohen; Sadie and Samuel)

Johanna Kinkel (July 8, 1810, Bonn–November 15, 1858, London) was a conductor and writer in addition to being a composer. She began composing when she was twenty, focusing primarily on lieder, duets and stage works for amateurs. She also wrote poetry, political articles and art criticism. She married, but the marriage was annulled very soon, although the divorce wasn't settled until 1839.

Johanna traveled to Frankfurt and Berlin in 1836. During this time she became acquainted with the Mendelssohn family; Felix admired her compositions. She remained in Berlin to study composition and piano and came to be friends with Fanny Mendelssohn and Bettina Brentano Arnim. Her stage works were known for their humor and irony, and they attracted good audiences.

In 1840 she met Gottfried Kinkel, a theologian and amateur poet who would later become an art historian. Three years later they were married. Gottfried Kinkel became prominent as a political leader in the turmoil of 1848; the following year he was imprisoned. Johanna, whose politics were no less critical than Gottfried's and who was active as a newspaper publisher and writer, found it expedient to move to Cologne. When Gottfried was finally freed they moved their family to London. Johanna stopped composing and became an advocate of women's rights. A victim of depression, she committed suicide.

Works

Before 1840 *Die Landpartie*, operetta

Books by or about Johanna Kinkel:

Burckhardt, Jacob. *Briefe Jacob Burckhardts an Gottfried und Johanna Kinkel*. Basel: Benno Schwabe, 1921.
Hans Ibeles in London. Stuttgart, 1860.
Kinkel, Johanna. *Piano Playing: Letters to a Friend*. Translated, edited and annotated by Winifred Glass and Hans Rosenwald. Chicago: Publishers Development, 1943(?)
(Sources: Cohen; Sadie and Samuel)

Elise Schmezer (1810–1856)

Works

1823 *Otto der Schütz*, opera
(Source: Cohen)

Caroline Wiseneder (Brunswick, Germany–August 25, 1868, Brunswick) founded singing societies and the Wiseneder Music School for the Blind, which became a model for other schools in Germany. She invented a moveable tactile chart for pupils to use. Her husband, Wiseneder, was an opera singer.

Works

1848 *Die Palastdame*, opera
1849 *Das Jubelfest* or *Die Drei Gefangenen*, opera
(Sources: Cohen; Laurence)

Italy

Marianna Bottini (November 7, 1802, Lucca, Italy–January 24, 1858, Lucca) was born into a noble family. Her *Stabat mater* and *Messa da Requiem*, written in 1819 in memory of her mother, attracted the attention of the Accad-mia Filarmonica in Bologna, who admitted her as "Maestra compositrice onoraria." She married Lorenzo Bottini, who was a marquis.

Although most of her works were written between the ages of 13 and 20, she provided compositions for the traditional Luccan festival in honor of St. Cecilia six times from 1822 to 1840. She was the only woman to do so.

In addition to her opera she wrote two cantatas and other vocal music, and music for orchestra and for various instruments.

Works

1822 *Elena e Gerardo*, operetta, unperformed
(Source: Sadie and Samuel)

Gabrielle Melia (19th century)

Works

1823 *Matilde nel castello delle Alpi*, opera
(Source: Cohen)

Adelaide Orsola Appignani (c. 1807–September 30, 1884, Rome) was a singer and conductor in addition to her composing. When her mother, a widow, married the violinist Andrea Aspri, Adelaide adopted her stepfather's surname and used Orsola as her first name.

She was a member of the Roman Accademia Filarmonica and sang in a performance of Donizetti's *Anna Bolena*. In 1842 she was offered an honorary membership of the Accademia di Santa Cecilia.

Works

1827 *Le avventure di una giornata*, melodrama, Rome
1834 *I riti indiani*, opera, not performed
1835 *Francesca da Rimini*, opera, not performed
1843 *Il pirati*, opera, librettist: G.E. Bidera
(Source: Sadie and Samuel)

Like many, if not all Italian composers of this time, **Carolina Uccelli** (1810, Florence–1885, Paris?) was born into a noble family. In 1830 she debuted in Florence with her opera *Saul*, for which she was librettist as well as composer.

Her husband died in 1843. Two years later she and her young daughter, who was a singer, moved to Paris. They gave concert tours in Belgium, Holland and Switzerland.

Works

1830 *Saul*, opera, librettist: Uccelli, Florence
1832 *Emma di Resburgo*, opera, librettist: Gaetano Rossi
(Sources: Sadie and Samuel; http://operadata.stanford.edu/)

Felicita Casella (c.1820, Bourges (?)–after 1865), an Italian composer of French birth, was sister of the composer and pianist Louis Lacombe. She married Cesare Casella, an Italian composer and cellist, before 1849. The two went to Oporto, and it was there that her Portuguese opera, *Haydee*, was given in 1849. She revised the opera, and four years later it was given in Lisbon, with her singing the principle role. She also wrote works for piano and for voice and piano.

Works

1849 *Haydée*, opera, after Dumas' *Count of Monte Cristo*, librettist: Luiz Felipe Leite
1865 *Cristoforo Colombo*, opera, librettist: Felice Romani, Nice
(Source: Sadie and Samuel)

Poland

Julia Grodzicka-Rzewuska (19th century)

Works

1821 *Obiadek z Magdusia*, comic opera
1825 *Malzonek swzystkich kobiet*, comic opera
(Source: Cohen)

Milaszewska (early 19th century) Poland

Works

1824 *Aspazja i Perykles*, opera, librettist: J. Mlocka
(Source: Cohen)

Spain

Ventura Sánchez de la Madrid (19th century)

Works

1841 *Ruggero*, opera
1842 *Iginia d'Asti*, opera

1850 *Malek-adel,* opera
1854 *La Maga,* opera
(Source: Cohen)

1850–1899

By mid-century, operetta, or *opéra comique,* was popular, and Jacques Offenbach was its best known composer. While operetta was associated with Paris, its popularity was more widespread. The sense of "operetta" has changed over the years. It is often thought of as a musical, but there's a difference. These were operas, but they were lighter in tone than opera, their production tended to be less complex and elaborate (and less expensive), and their vocal lines were less demanding. But to do operetta well required—and still requires—a high degree of professionalism in composing and singing.

Many women composed operettas, likely attracted to them by the fact that they were easier to have produced. And there was a marketing aspect as well: if the demand is high for operetta, it makes sense to write operettas, especially if opportunities are limited for having your grand operas performed. Although other developments were taking place in opera, operettas continued to be popular in parts of Europe throughout the rest of the century, particularly in England, with Gilbert and Sullivan.

Opera continued to flourish in the last half of the nineteenth century. Composers and librettists utilized a wide range of material for "plots," and composers continued to draw on the musical heritage of their country. There was heightened interest in traditional, folk, or indigenous music. Susie Harrison, Ella Adajewsky, and Stella Stocker were particularly interested in this music, an interest that often was reflected in their composing.

Opera during this period was marked by two extraordinary talents: Wagner and Verdi. Richard Wagner had unique gifts of composing, writing and a powerful sense of story and myth. His librettos and music developed together. While librettos almost always precede the music, at times Wagner reversed this, writing the libretto to fit his music. Difficult to emulate, difficult to imitate, he stood alone, and not without controversy. Giuseppe Verdi had a gift for melody and story, and a clear vision of composing opera. He was firmly committed to Italian nationalism. He drew from a range of sources, including Shakespeare and Shiller, for his opera librettos—and, he knew how to put on a good show for an audience. His operas can be easy to listen to, yet they're anything but simple. His popularity continues through the decades.

During this period many women wrote only one or two operas, and few wrote significantly more. Their operas tended to have lighter themes and might closely resemble operettas. As it was difficult to get operas produced, many composers, male and female, found the operetta stage more accessible.

Australia

Florence Menk-Mayer (b. ca. March 27, 1867, Melbourne) was a choir conductor and teacher, as well as a composer.

Works
1887 *Victorine*, opera
(Source: Cohen)

Austria

Henrietta Fahrbach (January 22, 1851, Vienna–February 24, 1923, Vienna) was a member of *the* Fahrbach family, which in 19th century Vienna was as well known as the Strauss family. Henrietta's father, Phillip Fahrbach, was a member of the Strauss orchestra for about ten years. Then in 1835 he formed his own orchestra, which rivalled the Strauss orchestra. After the death of Johann Strauss, Sr., Fahrbach was very successful, but Johann Strauss, Jr., eventually overshadowed him.

Henrietta's brother, also named Phillip Fahrbach, was a composer and conductor. His tours outside Austria and his appearance in Paris for the 1878 Exhibition spread his popularity and made his music more widely known, particularly in Britain.

Information about Henrietta is scant, but it is known she conducted a women's choir and was a music teacher in Vienna. In addition to her operettas she composed vocal music and music for piano, including waltzes, of course.

Several operettas
(Source: *New Grove Dictionary of Music and Musicians.* Edited by Stanley Sadie.)

Contessa Raffaela Rozwadowski (c1816, Graz–June 1906)

Works
1870 *Il Corsaro*, opera
(Source: Cohen)

Emilie Mayer (May 14, 1821, Mecklenburg–April 10, 1883, Berlin) was a notable sculptor as well as a composer. In 1847 she moved to Berlin to study privately. By this time she had composed songs, chamber music, symphonies and overtures. After she'd been in Berlin for three years she gave a very successful concert of her own works. One of her most successful compositions, *Sinfonia in B Minor*, had at least eight public performances by Karl Leibig.

Emilie traveled with her brothers to Vienna and was received by the Archduchess Sophie. She then travelled in Germany seeking to have her music performed and published. All this travel consumed a considerable amount of her resources and apparently affected her financial situation later.

During her lifetime her music was composed widely in parts of Europe, and received much acclaim. Her music is in the Berlin Staatsbibliothek. Although she was the most prolific German woman composer of the Romantic period, most of her music has remained unperformed since her death.

Works

Die Fischerin, operetta
1874 *Le Tonnelier de Nuremberg*, operetta, after E.T.A. Hoffman
(Sources: Sadie and Samuel; http://operadata.stanford.edu/)

Belgium

Eva Dell'Acqua (February 25, 1856, Brussels–February 12, 1930, Ixelles) was the daughter of a well-known Italian painter, Cesare Dell'Acqua, who had settled in Belgium.

Works

1882 *Le Prince Noir*, operetta
1884 *Le Tresor de l'Emir*, operetta
1888 *Le Feu de Paille*, operetta
1888 *Les Fiançailles de Pasquin*, operetta
1888 *Une Passion*, operetta
1888 *Le Secret de l'Alcade*, operetta
1889 *L'Oeillet Blanc*, operetta
1890 *Une Ruse de Pierette*, operetta, Librettist: Fritz van der Elst, Brussels
1896 *La Bachelette*, operetta, Librettist: Fritz van der Elst, Brussels
1900 *Tambour Battant*, operetta, Brussels
1906 *Zizi*, operetta, Librettists: Lannoy and André Leneka, Brussels
1918 *Pierrot Menteur*, operetta, Librettist: Fritz van der Elst *L'Oiseau Bleu*, operetta
(Sources: Cohen; Sadie and Samuel)

Juliette Folville (January 5, 1870, Liège–October 28, 1946) first studied with her father then continued at the Liège Conservatory. A child prodigy, she began her career as a violinist and pianist when she was about nine, touring many parts of Europe. When she was seventeen her work *Chant de Noel* was performed at the Liège Cathedral. She also became known for her interest in harpsichord and was a leader in its revival, playing it in concerts and promoting harpsichord music from the 15th to the 18th centuries. Her compositions cover a wide range, including music for theater, concertos for piano, orchestral suites, symphonic poems, music for orchestra and chorus, cantatas, and music for organ.

Works

1892 *Atala*, operetta, Lille
(Sources: Cohen; Sadie and Samuel)

Canada

Susie Frances Harrison (February 24, 1859, Toronto–May 5, 1935, Toronto) had a successful literary career in addition to her composing. After completing her schooling she was a pianist and singer. She married John W.F. Harrison, who was the organist of a church in Montreal. In 1887 John accepted a position of organist and choirmaster in Toronto; following the move Susan began her literary career, using the pseudonym "Seranus," and published articles in a variety of journals and periodicals. Many of her songs published in the United States and England were under the pseudonym "Seranus"; other songs in England were published under the name "Gilbert King."

She was also a music critic, writing for a variety of publications, and she wrote at least six books of poetry and three novels. She came to be considered an authority on folk music, and she used traditional Irish melodies in some of her compositions. Her opera, *Pipandor*, contains traditional French-Canadian melodies.

Works

Pipandor, opera, Librettist: F.A. Dixon
(Sources: Cohen; Sadie and Samuel; Wikipedia)

Czechoslovakia

Agnes Tyrrell (September 20, 1846, Brno–April 18, 1883, Brno) was the daughter of an English language teacher who had come to Brno. She first studied at the Vienna Conservatory, then with the director of the Brno Musikverein. She anticipated a career as a pianist, but her health restricted her to giving occasional concerts. Consequently she turned to composing, encouraged by Liszt, among others. In addition to her opera, she wrote for orchestra, choruses, piano, and an oratorio.

Works

Bertran de Born, opera, Librettist: F. Keim after L. Uhland, unperformed
(Source: Sadie and Samuel)

Denmark

Thekla Griebel Wandall (February 5, 1866–June 28, 1940) had her first lessons with her father, the composer Theodor Griebel, then studied at the Copenhagen Conservatory and in Germany. She wrote her first compositions when she was sixteen and continued to compose prolifically. By 1933 she had written over one hundred compositions. In addition to her operas she wrote music for chamber ensembles, piano, ballet, incidental music for stage, and vocal music.

Works

1885 *Don Juan de Marana*, opera
1895 *Schön Karin*, opera, Librettist: Eienar Christiansen, Breslau
(Source: Cohen)

England

When **Alice Mary Smith** (Mrs. Meadows-White) (May 19, 1839, London–December 4, 1884, London) was twenty-one, her first piano quartet was performed at a trial of new compositions by the London Musical Society, which subsequently premiered other orchestral works or hers. When she was twenty-eight she married Frederick Meadows White, who was in the legal profession. (Some sources state that he was director of the Royal Academy of Music.) That same year she was elected Female Professional Associate of the Royal Philharmonic Society and in 1884 was made an honorary member of the Royal Academy of Music.

She composed a significant amount of vocal music including cantatas, choral music, duets, and songs, as well as orchestral music, music for chamber ensembles and for piano. Her operetta, *Gisela of Rüdesheim*, was performed in 1865 at the Fitzwilliam Music Society at Cambridge.

Works

1865 *Rüdesheim*, or *Gisela*, operetta, Cambridge
(Source: Sadie and Samuel)

Maude Valerie White (June 23, 1855, Dieppe–November 2, 1937, London) first studied privately in Torquay and London, then at the Royal Academy of Music, where she studied with George A. Macfarren. In 1879 she was awarded the Mendelssohn Scholarship, the first woman to receive that honor. Ill health forced her to resign the scholarship after two years, and she went to South America in hopes of improving her health. By 1883 she was back in Europe, studying in Vienna. She was a skilled linguist, in part because she often traveled in search of an amenable climate. She translated her own song texts and several books.

Most of her compositions are vocal and sacred works; she was well known for her songs. She also wrote a ballet and some pieces for chamber ensembles.

Works

1868 *Figlia della Dora*, opera
Jocelyn, opera
Smaranda, opera

Books by or about Maude Valerie White:

White, Maude Valerie. *Friends and Memories*. London: E. Arnold: 1914.
_____. *My Indian Summer*. London: Grayson and Grayson, 1932.

(Sources: Cohen; Sadie and Samuel)

Florence Marian Skinner (fl. 1870s and 1880s) lived in Italy for many years. Both of her operas were performed in Italy; *Maria Regina di Scozia* was performed in London as well. Florence is sometimes listed as Fiorenza Steward-Stresa.

Works

1877 *Suocera*, opera
1883 *Maria Regina di Scozia*, opera
(Sources: Cohen; http://operadata.stanford.edu/)

Florence Ashton Marshall (March 30, 1843, Rome–1922) was a conductor and a writer in addition to her composing. She studied at the Royal Academy of Music in London. Her husband was Julian Marshall, who was a music collector as well as a writer and businessman. They each contributed to the first edition of Grove's *Dictionary of Music and Musicians*. She also wrote articles for periodicals and several biographies. Florence was an associate of the Philharmonic Society and conducted the South Hampstead Orchestra. Her compositions include vocal music and music for orchestra.

Works

1879 *The Masked Shepherd* operetta, Librettist: E. Simpson-Baikie
1897 *Prince Sprite*, fairy operetta, Librettist: B. Thomas

Books by or about Florence Marshall:

Marshall, Florence Ashton. *Handel*. Great Musicians Series. London: Sampson Low, 1883.
_____. *The Life and Letters of Mary Wollstonecraft Shelley*. 1889.
(Sources: Cohen; Sadie and Samuel)

Marian Ursula Arkwright (January 25, 1853, Norwich–March 23, 1922, Highclere, England) received her MusB in 1895 and her MusD in 1913 from Durham University. Subsequently she won the prize for an orchestral work by a woman sponsored by the magazine *Gentlewoman*. Her *Suite for Strings* was composed for the Australian Exhibition of Women's Work at Melbourne in 1907. She wrote primarily vocal music and chamber music.

Works

The Water Babies, children's operetta, from Charles Kingsley
(Source: Sadie and Samuel)

Ethel R. Harraden (1857, Islington, England–1917, Leamington Spa) grew up with music, as her father was an importer of musical instruments. She studied at the Royal Academy of Music, then worked as a pianist and composer. She married Frank Glover, and the couple settled in Leamington Spa. At that time Ethel became interested in composing for the stage. Her brother, Herbert Harraden, wrote the librettos for her operettas.

Works

1880s *All About a Bonnet*, opera, Librettist: Herbert Harraden, London
1891 *His Last Chance*, operetta, Librettist: Herbert Harraden, London
1895 *The Taboo*, opera, Librettist: Mason Carnes, London
Agatha's Doctor, opera
(Source: Sadie and Samuel)

Annie Fortescue Harrison (Lady Arthur Hill) (1851, Sussex–February 12, 1944, Berks.) was probably best known for her song "In the Gloaming," which she wrote in 1876. *The Ferry Girl* was very popular and was performed at the Gallery of Illustration, the Savoy Theatre and the Gaiety Theatre in London.

Works

1886 *The Lost Husband*, operetta, London
1883 *The Ferry Girl*, operetta, London
(Source: Sadie and Samuel)

Ida Walter (b. ca. 1886, London) studied at the Royal Academy of Music. In addition to her opera she composed some chamber music and songs.

Works

1886 *Florian*, opera
(Sources: http://operadata.stanford.edu/; Cohen)

Sophia Julia Woolf (1831, London–November 10, 1893, Hampstead) was King's Scholar at the Royal Academy of Music three times. She primarily wrote songs and piano pieces, some of which were used in theatrical productions or arranged for orchestra and used as theatrical entr'actes. In 1888 her opera, *Carina*, was produced at the Opera Comique in London and at the Crystal Palace.

Works

1888 *Carina*, comic opera, Librettists: E.L. Blanchard and C. Bridgman, London
(Source: Sadie and Samuel)

The parents of **Marie Wurm** (May 18, 1860, Southampton, England–January 21, 1938, Munich) were German; during her younger years the family was in England but Marie spent significant amounts of time in Germany. Her first teachers were her parents. She first studied in Germany at the Stuttgart Conservatory; subsequently she was a piano student of several noted teachers, including Clara Schumann. In England her composition teachers included Arthur Sullivan and C.V. Stanford. She was one of the few women who won the Mendelssohn Scholarship—and she won it three times in a row—which she used to study composition at Leipzig. Marie was much sought after as a pianist. She made her debut at the Crystal Palace in 1882, then performed in London and in Germany and eventually made her home in Germany. She established a woman's orchestra in Berlin in 1898.

She had three sisters, Adela, Alice and Matilde, who each changed the family name to Verne. All of them were pianists in England. Adela was particularly successful, and she traveled widely giving concerts. She made several very successful trips to the United States. In addition to operas Marie composed music for orchestra, chamber ensembles, and many works for piano; her vocal works include music for choral groups and partsongs.

Works

1890 *Prinzessin Lisa's Fee,* Japanese children's operetta, Lübeck
1921 *Die Mitschuldigen,* opera, after Goethe, Leipzig
(Source: Sadie and Samuel)

Lynedoch Moncrieff (Moncriff) (19th century)

Works

1898 *Pandora,* opera
(Source: Cohen)

The story of the life and career of **Dame Ethel Mary Smyth** (April 23, 1858, London–May 9, 1944, Woking, England) is among the best documented of all women composers, helped in large part by her numerous books of memoirs and her flair for publicity. At times her flamboyance worked to her disadvantage. She also had determination and perseverance—and excellent family connections. And she had talent.

Her earlier education consisted of private tutors and boarding schools. By the time she was seventeen she was determined to have a career in composing, and when she was nineteen, despite considerable opposition at home, she entered the Leipzig Conservatory to study composing. Grieg, Dvorak and Tchaikovsky were also students at the conservatory at that time. However, she felt the standards at the conservatory were low and left after one year to study privately. Through her instructor she met Clara Schumann and Brahms.

When she attempted to have her earlier compositions published she was told that only a few exceptional women had their songs published—namely Fanny Mendelssohn and Clara Schumann—and that was only because of their brother and husband. Still, the publisher said he would print her songs. After her orchestral debut at the Crystal Palace in April 1890, the critics spoke of her as a "promising young composer." The following year she finished her Mass in D. Her first opera, which premiered in Weimar, wasn't well received; however the critics did comment favorably on the orchestration. Her second opera, *Der Wald,* was performed at the royal opera in Berlin in 1902; three months later it was produced at Covent Garden. The following year it became the first opera by a woman to be performed at the Metropolitan Opera House in New York.

The Wreckers, her third opera, is often spoken of as her masterpiece. After being performed in a concert version by the London Symphony Orchestra, it was given its English stage premiere in June 1909. The following year she received an honorary DMus from the University of Durham. She continued to compose, but World War I closed opportunities for her works being performed in continental Europe. Ever enterprising, she decided to focus on writing. Her ten books are largely autobiographical, but since she had an extraordinary circle of friends and acquaintances the books have a broad scope and give a rich picture of the times and the people she knew. There is a CD of *The Wreckers* from Conifer Classics.

Works

1898 *Fantasio*, opera, Librettists: Henry Brewster and Smyth, after Alfred de Musset, Weimar
1902 *Der Wald*, opera, Librettists: Henry Brewster and Smyth, Berlin
1906 *The Wreckers*, lyrical drama, Librettists: Henry Brewster and Smyth, Leipzig
1913 *The Boatswain's Mate*, comedy, Librettist: Smyth, after W.W. Jacobs, London
1922 *Fête galante*, dance-dream, Librettists: E. Shanks and Smyth, London
1925 *Entente cordiale*, comedy, Librettist: Smyth, London

Books by or about Ethel Smyth:

St. John, Christopher. *Ethel Smyth: A Biography*. London: Longmans, 1959.
Smyth, Ethel. *As Time Went On*. London: Longmans, Green, 1936.
_____. *Beecham and Pharaoh*. London: Chapman and Hall, 1935.
_____. *Female Pipings in Eden*. London: Peter Davies, 1933.
_____. *A Final Burning of Boats*. London: Longmans, Green, 1928.
_____. *Impressions That Remained*. London: Longmans, Green, 1919.
_____. *Inordinate [?] Affection*. London: Cresset, 1936.
_____. *Streaks of Life*. London: Longmans, Green, 1921.
_____. *A Three-Legged Tour in Greece*. London, 1927.
_____. *What Happened Next*. London: Longmans, Green, 1940.
(Sources: Cohen; Sadie and Samuel)

Mary Grant Carmichael (1851, Birkenhead–March 17, 1935, London) was best known for the songs and piano pieces she composed; her Mass in E-flat was less successful than her other compositions.

Works

1898 *The Snow Queen or The Frozen Heart*, operetta, after Hans Christian Andersen
(Source: Sadie and Samuel)

In addition to her composing, **Mary Louisa White** (September 2, 1866, Sheffield–January 1935, London) was an English teacher. She wrote piano pieces and pieces for voice and often gave concerts of her works in London and Paris.

Works

1898 *The Babes in the Woods*, operetta
Beauty and the Beast, operetta
(Source: Cohen)

Edith Chamberlayne (19th century) studied at the Royal Conservatory of Music. She composed two symphonies, vocal music, and chamber music, including a Scherzo that was performed at the Crystal Palace in 1895. She wrote one opera, which has been lost.
(Source: Cohen)

Finland

Ida Georgina Moberg (February 13, 1859, Helsinki–August 2, 1947, Helsinki) was the first woman to be recognized as a composer in Finland. Her first studies were in Helsinki, where her teachers included Sibelius, at the Helsinki Orchestral School. She studied at the St. Petersburg Conservatory in 1893 and 1894, attended the Dresden Conservatory from 1901 to 1905, then was at the Dalcroze Institute in Berlin from 1911 to 1912. Subsequently she taught at the Helsinki Music Institute.

Works

Asiens Ljus [The Light of Asia], opera, never completed; fragments were performed
(Source: Sadie and Samuel)

France

Pauline-Marie-Elisa Thys (c1836, Paris–1909) was the daughter of Alphonse Thys, a successful composer of opera comique. Pauline began by composing salon music but soon turned her interest to larger works. She composed over a period of forty years, producing dramas, operettas, operas comique and operas. Many were staged at Paris theaters; others had concert performances. Under the pseudonym Mme. M. Du Coin she wrote at least one novel.

Works

1857 *La Pomme de Turquie*, operetta
1858 *L'Hériter sans le savior*, operetta
1860 *Dieu le garde*, operetta
1861 *La Perruque du Bailli*, operetta
1862 *Le Pays de cocagne*, operetta
1876 *Le Mariage de Tabarin ou La congiura di Chevreuse*, opera, Florence
1878 *Le Cabaret du pot-cassé*, operetta
1880 *Nedjeya*, operetta, Librettist: Pierre Nemo Naples
1881 *L'Éducation d'Achille*, operetta
1883 *Judith*
1887 *La Loi jaune*, operetta

Book by or about Pauline Thys:

Thys, Pauline (Writing as Mme. M Du Coin). *Les bonnes bêtes.*
(Sources: Sadie and Samuel; http://operadata.stanford.edu/)

Hermine Dejazet (1829–1880)

Works

1859 *Le Diable Rose* opera
(Source: http://operadata.stanford.edu/)

Marie (Felice Clemence) Grandval (January 21, 1830, Le Mans–January 15, 1907, Paris) was born into a family that was well-to-do and well connected. Her parents knew many composers and writers. Her father, who was in the Legion of Honor, was a talented pianist, and her mother wrote and published stories. Frederick Flotow, a family friend, taught Marie composition. Later, she studied with Frederic Chopin. Her marriage to the Vicomte de Grandval and the birth of two daughters didn't deter her from her music, and subsequently she studied with Camille Saint-Saëns for two years. In addition to her operas and operettas she composed symphonies, music for a ballet, piano music and vocal works. Her oratorio *La Fille de Jaïre* won the Concours Rossini. She also won the Cartier Prize, given by the Paris Conservatoire, for her chamber music. Because of her social position some of her works were published under pseudonyms.

Works

1859 *Le Sou de Lise*, operetta, Paris
1863 *Les Fiancées de Rosa*, opera comique, Librettist: Adolph Choler, Paris
1864 *La Comtesse Eva*, opera comique, Librettist: M. Carré, Baden-Baden
1868 *Donna Maria Infanta de Spagna*, opera, Librettist: Leiser
1868 *La Pénitente*, opera comique, Librettists: H. Meilhac and William Busnach, Paris
1869 *Piccolino*, opera, Librettist: de Lauzières, after V. Sardou, Paris
c1888 *Atala*, opera, Librettist: Louis Gallet
1899 *Mazeppa*, opera Librettists: C. Grandmougin and Georges Hartmann, Bordeaux
(Sources: Sadie and Samuel; http://operadata.stanford.edu/)

Charlotte Jacques (19th century) was a pianist, teacher and composer.

Works

1862 *La Veillée*, operetta
(Source: http://operadata.stanford.edu/)

Lagier, Suzanne (1833–1893)

Works

1865 *Jupiter et Léda*, opera
(Source: http://operadata.stanford.edu/)

Helene Santa Colona-Sourget (b. ca. February 8, 1827, Bordeaux) is sometimes listed under Santa-Colona-Sourget.

Works

1864 *L'Image*, opera, Librettist: Girard, Paris
(Source: Cohen)

Mme. Sabatier-Blot (19th century)

Works

1865 *Un Mariage per Quiproquo*, opera
(Source: http://operadata.stanford.edu/)

Little is known of the life of **Anaïs, Comtesse de Perrière-Pilté** (1836, Paris–December 1878, Paris). She was a wealthy woman; her town house had a salon for performing her smaller works and a *salle de spectacle* she had specially built for staging her larger works. Her two operas comique were performed privately. Her other three operettas, which were performed in public, were not favorably received.

Works

1866 *Le Sorcier*, operetta, Paris
1867 *Les Vacances de l'Amour*, opera comique, privately produced, Paris
1870 *La Dryade*, opera comique, privately produced, Paris
1873 *Jaloux de soi*, operetta, Paris
1875 *Le Talon d'Achille*, operetta
(Source: Sadie and Samuel)

Caroline de Sainte-Croix (b. ca. 1843)

Works

1873 *Les Rendez-vous galants*, Librettist: Ferdinand Langlé
1874 *Madame de Rabucor*, operetta, Librettist: Adolphe Jaime
1875 *Chanson du printemps*, Librettist: François Bouquet
1875 *Pygmalion*, Librettist: Eugène Hugot
(Source: http://operadata.stanford.edu/)

Louise Haenel de Cronenthall (June 18, 1839, Graz–c1876, Paris) was born in Austria but spent her professional life in France. When she was seventeen she entered the Paris Conservatoire. She was prolific and composed a broad range of music: symphonies, piano pieces, nocturnes, fugues, and dance forms. Louise also made transcriptions of ten pieces of Chinese music, drawing on music from 860 BC to the 18th century. The transcriptions were dedicated to the diplomats who were responsible for the Chinese pavilion at the Paris Exposition of 1867 and also to one of her relatives. She received an exhibition medal for the songs, which were performed daily at the exposition.

Works

1867 *La Nuit d'épreuve*, opera
(Sources: Sadie and Samuel; Cohen)

Daughter of the renowned opera singer Manuel García, **Pauline Viardot-García** (July 18, 1821, Paris–May 18, 1910, Paris) grew up with music and singing. She was her father's accompanist, and both her parents gave her vocal training. Her sister, Maria Malibran, was one of the most noted singers of her time. Pauline's education and musical training were notable. Her composition teacher was Anton Reicha, and her piano teachers were Meysenberg and Franz Liszt. She was fluent in Spanish, French, English and Italian, and in later life she was taken for a native speaker of Russian.

Her father died when she was eleven, and her mother took over her training. Pauline wanted to be a concert pianist, but her mother insisted that she focus on her singing. Her piano playing must have been remarkable. She was nineteen when she married Louis Viardot, who was a noted French writer; he was twenty-one years older than Pauline. Not surprisingly, their house attracted the most distinguished writers, musicians and artists in Paris. She continued to perform in opera; Meyerbeer wrote the role of Fidès for her. In 1859 she sang the role of Orpheus in a French version of Gluck's *Orfeo ed Euridice* (prepared for her by Berlioz). Apparently her performance was stunning; there were 150 performances in three years. Shortly after that, in 1863, she and her family retired to Baden-Baden. Seven years later, the Franco-Prussian War compelled them to move to London. A year later they returned to Paris.

Not surprisingly, many of her compositions are vocal music in various forms; however she did compose instrumental music as well. And of course she wrote opera and operettas. She seemed to know "everyone," and the number of writers and composers she intersected with is fascinating. It's said that Ivan Turgenev fell in love with her when he heard her sing in Russia. Two years later he left Russia and eventually he was part of the Viardot household and close to her children. He wrote the libretti for three of her operas. Pauline's daughter, Louise Pauline Héritte-Viardot (see entry), carried on the family tradition of opera, singing, and music.

Works

1867 *Trop de femmes*, operetta, Librettist: Ivan Turgenev
1868 *L'Ogre*, operetta, Librettist: Ivan Turgenev
1869 *Le Dernier Sorcier* [Der letzte Zauberer], operetta, Librettist: Ivan Turgenev
1879 *Le Conte de fées*, opera comique
1868? *Cendrillon*, opera comique

Books by or about Pauline Viardot:
(Note: The heroine in George Sand's novel *Consuela* was inspired by Viardot.)

Barry, Nicole. *Pauline Viardot*. Paris: Flammarion, 1991.
Fitzlyon, April. *The Price of Genius*. London: Calder: 1964.
Héritte de la Tour, Louise. *Memoires de Louise Héritte-Viardot* [her daughter]. Paris, Stock.
Steen, Michael. *Enchantress of Nations: Pauline Viardot, Soprano, Muse and Lover*. Thriplow: Icon, 2007.

(Source: Sadie and Samuel)

Baronne Almaury de Maistre (1840, Brussels–June 1875, Cannes) spent the last part of her life in seclusion, having never recovered from the death of one of her children. She wrote several religious works, including a "Stabat Mater," in addition to her operas.

Works

Ninive, opera
c1870 *Cleopatre, Reine d'Egypte*, opera, Librettist: M. Bogros
1870 *Les Roussalkas*, opera, Brussels
c1870 *Sardanapale*, opera
(Sources: Cohen; Laurence)

Gabrielle Ferrari (September 14, 1851, Paris–July 4, 1921, Paris) performed as a child prodigy when she was twelve. She studied at the Milan Conservatory, then in Naples, and eventually in France. Charles Gounod encouraged her composing. She continued her career as a pianist. After Gounod died she studied at Leipzig then returned to Paris. Beginning around 1895 her main focus was her composing. Her opera *Le Cobzar* was very successful in Monte Carlo, where it was first performed. However, in 1912, when it was revived in a two-act version in Paris, it aroused much debate and criticism by both pro- and anti-feminist writers. In addition to her operas Gabrielle composed orchestral pieces, piano works, and many songs.

Works

1874 *Sous le masque*, opera
1895 *Le Dernier Amour*, opera comique, Librettist: Paul Berlier
1896 *L'Âme en peine*, opera, Librettist: A. Bernede
1896 *Le Tartare*, opera, Librettist H. Vacaresco
1909 *Le Cobzar*, opera, Librettists: Paul Milliet and Helene Vacaresco, Monte Carlo
Le Captif, opera, incomplete
Lorenzo Salvieri, opera, incomplete
Le Corregidor, opera, incomplete

(Sources: Cohen; Sadie and Samuel)

The parents of **Augusta Holmés** (December 16, 1847, Paris–January 28, 1903, Paris) were Irish and Scottish but had settled in France. Alfred de Vigny was Augusta's godfather, and there is speculation that he may have been her father. Augusta grew up in Versailles. From an early age it was apparent she had an aptitude for poetry, painting and music, but her mother discouraged her musical interests. Only after the death of her mother when Augusta was eleven did she have her first music lessons, with the organist of the Versailles Cathedral. Eventually she became a pupil of César Franck.

Wagner—and her hearing *Das Rheingold*—had a strong influence on her and on her composing. She wrote music on a large scale; she was a strong orchestral composer, and her music often was based on classical and mythological subjects. Her first two operas, *Hero et Leandre* and *Lancelot du Lac*, weren't performed. Her next opera, *La Montagne noire*, was performed at the Paris Opéra but wasn't well received. Her dramatic symphonies and some of her choral works did better, but overall they weren't strongly successful either. Saint-Saens, commenting on her choral work *Les Argonautes*, said it was too noisily orchestrated.

Augusta Holmés had a strong personality in keeping with her composing style. She may have seemed larger than life at times. She dominated the salons, musical and literary, but she also mixed well with people and impressed them with her vitality and lively personality. Saint-Saens, who wanted to marry her (she declined), said, "We were all in love with her." And she did have the admiration of many of the personages of that time. Ethel Smyth, no shrinking violet herself when it came to personality—and who wasn't entirely taken with Augusta's music—said that her music contained "jewels wrought by one who was evidently not among the giants, but for all that knew how to cut a gem." Augusta was for years the mistress of the poet Catulle Mendès, with whom she had several children.

Works

1875 *Hero et Leandre*, opera, Librettist: Augusta Holmes, unperformed
c1880 *Lancelot du Lac*, opera, Librettist: Augusta Holmes, unperformed
1895 *La Montagne noire*, opera, Librettist: Augusta Holmes, Paris; *Astarte*, opera
      Librettist: Augusta Holmés
(Source: Sadie and Samuel)

Louise Pauline Héritte-Viardot (December 14, 1841, Paris–January 17, 1918, Heidelberg) was the oldest daughter of Pauline Viardot-García, the niece of Malibran and granddaughter of the great opera singer Manuel García. She grew up surrounded by music and singing and was taught singing by her mother. Louise continued the family "tradition," teaching singing at the Conservatory of St. Petersburg and the Hochschen Conservatory of Frankfurt and in Heidelberg. Her only opera, *Lindoro*, was produced at Weimar in 1879. She composed a cantata, *Das Baccusfest*, which was performed in Stockholm in 1880, as well as many songs and a string quartet. In 1881 Louise married Héritte, the French consul-general at the Cape of Good Hope, where they lived for several years. They then moved to Paris, and eventually settled in Berlin, in 1886.

Works

1879 *Lindoro* comic opera, Weimar

      Books by or about Louise Pauline Héritte-Viardot:

Héritte de la Tour, Louise. *Mémoires de Louise Héritte-Viardot: une famille de grands musiciens : notes et souvenirs anecdotiques sur Garcia, Pauline Viardot, La Malibran, Louise Héritte-Viardot et leur entourage.* Paris: Stock, 1923.
(Sources: New Grove; Cohen)

Marguerite Olagnier (1844, Paris–1906, Paris)

Works

1881 *Le Saïs*, opera
Le Persan opera, never performed
Lilipa, operetta, never performed
(Sources: Cohen; http://operadata.stanford.edu/)

Some composers are so closely associated with particular forms of music that it comes as a surprise to learn this woman composed an opera as well. **Cécile Chaminade** (August 8, 1857, Paris–April 18, 1944, Monte Carlo), so well known for her piano music in particular, is one such composer. As with so many composers, her mother, who was a pianist and a singer, was her earliest teacher. Her father was opposed to her attending the Paris Conservatoire, so she studied privately with various faculty members. When she was about 23 she began to compose seriously, and it was during this period that she composed her opera, which was performed privately.

Her compositions were very popular, particularly in England and the U.S., and Cécile made extensive concert tours to promote her music, performing regularly in England. Chaminade Clubs were formed in many cities around 1900, but not until 1908 did Cécile determine to make the trip to the U.S. She appeared in 12 cities, mainly on the East Coast and in the Midwest. They were successful financially; critically, though, the reception was lukewarm.

In 1901 she married Louis-Mathieu Carbonel, a music publisher who was considerably older than she and died in 1907. In 1913 she was awarded France's Legion of Honor, the first for a woman composer. Because of declining health and then the upheaval of World War I, Cécile was composing much less than in the past, and she'd reduced the number of public performance. However, between 1901 and 1914 she made several recordings. It appears that she never attempted another opera.

Works

1882 *La Sevillane*, opera comique, Librettist: Édouard Guinaud, privately performed
(Source: Sadie and Samuel)

Émilie Mathieu (19th century)

Works

1883 *Une Heure de liberté*, opera, Librettist: Émilie Mathieu. Paris
(Source: Cohen)

Célanie Carissan (b. ca. 1859, Nancy)

Works

1889 *La Jeunesse d'Haydn*, operetta
1892 *La Fiancée de Gael*, operetta
1895 *La Ballade de plongeur*
(Source: http://operadata.stanford.edu/)

In 1881 **Hedwige Chrétien** (1859–1944) won first prize in harmony and fugue at the Paris Conservatoire. That achievement and the fact that she later became a professor at the Conservatoire are about all that's known of her life. However her music leaves a significant track: a ballet, two comic operas, an operetta, vocal music, a number of orchestral pieces, and pieces for various instruments. The University of Michigan has copies of some of her works in their Woman Composers collection.

Works

1889 *Le Menuet de l'impératrice*
1891 *La Cinquantaine*
1904 *Petit Lunch*

(Sources: Sadie and Samuel; http://operadata.stanford.edu/)

In addition to composing **Amélie Pérronnet** (pseudo. Leon Bernoux) (c1831–October 1903, Paris) wrote poetry and, not surprisingly, the libretto to at least one of her operas.

Works

1906 *Je Reviens de Compiègne*, opera, Librettist: Amélie Pérronnet
1877 *Le Chanson d'Aubèpin*, operetta. Librettist: Amélie Pérronnet
St. Francois, opera
1881 *Le Sansonnet*
1884 *Les Révoltés de Lilline*
1887 *En cabine*, Librettist: Émile Mignot de Lyden
1898 *Cascarette*
1902 *Le Songe d'un soir d'été*

(Source: http://operadata.stanford.edu/)

Mme. Chevalier de Boisval (19th century)

Works

1894 *Le Champagne*, operetta. Librettist: Oscar de Créspy
1895 *Les Amoureux de Marinette*, opera. Librettist: Fabrice de Champville
1895 *Le Jeu de l'amour et du hasard*, opera, Literary source or librettist: Marivaux
1895 *Pierrot Pincé*, opera
1895 *Marivaudage*, operetta. Literary source or Librettist: Mérini
1896 *Assaut de valets*, opera. Librettist: Mérini
1896 *Pepita l'Andalouse*, operetta
1897 *Les Visites d'Yvonette*, operetta. Librettist: Jeanne Violet
1898 *Pan! Pan! C'est l'ésprit*, operetta. Librettist: Alfred de Besancenet
1903 *La Leçon imprévue*, operetta. Librettist: William Burtey
1904 *La Paix universelle*, operetta

(Source: http://operadata.stanford.edu/)

Durand de Fontmagne, Mme. Barone (19th century)

Works

1894 *Folies d'amour*, opera, Librettist/Literary source H. Dracy, Jean-François Regnard
1897 *Bianca Torella*, opera, Librettest: Armand Silvestre
1903 *Le Sergent Larose*, opera, Librettist: Charles Labor

(Source: http://operadata.stanford.edu/)

Mme. Lucy de Montgomery (19th century)

Works

1894 *Aréthuse*, opera, Librettist: Lucy de Montgomery
(Source: http://operadata.stanford.edu/)

Delphine Beauce Ugalde (Mme. Valcollier) (December 3, 1829, Paris–July 1910) began playing the piano when she was six and giving lessons when she was nine. She gave her first public performance, as a singer, when she was eleven. That performance led to solo appearances at the meetings of the Society of Classical Singing. In 1848, at age seventeen, she made her debut at the Opéra Comique, then sang at the Theatre-Lyrique until 1858. There, she was particularly successful in the operettas of Offenbach. Her husband was a musician; her daughter, Marguerite, was a singer.

Works

1867 *Une Halte au Moulin*, opera comique, Librettist: Constant Jardry
1895 *Le Page de Stella*, operetta, Librettist: L. Charley

(Sources: Cohen; http://operadata.stanford.edu/)

Raffaela Franchino (19th–20th centuries)

Works

1899 *Le Mariage par ruses*, opera
1905 *Babet et Colin*, opera

(Source: http://operadata.stanford.edu/)

Germany

By the time **Ingeborg von Bronsart** (August 12 or 24, 1840, St. Petersburg–June 7, 1913, Munich) was eight she was showing outstanding talent as a pianist and in composing. When she was fifteen she studied at St. Petersburg, then in 1858 she moved to Weimar to study with Liszt, who held her in high regard as a pianist and a composer. Late in 1858 she began a successful career as a travelling virtuoso, an activity that lasted for ten years. Her husband whom she had married in 1861 was often her accompanist. When Hans was appointed Intendant at the court theaters in Hanover and then in Weimar, Ingeborg had to end her career as a pianist. She then concentrated on composing, primarily songs and operas.

Her *Kaiser-Wilhelm-Marsch*, composed in 1871, was featured at the 1893 World Columbian Exposition in Chicago, where women composers were one of the many focuses of the Exposition. She wrote widely, particularly vocal music and music for piano.

Works

1867 *Die Göttin von Sais, oder Linas und Liane*, opera, Librettist: Friedrich Meyer, Berlin, lost
1873 *Jery und Bätely*, operetta, after Goethe, Librettist: Kahnt, Leipzig
1891 *Koenig Hiarne*, opera, Berlin, Librettist: Hans von Bronsart, Friedrich von Bodenstedt
1909 *Die Sühne* Dessau Hoftheater, Librettist: Ingeborg von Bronsart, possibly with Theodore Korner

(Sources: Sadie and Samuel; http://operadata.stanford.edu/)

Georgine Christine Maria Anna Eschborn (May 13, 1828, Mannheim–1911, Lubbichow) was from a musical family. She, her sister Nathalie, and her brother Karl sang in Amsterdam in Mozart's *Magic Flute* as the three Genies when Georgine was nine. It's likely the three received their musical education from their father. Georgine was the most prolific composer in the family, but few of her works were performed.

Works

Alpenrose, operetta
(Source: Cohen)

Auguste Goetze (February 24, 1840, Weimer–April 29, 1908, Leipzig) was considered a very talented singer; her father, Franz Goetze, was a vocal teacher. Auguste began an opera school in Dresden in 1875.

Works

Susanna Monfort, opera
Magdalena, opera
Eine Heimfahrt, opera
Vittori Accoramboni, opera
(Sources: Cohen; Laurence)

Louise Japha Langhans (February 2, 1826, Hamburg–October 13, 1910, Wiesbden) is variously listed under "Japha" and "Langhans." A pianist from an early age, Louise gave her first concert at age twelve. About that time she met Johannes Brahms, who was seven years younger than Louise. They practiced together and discussed his early compositions. This became a long-lasting friendship; Brahms dedicated one of his early works to Louise and her sister Minna.

Louise was invited by Clara Schumann to come to Dusseldorf with her sister to study with the Schumanns—and there she met up again with Brahms. Her husband, Wilhelm Langhans, whom she married in 1858, was a composer and a music writer. After her marriage Louise continued her performing career, particularly in Paris. She came to know many of the celebrated composers of that time, including Liszt, Heller, Saint-Saëns, Franck and Rossini. In 1874 she and her husband divorced, and Louise settled in Wiesbaden. She wrote one opera, which is lost.

(Sources: Cohen; Wikipedia)

Luise Adolpha Le Beau (April 25, 1850, Rastatt, Germany–1927, Baden-Baden) was also a student of Clara Schumann for a brief period of time. Luise's main teacher was Joseph Rheinberger; the family moved to Munich in 1874 for the express purpose of her being able to study with him. She made a strong beginning and achieved much success; her compositions were well reviewed and they often won prizes. Her Op. 24 Cello Pieces won an international competition; the certificate of winning already having been printed with "Herr," this had to be crossed out and replaced with "Fraulein."

But matters went awry. Luise got on the wrong side of people with some frequency throughout her life. She became estranged from Rheinberger and increasingly had trouble arranging performances of her works in Munich, a development she blamed on the estrangement. Her family, who was certainly supportive, moved to Wiesbaden seeking opportunities for Luise, then five years later to Berlin, and finally to Baden-Baden. But opportunities didn't seem to pan out for her. She was, however, one of the composers featured at the World Columbian Exposition in Chicago in 1893.

Works

1888 *Hadumoth*, opera
1901 *Der verzauberte Kalif*, fantasy opera, Librettists: Le Beau and L. Hitz

Books by or about Luise Le Beau:

Le Beau, Luise. *Lebenserinnerungen einer Komponistin* [autobiography]. Baden-Baden, 1910.

(Sources: Glickman and Schleifer; Sadie and Samuel)

Louisa Mars (b. ca. 1880s)

Works

1889 *Leoni, the Gypsy Queen*, operetta
(Source: http://operadata.stanford.edu/)

Many composers had careers or avocations in addition to their composing. The "other life" of **Emilie Mayer** (May 14, 1821, Mecklenburg–April 10, 1883, Berlin) was one of the more unusual. She first composed dances and variations but soon branched out into other areas. She moved to Berlin in 1847 to continue her studies and broaden her composing. In 1850 she gave a concert of her own works that included a concert overture, string quartet, choral setting for chorus and orchestra, two symphonies, and several piano solos. She was a remarkably prolific composer, with many orchestral pieces, music for chamber ensembles, music for piano and vocal music to her credit. Her artistic endeavors were not slighted: her sculptures out of bread were highly sought after.

Works

Die Fischerin, operetta
Le Tonnelier de Nuremberg, operetta
(Source: Sadie and Samuel)

Julie von Pfeilschifter (b. ca. April 15, 1840, Mannheim) composed ballet and opera.

Works

Agneta, opera
(Source: Cohen)

Hendrika van Tussenbroek (December 2, 1854, Utrecht–June 22, 1935) was known for her music for children.

Works

Three Little Lute Players, children's opera, Librettist: Tussenbroeck
Several miniature operas
(Sources: Cohen; Laurence)

Elsa Laura von Wolzogen (b. ca. August 5, 1876, Dresden) was a lutenist in addition to her composing. She and her husband, Ernst Wolzogen, toured the United States in 1910 and 1911.

Works

Der Heiligenschein, opera
(Source: Cohen)

Hawaii

Lili'uokalani, Queen of Hawaii (September 2, 1838, Honolulu–November 11, 1917, Honolulu), in terms of musical fame was perhaps best known for her song "Aloha'oe." She was knowledgeable about both western European music and Hawaiian music, and was likely the first Hawaiian to bring the two traditions together. She played piano, organ, and several plucked string instruments. Her musical training began at Chiefs' Children's School. In 1866 her composition *He mele lāhui Hawai'i* was published; it was her first music publication and was the Hawaiian national anthem for ten years. She was designated heir apparent by her brother (King) David Kalakaua in 1877; at that time she received the name Lili'uokalani. In 1891 she became queen. Two years later she was deposed.

Works

Mohailani, comic opera, incomplete

Books by or about Lili'uokalani:

Lili'uokalani, Queen of Hawaii. *Hawaii's Story by Hawaii's Queen*, 1898. Boston: Lee and Shepard, 1899, c1898.
_____. *Music of Hawaii*, 1898.
Stone, Adrienne. *Hawaii's Queen, Liliuokalani*. New York: Messner, 1947.
(Source: Sadie and Samuel)

Ireland

Annie Wilson Patterson (October 27, 1868, Lurgan–January 16, 1934, Cork) was the first woman to earn—and receive—the DMus from the Royal University of Ireland. She had a strong interest in traditional Irish music, collecting, arranging and publishing the traditional music. In 1897 she was an organizer and founder of the Feis Ceoil, the Irish Musical Festival. She gave radio talks and lectures and wrote on Irish music and music appreciation. Annie was appointed lecturer in music, with a specialty in Irish music, at University College in Cork. Her compositions include songs, choral works and cantatas, and symphonic pieces. Reputedly she composed at least two operas; Norton Grove comments that there is no record of publication or performance.

Works

The High-King's Daughter, opera, Librettist: Annie Patterson
Oisín, opera, Librettist: Annie Patterson

Books by or about Annie Patterson:

Patterson, Annie Wilson. *Chats with Music Lovers*. London: T.W. Laurie, 1907.
_____. *Great Minds in Music*.
_____. *How to Listen to an Orchestra*. London: Hutchinson, 1913.
_____. *The Music of Ireland*.
_____. *The Profession of Music*. London: W. Gardner, Darton, 1926.
_____. *Schumann*. Master Musician Series. London: J.M. Dent, 1903.
_____. *The Story of Oratorio*. London: Walter Scott, 1902.

(Source: Sadie and Samuel)

Hope Temple (December 27, 1859, Dublin–May 10, 1938, Folkestone) used several pseudonyms, including Alice Maude Davis and Dotie Davis. Hope Temple was the name on the publications of all her compositions. From the age of thirteen she studied in London; her studies included piano, harmony and counterpoint. She intended to have a career as a concert pianist but injured her hand when she was seventeen. Subsequently she moved to Paris for further study. André Messager was one of her teachers. They married in 1895. He was at the Opéra Comique from 1898 to 1904. Hope left her composing and became involved in society and social events. Most of her compositions are songs.

Works

1892–93 *The Wooden Spoon*, operetta, London
(Source: Sadie and Samuel)

Italy

Elisa Ziliotto (1825–c1855?)

Works

1855 *La cena magica*, opera, Librettist: R.G. Spinelli
(Source: http://operadata.stanford.edu/)

Carlotta Ferrari (January 27, 1837, Lodi, Italy–November 23, 1907, Bologna) was a poet as well as a composer. She studied at the Milan conservatory; subsequently she lived in Bologna, where she taught piano and singing. Writing was a strong focus for her, and she wrote her librettos and texts for her songs. She published four volumes of her poetic and prose works.

In addition to her operas she wrote a Requiem Mass, at least one musical drama, and numerous other works and songs. Perhaps it was her interest in literature that led her to choose Oliver Goldsmith's *The Vicar of Wakefield* as the basis for a four-act drama.

Works

1857 *Ugo*, opera, Librettist: Ferrari, Milan
1866 *Sofia*, opera, Librettist: Ferrari, Lodi
1871 *Eleonora d'Arborea*, opera, Librettist: Ferrari, Cagliari

Books by or about Carlotta Ferrari:

Ferrari, Carlotta (Ferrari da Lodi). *Dante Alighieri : poemetto in terza rima.* Lodi: Tipografia di Enrico Wilmant, 1867.
_____. *Roma: poemetta in tre canti.* Roma: Tipografia di Giovanni Polizzi e C., 1871.

(Source: Sadie and Samuel)

Teresa Seneke (1848–1875)

Works

1866 *Le due amiche*, opera, Rome
(Source: http://operadata.stanford.edu/)

Alceste Gambaro (19th century)

Works

1882 *Alceste*, opera
1882 *La perla del villaggio*, opera, Librettist: Egisto Gerunzi
(Source: http://operadata.stanford.edu/)

Adelina Marra (b. ca. 1858, Catanzaro) was a singer as well as a composer.

Works

1888 *Sara*, opera, Librettist: Vito de Mercurio
(Source: http://operadata.stanford.edu/)

Mary Rosselli-Nissim (June 9, 1864, Florence–September 26, 1937, Viareggio) was talented both in music and art; she was a painter and sculptor and in her later years focused on industrial design. She won first prize at the

1911 Turin International Exhibition. In the 1890s she became well known for her drawing-room songs. Her one-act opera *Nephta* (which she had composed in 1891) won honorable mention at the Vienna Steiner contest. After the 1890s she focused more on her painting, sculpture and industrial design, but she also composed at least two more operas.

Works

1891 *Nephta*, opera
1898 *Max*, opera, in collaboration with Menichetti, Librettist: Enrico Golisciani
1915 *Fiamme*, opera, Librettist: Biovacchino Forzano
1931 *Andrea del Sarto*, opera, Librettist: Antonio Lega, after Alfred de Musset
(Source: Sadie and Samuel)

Gisella Delle Grazie (1868–fl. 1894–1895)

Works

1894 *Atala*, opera, Turin, under a pseudonym
1895 *La trecciaiuola di Firenze*, opera, Trieste
1896 *Il Passaporto del Droghiere* or *Passaporto*, opera
(Sources: Cohen; Sadie and Samuel)

Contessa Ida Correr (b. ca. 1855, Padua)

Works

1809 *La gondoliere*, opera, three acts
(Source: http://operadata.stanford.edu/)

In addition to her opera, **Virginia Mariani Campolieti** (December 4, 1869, Genoa–1941, Milan) composed a cantata, *Apoteosi di Rossini*, which won the Bodoi Prize, chamber music and songs.

Works

1898 *Dal sogno alla vita*, opera, Librettist: Fulvio Fulgonio
(Sources: Sadie and Samuel; http://operadata.stanford.edu/)

Lucia Contini Anselmi (October 15, 1876–after 1913), who had a career as a concert pianist in addition to being a composer, studied at the Rome Conservatory. She often performed outside of Italy. Many of her compositions are for piano, as solo instrument or with orchestra, with cello, or with violin. Her piano work *Ludentia* won a gold medal in 1913 at the International Composers' Competition in Perugia.

Works

La sponda magica, fairy opera
(Source: Sadie and Samuel)

The parents of **Countess Gilda Ruta** (October 13, 1856, Naples–1932?, New York) were well placed in music: her mother was an English singer, and her father was a composer and codirector of the Naples Conservatory. After studying with her father she went to Rome and studied with Liszt. She sang in at least one opera, but it was her career as a concert pianist that distinguished her. She toured widely and eventually settled in New York, where she taught piano and composition. In 1890 she was awarded a gold medal for her vocal and orchestral works at the international exhibition of Florence.

Works

The Fire-Worshippers
(Source: Sadie and Samuel)

Poland

Ludmila Jeske-Choinska-Mikorska (1849, Malachów, near Poznan–November 2, 1898, Warsaw) first studied in Vienna, then continued in Milan, at the Paris Conservatoire, and in Frankfurt. She began teaching in 1877, first in Poznan then in Warsaw. Her composing attracted much favorable attention, particularly her songs and comic operas. She was awarded a special diploma at the World Columbian Exposition in Chicago, 1893, for her ballad "Rusalka" and her operatic overtures. The next year she received a medal at the 1894 exhibition at Amsterdam.

Works

1884 *Zuch dziewczyna*, operetta, Librettist: K. Kazeski, Warsaw
1892 *Markiz de Créqui*, operetta, Warsaw

Books by or about Ludmila Jeske-choinska-Mikorska:

Jeske-Choinska-Mikorka, Ludmilla. *Muzykanci* [a novel]. Warsaw, 1884.
(Sources: Sadie and Samuel; http://operadata.stanford.edu/)

Russia

Ella Adajewsky (February 10/22, 1846, St. Petersburg–July 26, 1926, Bonn). The spelling of her last name varies. Cohen lists her as "Adajewsky";

Norton Grove lists her under "Adayevskaya," identified as a pseudonym. After attending the St. Petersburg Conservatory from 1862 to 1866, Ella was a concert pianist touring in Russia and Europe. Her composing career began about 1870 when she started composing choruses for the Imperial Chapel Choir. She dedicated *Zarya Svobodi* to Alexander II, but the censor rejected the opera because of a scene of peasant uprising.

Ella was very interested in the music of ancient Greece, the Greek chuh, and Slavonic folksong. This led to her composing a fantasia, *Greek Sonata*, using quarter tones for clarinet and piano. She moved to Venice about 1891, then twenty years later moved to Germany with her friend Baroness von Loë. They became part of the artistic circle around the poet Carmen Sylva. Ella increasingly became involved in her research on folk music and published widely. She is considered to be among the pioneers of modern ethnomusicology.

Works

Neprigozhaya [The Homely Girl], opera
1873 *Doch' boyarina* [The Boyar's Daughter], opera
1877 *Zarya svobodi* [The Dawn of Freedom], opera
Solomonida Saburova, comic opera, in manuscript

(Sources: Cohen; Sadie and Samuel)

In 1862 **Valentina Serova** (1846, Moscow–June 24, 1924, Moscow) began studying at the St. Petersburg Conservatory, having been awarded a scholarship to study piano with Anton Rubinstein. The composer Alexander Serov heard her improvising—at which she was very skillful—and remarked, "Too bad you're not a boy!" Valentina rejoined, "And why can't a girl be a composer?" Subsequently she left the conservatory to study privately with Serov. They married in 1863. About four years later they published a book on music and theater that included Valentina's earliest writings on music.

Serov died in early 1871, leaving incomplete his latest opera, which was scheduled to premiere in late spring. Valentina, with help from Nikolay Solov'yov, finished the opera in time for the opening. This rejuvenated her interest in composing, and she went on to compose four operas of her own. She continued writing, primarily music criticism, and was a strong supporter of music education for people. Valentina and Alexander's son, Valentin Serov, became a noted portrait painter.

Works

1885 *Uriel Acosta*, opera, Librettist: Serova and P. Blaramberg, after C. von Gutschow's novel, *Moscow*
1880s *Marie d'Orval*, opera, Librettist: Serova, music is lost

1899 *Il'ya Muromets*, opera, Librettist: Serova, Moscow
1904–05 *Vstrepenulis* [They Roused Themselves Up], opera, Librettist: Serova, lost

Books by or about Valentina Serova:

Pushnova, Natalia. *Valentina Serova: krugotchuzhdeniia.*
(Sources: Sadie and Samuel; http://operadata.stanford.edu/)

Scotland

The family of **Mildred Marion Jessup** (October 6, 1868–June 9, 1897), who was born at Glamis Castle, was of noble heritage. Mildred was in delicate health, and her sister Maude, a violinist, occupied the musical spotlight in the family. According to the press, Mildred's health was such that medical advisors "practically ordered" the family to leave Glamis Castle and winter in Egypt.

Mildred's husband, Augustus Jessup, was a wealthy American businessman. He bought the Schloss Lenzburg in Switzerland, which dated from the twelfth century. The reconstruction he undertook was formidable—and expensive. He wrote the libretto to her opera *Etelinda*. The opening was a considerable success; at that point the audience didn't know the name of the opera. After the next performance, which was followed by much cheering and acclaim, Lady Mildred made a curtain call. The press commented favorably on her success with the "fastidious musical public of Florence." Cohen erroneously lists her as "American."

Works
1894 *Etelinda*, opera
(Sources: http://www.scottishmusiccentre.com/directory/r50240/; http://operadata. stanford.edu/)

Spain

As a child, **Soledad Bengoecha de Cármena** (March 21, 1849, Madrid–1893, Madrid) took part in concerts her father organized at home. When she was eighteen her Mass was performed to much acclaim by the public and critics. In 1874 her zarzuelas were produced in Madrid, also to favorable critical review.

Works
1874 *Flor de los cielos*, zarzuela, Madrid
1874 *El gran día*, zarzuela, Madrid
1876 *A la fuerza ahorcan*, zarzuelea, Madrid
(Source: Sadie and Samuel)

Luisa Casagemas (December 13, 1863, Barcelona–after 1894) began the opera *Schiava e Regina* when she was sixteen and finished it when she was eighteen. It received a prize at the 1893 World Columbian Exposition. The opera had a rather checkered career in production. In 1893 it was to have been performed at the Liceu Theater in Barcelona, but an earlier anarchist attack on the Liceu caused the performance to be cancelled. The royal family then arranged for a performance of excerpts at the royal palace in Madrid the next year. In addition, some of the numbers were arranged for voice and piano and published. There was also a soirée performance with Casagemas performing passages on the piano. Luisa is credited with numerous pieces for voice and piano, pieces for various instruments, and another opera.

Works

1881 *Schiava e regina*, opera, Librettist: J. Barrett. This won a prize at the World's Columbian Exposition
I briganti Monserrat, opera
(Source: Sadie and Samuel)

Sweden

Elfrida Andrée (February 19, 1844, Visby, Sweden–January 11, 1929, Stockholm) was the first woman organist in Sweden, the first to compose chamber and orchestral music, and the first to conduct a symphony orchestra. She also was also the first woman telegraphist in Sweden.

Elfrida and her sister, Fredrika Stenhammar, learned music from their father. (Fredrika went on to be a famous opera singer). Elfrida was fourteen when she passed the examination that would allow her to be an organist, having had to prepare for it on her own when the school involved blocked her from doing the customary preparatory work in hopes she wouldn't succeed in the exam, or even take it. Elfrida later was influential in the revision of the law to allow women to hold the office of organist.

In 1867 she moved to Göteborg and was organist at the cathedral until her death. She organized a series of people's concerts that were very popular and through the years gave about eight hundred such concerts. Her motto was "the education of womankind." In 1879 she was made a member of the Swedish Academy of Music. She composed widely, her works including orchestral symphonies, organ symphonies, chamber music, choral music and music for organ.

Works

1899 *Frithiof's saga*, opera, unperformed, Librettist: Selma Lagerlöf
(Sources: GDM&M-1954; Sadie and Samuel)

Helen Munktell (November 24, 1852, Brycksbo, Sweden–September 10, 1919, Stockholm) first studied in Stockholm. In 1877 she went to Paris to study. She was a pupil and close friend of Vincent d'Indy. In 1910 she returned to Sweden to live, spending winters in Paris.

I Firenze was performed for three seasons in Stockholm. Other works of hers were frequently played by the Société National de Musique in Paris. In 1919 she became a member of the Swedish Academy of Music.

Works

1889 *I Firenze*, opera comique, Librettist: Daniel Fallstrom
(Source: Sadie and Samuel)

United States

Emma Roberto Steiner (1850, Baltimore–February 27, 1928, New York) wrote part (one-and-a-half acts) of a grand opera (*Aminade*) when she was eleven. At the age of twenty-three she was assistant music director for the Rice and Collier Iolanthe Company in Chicago. She turned her attention to conducting, working with several companies and producing Gilbert and Sullivan and other light operas. Soon she became known for her own operatic works. In 1894 she conducted a program of her works with the Anton Seidl Orchestra in New York. In 1903 she became the manager of the Metropolitan Opera, which reputedly wanted to appoint her conductor as well. In all, she conducted over 6,000 performances, more than 50 operas and operettas.

Her compositions include music for orchestra, orchestral arrangements, and piano and vocal music. Theodore Thomas chose four of her works to be performed at the World Columbian Exposition in Chicago in 1893. She conducted concerts of her own works in several venues, including the Metropolitan Opera House and the Museum of Natural History. Emma Steiner had a remarkable career. She and Caroline B. Nichols (1864–1939) were the earliest women to have a full career as conductors.

The early 1900s was a difficult time for Emma. A fire destroyed many of her works, including the only copy of her first opera. A severe illness affected her eyesight. Her father died, leaving a will that excluded Emma in preference of his stepdaughter. Around 1910 she abandoned her career and moved to Alaska, traveling and prospecting in the tin mining fields. She was the first white woman to enter the particular region where she discovered important tin deposits. She returned to the United States after about ten years in Alaska and gave talks about Alaska, then turned to music, writing and performing into the 1920s. In 1925 the Metropolitan Opera had a special performance of her works; this was the last time a woman would conduct there until 1976. Emma helped found a home for elderly and infirm musicians, dedicating some of the proceeds from her music to the home.

Works

1877 *Fleurette*, operetta, San Francisco
1894 *Brigands*, operetta
1894 *Day Dreams*, operetta
1900 *The Man from Paris*, operetta, Librettists: M.I. Macdonald and J. W. Castle
1907 *Burra Pundit*, operetta, Librettist: Katherine Stagg and "Joe-Ker"
The Alchemist, operetta
La Belle Marguerite, operetta
Little Hussar, operetta

(Sources: Sadie and Samuel; Wikipedia)

The father of **Eliza Mazzucato Young** (b. ca. 1858) was Chevalier Alberto Mazzucato, who was the director of the conservatory and the conductor at La Scala, Milan. Eliza composed chamber works and vocal pieces.

Works

1880 *Mr. Samson of Omaha*, opera
The Maid and the Reaper, opera
(Sources: http://operadata.stanford.edu/; Cohen)

The birth name of **Caroline Richings** (1827, England–1882, Richmond, Virginia) was Mary Caroline Reynoldson. As a very young girl, she was adopted by Peter Richings, an American actor. Caroline began as a concert pianist, making her debut in Philadelphia in 1847. Her operatic debut was in 1852 as Marie in Donizetti's *La Fille du Régiment*. Her father formed the Richings Opera Company in 1859; that same year Caroline married Peter Bernard, who was with the company. When her father retired in 1867 Caroline, who had been a pianist and singer, took over as director, and the Richings-Bernard Company performed throughout the United States. Later the company became the Caroline-Richings-Barnard company. Caroline founded The Caroline Richings Old Folks Company in 1874–75, which performed light opera and concerts. Her final appearance was in *The Duchess* in 1881.

Works

1881 *The Duchess*, operetta
(Sources: Cohen; http://www.picturehistory.com/product/id/21952)

Caro Roma (September 10, 1869, East Oakland, California–September 23, 1937, East Oakland, California) began performing as a child. As a teenager she directed an opera company that toured Canada. She attended the New England Conservatory, graduating in 1890. Subsequently she appeared with the Castle Square Opera Company in Boston and the Tivoli Opera House in San Francisco. In 1906 she sang with the Turner Grand Opera in London. Caro also sang in vaudeville. She relocated to Miami and was on the faculty of the Florida Conservatory of Music. A prolific songwriter, Caro had over 1,000 published songs to her credit.

Works

God of the Sea, opera, unperformed

Books by or about Caro Roma:

Roma, Caro. *Some Idle Moments*. 1901?
(Source: Sadie and Samuel)

Constance Fauntleroy Runcie (January 11, 1836, Indianapolis–May 17, 1911, Winnetka, Illinois) grew up in New Harmony, Indiana. Her maternal grandfather was Robert Owen. Both her parents were musicians, and her father was also a composer. In 1852 her father died, and the family moved to Germany, where Constance stayed for six years. She intended to study piano and harp but shifted her focus to composition. She married James Runcie, a minister in New Harmony, in 1861. Constance composed in large forms, which was unusual for American women composers at that time. Her compositions include a symphony, a piano concerto, a violin concerto, the opera *The Prince of Asturia*, chamber music, and songs for which she wrote the text. She also wrote poetry, two novels that were unpublished, and a biography of Felix Mendelssohn. She also founded the Minerva Society in New Harmony in 1859, one of the first women's clubs in the United States.

Works

The Prince of Asturia, opera

Books by or about Constance Runcie:

Runcie, Constance. *Poems, Dramatic and Lyric*. New York, London: G.P. Putnam's Sons, 1888.
(Sources: Sadie and Samuel; Cohen)

Abbie Gerrish-Jones (September 10, 1863, Vallejo, California–February 5, 1929, Seattle) was part of a musical family. She began her music study early and at fourteen was a church organist. Her interests were broad, and she studied languages, psychology and philosophy as well as writing and verse. Abbie wrote *Priscilla* when she was in her early teens, which is considered to be the first complete opera—libretto and score—to be written by an American woman. In addition to opera she wrote music for piano, teaching pieces and vocal music. Her articles and work as a music critic won various prizes and awards.

Works

1885 *Priscilla*, opera, Librettist: Abbie Gerrish-Jones
1917 *The Snow Queen*, opera, Librettist: Gerda Wismer Hoffman, based on Hans Christian Andersen
Abou Hassan, opera, Librettist: Abbie Gerrish-Jones
The Milkmaid's Fair, opera, Librettist: Abbie Gerrish-Jones
The Andalusians, opera, Librettist: Percy Friars
Two Roses, opera, Librettist: Abbie Gerrish-Jones
Sakura-San, opera, Librettist: Gerda Wismer Hoffman
The Aztec Princess, opera, Librettist: Abbie Gerrish-Jones
(Source: Sadie and Samuel)

Louisa Melvin Delos Mars (no information) was the first African-American woman to compose a produced opera, *Leoni, the Gypsy Queen*.

Works

1889 *Leoni, the Gypsy Queen*, operetta
(Source: http://en.wikipedia.org/wiki/Timeline_of_music_in_the_United_States_1880%E2%80%93191#1889)

Emma Marcy Raymond (March 16, 1856, New York City–November 1913) composed chamber music and vocal pieces.

Works

1889 *Dovetta*, opera, New York
(Sources: http://operadata.stanford.edu/; Cohen)

Stella Prince Stocker (April 3, 1858, Jacksonville, Illinois–1925) graduated from the University of Michigan, then studied at Wellesley College and the Sorbonne. She was particularly interested in Native American music and legends, an interest reflected in some of her compositions, and she frequently lectured on Native American music in the United States and abroad. She composed music for piano, vocal music and music for theater.

Works

Beulah, operetta
Queen of Hearts, operetta

1893 *Ganymede*, operetta, performed at the Chicago World's Fair
Raoul, operetta
(Sources: Sadie and Samuel; Cohen)

Mary Carr Moore (August 6, 1873, Memphis–January 9, 1957, California) had a remarkable career, and opera had a significant place in that career. She first studied in San Francisco, and by the time she was twenty-six she was teaching and composing. In 1894 she sang the leading role in *The Oracle*, her first opera. She then decided not to pursue a singing career but instead to focus on her composing and teaching. For the rest of her life she lived on the West Coast and taught. From 1926 to 1943 she was professor of theory and professor of composition (concurrently) at Chapman College in Orange, California. Chapman awarded her an honorary DMus in 1936.

Narcissa is considered to have a strong claim to be the first major "American" opera, but critics denied it that honor for several reasons including these: it doesn't have a romantic interest; the composer wasn't on the East Coast; such an opera should be set on the East Coast during colonial times—setting it on the West Coast was apparently beyond the pale. In 1930 *Narcissa* was belatedly awarded a David Bispham Memorial Medal.

Mary was a prolific composer in areas other than opera: music for orchestra, choral music, chamber music, and music for piano and for organ. Many of her librettos were written by her mother.

Works

1894 *The Oracle*, operetta, Librettist: Moore, San Francisco
1909 *Narcissa or The Cost of Empire*, opera, Librettist: Sarah Pratt Carr, Seattle
1912 *The Leper*, opera, unperformed
1917 *Harmony*, opera, San Francisco
1919 *The Flaming Arrow or The Shaft of Ku'pish-ta-ya*, operetta, Librettist: Carr, San Francisco
1927 *David Rizzio*, opera, Librettist: E.M. Browne, Los Angeles
1929 *Legende provencale*, opera, Librettist: E. Flaig, unperformed
1931 *Los rubios*, opera, Librettist: Nieta Marquis, Los Angeles
1932 *Flutes of Jade Happiness*, operetta, Librettist: L.S. Moore, Los Angeles
(Sources: Cohen; Sadie and Samuel)

Edith Rowena Noyes (b. ca. March 26, 1875, Cambridge, Massachusetts) studied piano under Edward MacDowell in Boston from 1891 to 1896; at the same time, she was studying theory under George Chadwick. She was eighteen when she made her debut as a concert pianist, and she gave concerts of American music throughout Europe from 1899 to 1919. Her compositions include music for orchestra, chamber ensembles, and some vocal and sacred music.

Works
1898 *Last Summer*, operetta
1917 *Osseo*
(Source: Cohen; http://operadata.stanford.edu/)

1900–1939

A change in opera set in almost immediately after the turn of the twentieth century with Debussy's *Pelléas et Mélisande* in 1902. His music was impressionistic and used different harmonies and rhythms. In 1918 Bela Bartók's opera, *Bluebeard's Castle*, premiered in Budapest. Bartok, a Hungarian composer, also used rhythms and harmonies different from the more classical modes. Bartók and Debussy weren't alone in their musical explorations, but their music stands out.

The late 1800s and early 1900s were significant times of musical exploration. Of course such changes didn't come from nowhere. Opera, along with music in general, and art, architecture, and literature had been changing rapidly during the later 1800s. But now, with the new century, there was a particularly strong energy for change. And change was indeed in the air—with different opportunities, inventions, and conveniences. Not all changes were good. World War I was unlike any war the world had ever seen. Music took on a more unsettled aspect. The Jazz Age reflected upheaval and new energy and change, and it resonated in opera.

Interest in traditional music, folk songs, and songs of indigenous people continued. Perhaps the war led to an increased sense of the fragility of peoples and their music. Varvara Gaigerova, Mirrie Hill, Berta Bock, Marguerite Béclard d'Harcourt, Elizabeth Poston, Lily Strickland, and Elisabetta Oddone Sulli-Rao sought out this music and often utilized it in their own composing.

Women were studying in the conservatories, universities, and music academies and institutes, earning degrees, receiving prestigious prizes and scholarships, and being offered significant opportunities in music, all at the international level. There were opportunities to conduct as well. This was also a time when many professional societies and associations for women were formed. Lili Boulanger won the Prix de Rome, the first woman to do so. Les Six, a group of promising music/composition students in France, included Germaine Tailleferre. Giulia Recli was the first Italian woman to enter the symphonic repertory.

More change was to come. The arts are always sensitive to economics, and the Great Depression had an effect that rippled throughout Europe and the Americas. The tensions and changes wrought by the economic upheaval contributed to political upheaval. Music increasingly reflected the unsettled times.

Australia

Florence Maud Ewart (November 16, 1864, London–November 8, 1949, Melbourne) studied in Birmingham and London, receiving her diploma from the National Training School for Music in 1882. She went on to study violin at the Hochschule für Musik in Leipzig. There she was sponsored by Adolph Brodsky, and she worked for him as a tutor. After more study in Berlin she went back to Birmingham, where she gave violin recitals and conducted an orchestra for musical societies. She married Alfred James Ewart, a botanist, in 1898. Upon his appointment as the first professor of botany at the University of Melbourne and government botanist the family moved the Australia.

Florence's *Ode to Australia* for chorus and orchestra was performed at the 1907 Exhibition of Women's Works and met with great success. That led to commissions and requests for compositions from musical and literary societies. Although Florence traveled to England and Europe three times in an effort to have her larger works performed, she was unsuccessful in that endeavor, and her success rested with her songs and smaller-scale works. In the 1920s Florence spent three years in Europe where she studied with Ottorino Respighi. In 1927 she and her husband divorced and Florence began composing again.

Works

c1910 *Ekkehard*, opera, Librettist: Ewart, after J.V. von Scheffel, Melbourne
1930 *The Courtship of Miles Standish*, opera, Librettist: Ewart, after H. Longfellow, concert performance
1933 *Mateo Falconé*, opera, Librettist: Ewart, after P. Merimee, unperformed
1933 *Nala's Wooing*, opera, after *The Mahabharata*, unperformed
c1945 *Pepita's Miracle*, opera, after A. Bridge, unperformed
1949 *A Game of Chess*, opera, after G. Gaicosa, incomplete

(Source: Sadie and Samuel)

Mirrie Solomon Hill (sometimes under Solomon) (December 1, 1892, Sydney–May 1, 1986, Sydney) was one of the first students at the Sydney Conservatorium, which opened in 1916. After graduating she taught at the conservatorium. Her husband, Alfred Hill, also was a composer. Mirrie was interested in music of aboriginal peoples and used those themes in some of her music, particularly *Arnhem Land Symphony*. Her compositions include orchestra pieces, music for various instruments, and vocal music.

Works

1935 *Old Mr. Sundown*, children's operetta
(Sources: Sadie and Samuel; Cohen)

Peggy Glanville-Hicks (December 29, 1912, Melbourne–June 25, 1990, Sydney) had a particularly prolific life in music. She first studied at the Melbourne Conservatorium. When she was nineteen she won the Carlotta Rowe Open Scholarship, which allowed her to study at the Royal College of Music from 1932 to 1936. There, her teachers included Vaughan Williams for composition and Constant Lambert and Sir Malcolm Sargent for conducting. She was awarded the Octavia traveling scholarship in 1936, which she used to study in Vienna and then with Nadia Boulanger in Paris. She married Stanley Bates in 1938; they divorced in 1949.

Her *Choral Suite*, from John Donne, was performed at the ISCM Festival in London, the first time Australia was featured in this festival. In 1940 she and Stanley Bates founded Les Trois Arts, a ballet company. Two years later she settled in the United States, where she lived until 1959 when she settled in Athens. She was cofounder of the International Music Fund to help reestablish European artists after World War II.

Peggy also wrote music criticism, essay entries for the *Grove Dictionary of Music and Musicians*, and numerous articles. With Yehudi Menuhin she was music consultant for concerts of Indian Music at the Museum of Modern Art. She was the recipient of numerous awards and grants throughout her career, including two Guggenheim Fellowships and a Fulbright Fellowship. She composed much orchestral music, music for chamber ensembles, vocal music, ballets, and film music. Her interests in traditional Greek music and Far Eastern folklore are reflected in some of her operas and compositions.

Works

1933 *Caedmon*, opera, Librettist: Peggy Glanville-Hicks, unperformed
1954 *The Transposed Heads*, opera, Librettist: Peggy Glanville-Hicks after Thomas Mann: *Die vertauschten Köpfe*, opera, Louisville
1959 *The Glittering Gate*, opera, Librettist: Peggy Glanville-Hicks after Lord Dunsany, New York
1961 *Nausicaa*, opera, Librettists: Robert. Graves and A. Reid, after Graves' *Homer's Daughter*, New York
1962 *Carlos Among the Candles*, opera, unperformed
1965 *Sappho*, opera, based on Lawrence Durrell's verse play, composed for Maria Callas but unperformed.
(Source: Sadie and Samuel)

Austria

Maria Bach (1896–1978), whose ancestors were members of *the* Bach family, grew up in a musical family. Maria studied violin and piano privately then later attended the Vienna Academy of Music and Performing Arts, where she studied music theory, composition and conducting. Her song cycle was published in 1921. Maria had a successful career as a composer, but the family encountered financial difficulties when her father died. In 1940 she went to Italy with Arturo Ciacelli, a painter, and took up painting. The exhibits of her paintings were very successful, and for a time she had a dual career as a painter and a composer. After Ciacelli died in 1966, Maria gave up both careers but eventually returned to composing. Her papers are in the City Hall Library in Vienna.

Works
Glaukus, lost
(Sources: Sadie and Samuel; Wikipedia; Cohen)

Mathilde Kralik von Meyrswalden (December 3, 1857, Linz–March 8, 1944, Vienna) studied in Vienna beginning in 1876, under Julius Epstein and Anton Bruckner. She then attended the Vienna Conservatory. She belonged to the Austrian Composers' Union and the Vienna Bach Society and was president of the Vienna Women's Choral Society, often composing works for the various groups. In addition to her operas she composed melodramas, masses and other sacred vocal and choral music, leider, an orchestral piece, and music for chamber ensembles and solo instruments. In her vocal works she often utilized texts by her brother Richard Kralik.

Works
Blume und Weissblume, opera
1907 *Der Heilige Gral*, opera, Librettist: R. Kralik
(Source: Sadie and Samuel)

Irma von Halácsy (Vienna December 31, 1880–March 7, 1953, Vienna) was the daughter of a well-known botanist, Eugen Halácsy. Irma studied violin at the Vienna Conservatory. In 1900 she began touring as a professional violinist, continuing until 1912, when she gave up performing and instead focused on teaching and composing. She composed an orchestral piece, chamber music, and vocal music, including many leider, a ballet, and film music. In 1986 original manuscripts of her music were discovered. These are now in a private collection.

Works

1909 *Antinoos*, opera, never performed in a complete form
1921 *Abbé Mouret*, opera, never performed in a complete form
1922 *Der Puppenspieler*, opera, never performed in a complete form
1923 *Herz atout*, opera, never performed in a complete form
1943 *Schelmenrbshaft*, opera, never performed in a complete form
1948 *Salambo*, opera, never performed in a complete form
(Source: Sadie and Samuel)

Vilma (Wilma) von Webenau (February 15, 1875, Constantinople–October 9, 1953, Vienna) was the first student of Arnold Schoenberg. Her grandmother Julia von Webenau (1813–1867) was also a composer. Julia von Webenau, who often is listed as Julia Baroni-Cavalcabò, had studied with Franz Xaver Wolfgang, Mozart's son.

Works

Mysterium, opera
Don Antonio, opera
Der Fakir, opera
Der Poldl, opera
Der Prinzessin, opera
Der Schatz, opera

(Sources: Sadie and Samuel; Wikipedia; Dehardi, thesis, sophie.byu.edu)

Lise Maria Mayer (May 22, 1894, Vienna–March 13, 1968) had a notable career as a conductor and professor. She was professor at the New Conservatory in Vienna. According to the *Chicago Tribune* she conducted operas in Vienna. The article (which includes a picture) also notes "a distinguished composer, her latest symphonic work, Kokain, has been warmly acclaimed." She composed orchestral works, pieces for chamber ensembles, piano music, choral music with orchestra, vocal music, and, reputedly, one opera.

(Sources: Cohen; http://archives.chicagotribune.com/1929/01/06/page/54/article/doing-mens-work-in-europe)

Brazil

Chiquinha Gonzaga (Francisca Edwiges Neves) October 17, 1847, Rio de Janeiro–February 28, 1935, Rio de Janeiro) studied piano in Rio de Janeiro. She married in 1863, but her husband wasn't amenable to her having a music career and she separated from him four years later. She married again but separated from that husband as well.

In 1877 she had her first success as a composer when several of her dances were published. Her operettas were immediately successful; the first led to her being known as "the feminine Offenbach." She was immensely prolific, with seventy-seven stage works. She also composed over three hundred works in dance and song forms, music for band, chamber groups, piano, and vocal music. *Forrobodó* had 1,500 performances. In 1885 she was the first woman to conduct a theater orchestra in Brazil. She was also active in the slave freedom movement.

Works

A corte na roça, operetta, Librettist: Francisco Sodre
1912 *Forrobodó*, operetta, Librettists L. Peixoto and C. Bettencourt
1933 *Maria*, operetta, Librettist Viriato Correa
(Sources: Sadie and Samuel; Cohen)

Cinira Polonio (1861, Rio de Janeiro–1948) was an actress and a singer, having studied in France and Italy. Her debut was in Rio de Janeiro in 1878 when she sang Marguerite in *Faust*.

Works

1919 *O Relogho de cardeal*, operetta
(Sources: Cohen; http://operadata.stanford.edu/)

Griselda Lazzaro Schleder (b. ca. 1889, Sao Paulo) was a choral conductor, teacher and writer in addition to her composing. She graduated from the National School of Music in Rio de Janeiro. Subsequently she directed the First Brazilian Choir, which performed during the opera seasons at the Rio de Janeiro Municipal Theatre. The National School of Music awarded her their gold medal.

Works

E o teu amor, operetta
(Source: Cohen)

Lycia de Biase Bidart (sometimes listed under de Biase) (b. ca. February 18, 1910, Espirito Santo) was a pianist, violinist, conductor, and teacher, as well as a composer. She was a prolific composer, with many works for orchestra, chamber ensembles, piano, music for voice and choral groups, and two ballets. Her Sonata Fantasia no. 1 won a prize in the Viotti international competition in Italy in 1975. In 1978 a catalogue of her works was published by the Ministério das Relações Exteriores in Brazil.

Works

1939 *A noiva do mar*, opera, from the novel by Xavier Marques, *A Noiva do Golfinho*
(Sources: Sadie and Samuel; Cohen)

Canada

Roberta Geddes-Harvey (December 25, 1849, Hamilton, Ontario–April 22, 1930, Guelph, Ontario) earned her BMus in 1899 (at the age of fifty) from Trinity College at the University of Toronto. She was an organist and choirmaster in Guelph from 1876 to 1926. She wrote music for orchestra, many vocal pieces and pieces for piano, and an oratorio, *Salvator*. Her opera was first performed at the Royal Opera House in Guelph.

Works

1903 *La Terre bonne*, also known as *The Land of the Maple Leaf*, opera, Librettist: A. Klugh

(Sources: Cohen; Sadie and Samuel; http://operadata.stanford.edu/)

Albertine Morin-Labrecque (June 8, 1896, Montreal–September 25, 1957), a concert pianist and professor, studied first in Montreal then studied harmony and composition in Paris. She returned to Montreal and attended Montreal University, earning her MusDoc. She then became professor of pedagogy. Her compositions include music for orchestra, band, chamber ensembles, piano vocal music, and a ballet.

Works

1930 *Francine*, opera comique

(Sources: Cohen; http://operadata.stanford.edu/)

Cuba

Maria de las Mercedes Adam de Aróstegui (September 24, 1873, Camaguey, Cuba–October 20, 1957, Madrid) moved to Spain when she was nine. She studied at the Conservatorio Real in Madrid, where she received first prize in piano in 1888. She then studied in Paris; there her instructors included Jules Massenet and Vincent d'Indy. Her music was performed in Paris. She spent time in Spain, giving recitals and playing in chamber concerts with Pablo Casals. Her music also was performed in Cuba, and her opera was given in Havana in the 1930s.

Most of her compositions are orchestral works and songs.

Works

1921 *The National Flower*, opera, Librettist J. Church

(Source: Sadie and Samuel)

Czechoslovakia

Maria Drdova (pseud Constans Konstantin) (September 9, 1889, Blanski–1970) first studied in Vienna. From 1923 to 1925 she studied at the Sorbonne, then she studied in Rome under Respighi for a year. Her compositions include orchestral music, chamber music and a ballet. The Kapralova site credits her with twelve operas.

Works

Six part cycle: *Zeme; Indrani; Drahomira; Ohen; Vzpoura; Vzlet Cil, Vestalka*, opera
(Sources: http://www.kapralova.org/WOMEN.htm; Cohen)

Marie Kucerova-Hersoa (b. ca. February 20, 1896, Kutna Hora) graduated from the Prague Conservatory in 1915. From 1921 until World War II she conducted in theaters and taught at music schools in Tabora and Kutná Hora. She remained active in musical life in Kutná Hora, teaching privately and conducting choirs. Her compositions include music for orchestra, piano, vocal music, music for theater and a ballet.

Works

1938 *Broucci*, opera for children
1938 *Mlady genius*, opera for children
1956 *Tri tovarysi*, opera for children
1956 *Ulicnik Pericko*, opera children
(Sources: http://www.kapralova.org/WOMEN.htm; Cohen)

Denmark

Hilda Sehested (April 27, 1858, Fyn–April 15, 1936, Copenhagen) graduated from the Kongelige Danske Musikkonservatorium in 1901. She was an organist but never pursued a professional career, instead focusing on composing. In 1895 there was a Women's Exhibition in Copenhagen; Hilda, an anti-feminist, refused to take part in the music events of the Exhibition. However in 1916 she wrote and conducted a cantata for Dansk Kvindesamfund, a Danish women's organization. Her compositions include pieces for orchestra, chamber music, and music for piano.

Works

1913 *Agnete og Havmanden*, opera, Librettist: S. Michaelis, accepted at the Kongelige Theater in Copenhagen, never performed.
(Source: Sadie and Samuel)

England

Liza Lehmann (July 11, 1862, London–September 19, 1918, Pinner) initially intended to be an opera singer; Jenny Lind was among her singing teachers. She also studied composition in Rome, Wiesbaden and London. Her vocal range was impressive, but she realized she didn't have the stamina and powerful voice for a career in opera. Liza then turned to performing in recitals and followed a successful career until 1894, when she married Herbert Bedford, a painter. She began publishing her songs. Her most famous one is "In a Persian Garden" based on the *Rubaiyat of Omar Khayyam.*

She made her first tour of the United States in 1910 giving recitals at which she accompanied her own songs. She then became the first president of the Society of Women Musicians, then a professor of singing at the Guildhall School of Music. In addition to her many songs, she wrote several vocal works with orchestra. She also wrote chamber and instrumental works.

Works

1904 *Sergeant Brue*, operetta, Librettists: Owen Hall [pseudonym of J. Davis and J. Hickory Wood], London
1906 *The Vicar of Wakefield*, romantic light opera, Librettist: O.L. Housman, after Oliver Goldsmith, Manchester and London
1907 *Warum der Frühling kommen muss*, opera, Librettist: Therese Lehmann-Haupt
1915 *Everyman*, opera, London

Books by or about Liza Lehmann:

Lehmann, Liza. *The Life of Liza Lehmann, by Herself.* New York, E.P. Dutton, 1919.
(Sources: Sadie and Samuel; http://operadata.stanford.edu/)

Louisa Emily Lomax (June 22, 1873, Brighton–August 29, 1963, Brighton) spent three years at the Royal Academy of Music, where she was a Goring Thomas Scholar. She also won the Lucas Silver Medal and was made an associate of the RAM in recognition to her contributions in music. Eight years later she was made a professor of composition, a position she held for twenty years. Although she received much favorable recognition for the music and librettos of her stage works, her opera never was fully performed.

Works

The Marsh of Vervais, opera, never performed
1905 *The House of Shadows*, opera/stage work, Librettist: Louisa Lomax
1906 *The Wolf*, opera/stage work, Librettist: Louisa Lomax
1907 *The Brownie and the Piano-tuner*, opera/stage work, Librettist: Louisa Lomax

Louisa was also librettist for Walton O'Donnell's comic opera *The Demon's Bride.*
(Source: Sadie and Samuel)

The first published works of **Adela Maddison** (December 15, 1866, sometimes given as 1862, London–June 12, 1929, Ealing) are dated 1882. The following year she married Frederick Brunning Maddison. When Gabriel Fauré came to London in 1894, she and her husband supported him and helped him settle into the musical life of London. By that time her husband was working for a music publishing company; subsequently the company had a contract to publish Fauré's work for five years. The three became close friends, and Adela studied with him.

When Adela moved to Paris in the late 1890s her husband remained in England. She stayed in Paris until about 1905, much involved with the musical life of Paris, meeting Delius, Debussy and Ravel. She then spent several years in Germany, where she composed *Der Talisman*, which was performed in Leipzig and received excellent reviews. During World War I she was in England. Eventually she moved to Glastonbury, where she was involved with the Glastonbury Festivals for many years, creating much of the music.

Works

1910 *Der Talisman*, opera, after L. Fulda, Leipzig
1920 *The Children of Lir*, opera
1920s *Ippolita in the Hills*, opera, Librettist: M. Hewlett
(Sources: Sadie and Samuel; Wikipedia)

Dora Estella Bright (Mrs. Windham Knatchbull) (August 16, 1863, Sheffield–November 16, 1951, Somerset) had several significant "firsts" in her career as a composer. She studied at the Royal Academy of Music; in 1888 she was the first woman to win the Lucas Medal for composition. A noted pianist, she launched her recital career in 1889. That same year she gave concerts in several cities in Germany, playing her Piano Concerto in A minor. The following year the concerto was performed at a Crystal Palace concert. In 1892 she was the first woman to have a composition played in concert by the Philharmonic Society—her *Fantasia in G*—which she played. That was also the year where she gave a recital of English keyboard music, surprisingly the first such recital ever. And, to top off the year, she married Captain Knatchbull. After her marriage she focused more on composition, particularly ballet. She also wrote more orchestral music, choral music, music for piano, and three operas.

Works

1911 *The Portrait*, opera, Librettist: Dora Estella Bright
Quong Lung's Shadow, opera
One other opera
(Source: Sadie and Samuel)

The father of **Frances Allitsen** ("Allitsen" was a pseudonym) (December 30, 1848, London–September 30, 1912, London) was the famous bookseller John Bumpus; her two brothers, John and Edward Bumpus, were music distributors. She studied at the Guildhall School of Music and made her singing debut in 1882, but she was most involved in composing, and her songs became very popular. She also wrote song cycles, dramatic cantatas, and musical dramas. Her opera was published in 1912 but wasn't performed. She kept a detailed diary, with comments, of her dealings with music publishers.

Works

1912 *Bindra the Minstrel*, romantic opera, Librettist: Allitsen, published, not performed
(Source: Sadie and Samuel)

Ellen Coleman (c1886, London–February 5, 1973, London) was composing sonatas when she was fourteen; however she didn't study composition until 1921, when she was about thirty-five. She was well traveled and became friends with many notable musicians of her time. In 1937 and 1938 she had three concerts of her works at the Salle Pleyel-Chopin in Paris. One of her operas, *The Walled Garden* was broadcast twice by the BBC. In addition to her operas she wrote masses, chamber music and many songs. Her archive is at the University of Reading.

Works

The Walled Garden, opera
One other opera
(Source: Sadie and Samuel)

Elizabeth Poston (October 24, 1905, Highfield, Herts.–March 18, 1987, Highfield) studied at the Royal Academy of Music and privately with the organist of St. Paul's Cathedral. Seven of her songs were published when she was twenty. From 1930 to 1939 she toured, particularly in Italy. Her strong interest in art was a factor in her travels; she also collected folksongs. In 1939 she returned to England, where she joined the staff of the BBC, often working with the direction of music in the European Service. During the war years she also was a pianist at the National Gallery Concerts. In 1945 she resigned from the BBC in order to spend her time on composition, in which she was helped by Vaughan Williams. She was president of the Society of Women Musicians from 1955 to 1961. She composed for orchestra, chamber ensembles, and piano, and wrote a large amount of vocal and sacred music. She also composed much incidental music for radio.

Works

The Briary Bush, opera
(Sources: Sadie and Samuel; Cohen)

Phyllis Tate (April 6, 1911, Gerrards Cross–May 29, 1987, London) was a teenager when she began composing foxtrots for her ukulele. She studied at the Royal Academy of Music from 1928 to 1932; her early works, including her first operetta, were performed at the RAM and other venues. She continuously worked as a freelance composer. In 1935 she married Alan Frank, a music publisher, after which time she lived in London. Over a period of years she was involved with a variety of musical organizations.

Works

1932 *The Policeman's Serenade*, operetta, Librettist: A.P. Herbert
1960 *The Lodger*, opera, Librettist: David Franklin, after B. Lowndes, London
1962 *Dark Pilgrimage*, television opera, Librettist: David Franklin
1966 *The What D'ye Call It*, opera, Librettist: V.C. Clinton-Baddeley
1968 *The Story of Lieutenant Cockatoo*, opera, Librettist: Ronald Eyre
1971 *Twice in a Blue Moon*, opera, Librettist: Christopher Hassell
1971 *A Pride of Lions*, operetta
The Scarecrow, operetta for children, Librettist; Michael Morpurgo
Additional operettas for young people

(Sources: Cohen; Sadie and Samuel; http://operadata.stanford.edu/)

Ethel Leginska ("Ethel Liggins") (April 13, 1886, Hull, England–February 26, 1970, Los Angeles) adopted the name "Leginska" early in her professional career. She was a pianist, teacher and conductor as well as a composer. Early on she showed exceptional skill as a pianist and was sent to the Hoch Conservatory in Frankfurt, then to Berlin. Her official debut was with the Queen's Hall Orchestra in London when she was sixteen. She then gave concert tours in Europe and in 1913 toured in the United States, where she was a great favorite.

Ethel began composing the next year. In 1918 she studied with Ernest Bloch in New York. She continued her career as a concert pianist until 1926, when she turned her full attention to composing and conducting. She was extraordinarily successful, directing major orchestras in Munich, Paris, London and Berlin in 1924 and in New York the following year. She stayed in the United States and made many national tours, conducting in major cities. This was the era of Women's Symphony Orchestras, and she was invited to conduct the Women's Symphony Orchestras in Boston and Chicago, as well as symphony orchestras in many other major cities.

She was back in Europe in 1930, conducting at leading opera houses in

Europe. She then returned to the United States. In 1935 she was invited to conduct the premiere of her opera *Gale* at the Chicago City Opera. She moved to Los Angeles in 1940 and began teaching piano. In 1957 she conducted her opera *The Rose and the Ring*, which had been composed in 1932. Most of her composing was done early in her career, by the end of the 1920s. In addition to her operas she composed symphonic poems, songs and piano music.

Works

1932 *The Rose and the Ring*, alternative title *The Haunting*, Librettist: Edith Emilie Ohlson, after William Makepeace Thackeray
1935 *Gale*, one act, Librettist: Catherine Amy Dawson-Scott (Leginska directed)
1969 *Joan of Arc*
(Sources: Cohen; Sadie and Samuel; http://operadata.stanford.edu/)

France

In addition to writing opera **Marcelle Biasini** (Early 20th century) composed ballets.

Works

1904 *Cyr à Nice*, opera
1904 *La Reine des reines*, opera
(Source: http://operadata.stanford.edu/)

Jane Vieu (1871–April 8, 1955, Paris) wrote in many genres: opera, orchestral works, chamber music, piano and vocal music (some are under the pseudonym Pierre Valette). She may have been married to Maurice Vieu. The two formed a publishing house, Maurice Vieu and Jane Vieu, in Paris.

Works

1905 *Arlette*, operetta, Librettists: Roland and L. Bouvet, Brussels
1937 *Sur le pont d'Avignon*, fantasie-operétte, Librettist: L. de Lahitte
Piège d'Amour, operetta
(Sources: Sadie and Samuel; Cohen; http://operadata.stanford.edu/)

Armande de Polignac, Countess of Chabannes (January 1, 1876, Paris– April 29, 1962, Seine-et-Oise) studied with Fauré and d'Indy. In addition to her operas and operetta she composed ballet music, vocal music, at least one symphony and chamber music.

Works

1907 *La Petite Sirène*, opera, Librettist: Henry Gauthier-Villars

1910 *Les Roses du calife*, opera, Librettist: Georges de Dubor
(Sources: Cohen; http://operadata.stanford.edu/)

Irénée Berge (February 1, 1867, Toulouse–July 30, 1926, Jersey City) was primarily known for his piano and vocal compositions. He also composed at least one chamber piece.

Works

1910 *Corsica*, opera
(Sources: Cohen; http://operadata.stanford.edu/)

Nadia Boulanger (September 16, 1887, Paris–October 22, 1979, Paris) was one of the most outstanding teachers over a period of decades that extended well into the 20th century. Seemingly "everyone" studied with her if possible. She was also a conductor, and she devoted a good part of her life and energy to conducting.

Her father, Ernest Boulanger, who had won the Prix de Rome, composed operas and taught at the Paris Conservatoire (her mother had studied there as one of his students). Nadia entered the conservatoire when she was ten. She sought the Prix de Rome, and for the 1908 competition her preliminary submissions included an instrumental fugue, although a vocal fugue was required. She placed second in the competition. Generally, the person who placed second would likely be the winner the next year, but Nadia declined to enter again.

Nadia's younger sister Lili (see entry) was the focal point of her life. Immensely talented and a gifted composer, Lili was very fragile. Her health declined markedly as she grew older. Lili was the first woman to win the Prix de Rome, in July 1913. Her death in 1918 affected Nadia deeply. After Lili's death Nadia no longer composed but turned her attention and energy to teaching and conducting.

Works

1911 *La Ville morte*, opera, after d'Annunzio, *La città morta*
(Source: Sadie and Samuel)

Lili Juliette Marie Olga Boulanager (August 21, 1893, Paris–March 15, 1918, Mazy, France) is one of those tragic, extremely talented people who often generate this speculation: What would she have achieved had she lived or had good health? When she was two years old her immune system was damaged, and throughout her life she struggled with Crohn's disease. Lili's talent was obvious from an early age, and her mother and her sister Nadia watched over her and cared for her. She composed during her sporadic intervals of good health.

Her father, Ernest, had won the Prix de Rome in 1835 and was a composer of comic operas. His death in 1900 left the family badly off, and much responsibility fell on Nadia, who was Lili's teacher. When she was sixteen, Lili determined she would win the Prix de Rome and turned all her energies toward studying and working toward the Prix. And she did it! In July 1913 she won the Prix de Rome, the first woman to do so. The cost to her health and energy was high, and there were special provisions for her residency during the competition (which some objected to), but the accommodations that were made for Lili's medical needs were decidedly not a factor in her winning.

Subsequently, she received a publishing contract with the publisher Ricordi for two full-length operas. She'd always been taken with Maurice Maeterlinck's writings, and in 1916 she got his permission to use *La Princesse Maleine* for one of the operas, but she wasn't able to complete the opera. Lili composed choral works, and instrumental pieces. Unfortunately, many of her compositions were either lost or destroyed.

Works

1912 *La Princesse Maleine*, opera, Librettist: Maeterlinck (one complete scene survives)
(Source: Sadie and Samuel)

Hanna Marie Hansen (1875, Trondheim–1954) was a noted organist, pianist and teacher as well as a composer. She began studying at the École Normale in Paris when she was five, and at the age of seven she made her debut in Oslo and Paris. In 1894 she graduated from the Paris Conservatoire with highest honors; she also studied composition in Berlin.

In addition to her opera she composed chamber music, music for piano, and at least one orchestral piece. In 1927 she became a French citizen.

Works

Kleon, opera
(Source: Cohen)

Henriette Descat (20th century)

Works

1914 *Les Menhirs de Carnac*, opera, Librettist: Raymond Labruyère
(Sources: Cohen; http://operadata.stanford.edu/)

Charlotte Sohy Labey (July 12, 1887, Paris–December 19, 1956, Paris) composed a symphony and a sinfonia for orchestra, chamber music, music for piano, vocal music, and three masses.

Works

1917–1920 *L'Esclave*, opera
Astrid, opera, from Scandinavian legend of Selma Lagerlof
(Sources: Cohen; http://www.musimem.com/labey.htm)

Germaine Raynal (20th century)

Works

1920 *La Belle du Far-West*, operetta, Librettist: Maurice de Marsan
1920 *La Reine ardente*, operetta, Librettist: Edmond Pingrin
1922 *Pouick!*, operetta, Librettist: Maurice de Marsan
(Source: http://operadata.stanford.edu/)

Marguerite Canal (January 29, 1890, Toulouse, France–January 27, 1978, near Toulouse) attended the Paris Conservatoire, receiving firsts in harmony in 1911, piano accompaniment in 1912, and fugue in 1915. Subsequently, in 1917 and 1918, she conducted orchestral concerts, the first woman to do so in France. The next year she was appointed to teach at the conservatoire. In 1920 she received the Prix de Rome for her opera *Don Juan*. During her residency at the Villa Medici in conjunction with the Prix de Rome she had to leave her conservatoire appointment. Returning to the conservatoire in 1932, she taught until her retirement. She wrote for chorus and orchestra, and many songs.

Works

1920 *Don Juan*, opera
c1922 *Tlass Atka*, opera, from Jack London, orchestration incomplete
(Source: Sadie and Samuel)

Marguerite Bélard d'Harcourt (February 24, 1884, Paris–August 2, 1964, Paris) was an ethnomusicologist as well as a composer. Her studies at the Schola Cantorum stirred her interest in Gregorian chant, music of ancient Greece, and folk songs. She and her husband, Raoul d'Harcourt, who was an ethnomusicologist, traveled widely, making several trips to South America. This led to a book on the music of the Incas. Marguerite was also interested in folk songs of Canada and music of native peoples. Her compositions include music for orchestra, chamber music, and songs.

Works

1925 *Raimi ou fête du soleil*, opera
1937 *Dierdane*, opera, after Synge's *Deirdre of the Sorrows*

Books by or about Marguerite Beclard d'Harcourt:

d'Harcourt, Marguerite Beclard. *Chansons populaire françoises du Canada: leur langue musicale*. With Raoul d'Harcourt. Québec: Presses Universitaires Laval, 1956.

_____. *Las Musique des Incas et ses survivances*. Lima, Peru?: Occidental Petroleum Corp. of Peru, 1990.

_____. *Les Tissus indiens du vieux Pérou*. Series: Documents d'art. Art ornamental. Paris: A. Morancé, 1924.

(Source: Sadie and Samuel)

Germaine Tailleferre (April 19, 1892, Pau-St.-Maur, France–November 7, 1983, Paris) was a prodigy at the piano, and it is said she had a remarkable talent in art as well. From an early age she knew her own mind. When she was twelve she began studies at the Paris Conservatoire, which her father strongly opposed. Her response was to give piano lessons to pay her professors and support herself. She was awarded numerous prizes at the conservatoire.

In 1917 her two-piano piece *Jeux de plein air* so impressed Erik Satie that he christened her his "musical daughter." Satie was a strong influence in her career, and her inclusion in his group of Nouveaux Jeunes brought her public attention. Nouveaux Jeunes, formed during student days at the conservatoire, was the forerunner of Les Six, which was formed in 1920. Germaine was the only female member of Les Six, the other members being Arthur Honegger, Darius Milhaud, Georges Auric, Francis Poulenc and Louis Durey. Les Six was created as a "political reply" to the Russian composers known as The Five, consisting of Mily Balakirev (the leader), César Cui, Modest Mussorgsky, Nikolay Rimsky-Korsakov, and Aleksandr Borodin, who wanted to focus on producing a specifically Russian kind of art music.

In contrast, Les Six was never a cohesive group, nor did they have a fixed agenda as a group. They were autonomous in their own works. However, they did collaborate on *Les Mariés de la tour Eiffel*, a ballet with two speaking voices with text and choreography by Jean Cocteau, which premiered in 1921. They also made an album of piano pieces. This time marked the peak of Germaine's career. She composed throughout her life but never had the acclaim she'd had when younger, and particularly when she was a member of Les Six.

Two unhappy marriages—to caricaturist Ralph Barton in 1926, and to the lawyer Jean Lageat in 1931—drained much of her creative energies. But her composing also tended to be too hurried, in part from trying to earn money from commissions as quickly as she could. She also would borrow from herself, and her works often sounded repetitious and ordinary. However, the concertos she composed in the 1930s were successful, as was her *Cantate de Narcissei* in 1938.

She found a niche in composing film music, a form she did well.

Eventually she focused on opera and stage works. She spent 1942 to 1946 in the United States, after which she produced the Second Violin Sonata. She then turned her attention to operas, primarily opera bouffé, many of which were produced over the radio, particularly in the 1950s.

Works

1930 *Zoulaina*, opera comique, Librettist: C.-H. Hirsch, unperformed
1937 *Le Marin du Bolivar*, opera, Librettist: Henri Jeanson, Paris Exhibition
1950 *Dolores* operetta, Paris
1951 *Il Était un petit navire*, operetta, Librettist: H. Jeanson, Paris
1951 *Parfums* operetta, Librettists: G. Hirsch and J. Bouchor, Monte Carlo
1955 *La Fille d'opéra*, radio opera, Librettist: D. Centore, Radiodiffusion-Télévision Français
1955 *Le Bel Ambitieux*, radio opera, Librettist: D. Centore, Radiodiffusion-Télévision Français
1955 *Monsieur Petitpois achète un château*, radio opera, Librettist: D. Centore, Radiodiffusion-Télévision Français
1955 *La Pauvre Eugénie*, radio opera, Librettist: D. Centore, Radiodiffusion-Télévision Français
1959 *Mémoires d'une bergère*, radio opera, Librettist: P. Jullian, Radiodiffusion-Télévision Français
1960 *Le Maître*, chamber opera, based on E. Ionesco, Radiodiffusion-Télévision Français
1960 *La Petite Sirène*, radio opera, Librettist: P. Soupault, Radiodiffusion-Télévision Français

Books by or about Germaine Tailleferre:

Tailleferre, Germaine. *Les Mémoires de G. Tailleferre: dossier*. Series: Revue internationale de musique française, no. 19. Paris: Champion, 1986.

(Source: Sadie and Samuel)

Suzanne Demarquez (July 5, 1899, Paris–October 23, 1965, Paris) won first prizes at the Paris Conservatoire for history of music and score reading. She composed a Sonatine for orchestra, much chamber music, music for piano and vocal music in addition to her opera. She was also a music critic.

Works

Thesée à Marseille, opera

Books by or about Suzanne Demarquez:

Demarquez, Suzanne. *Hector Berlioz*. Lausanne: La Guilde du livre, 1969.

_____. *Manuel de Falla*. Translated from the French by Salvator Attanasio. New York: Da Capo, 1983, c1968.
_____. *Purcell*. Paris, Éditions du Vieux Colombier, 1951.
_____. *André Jolivet*. Paris, Ventadour, coll. Musiciens d'aujourd'hui, 1958.
(Source: Cohen)

Elsa Barraine (February 13, 1910, Paris–March 20, 1999) grew up in a musical family. She attended the Paris Conservatoire, winning prizes in harmony and accompaniment and the Prix de Rome in 1929 for her cantata *La fierge guerrière*. From 1936 to 1940 she worked for French Radio. She became a professor at the Conservatoire in 1953.

Works

1932 *Le Roi Bossu*, opera, Librettist: Albert Carré
(Source: Sadie and Samuel)

Claude Arrieu (November 30, 1903, Paris–March 7, 1990, Paris) was awarded first prize for composition in 1932 at the Paris Conservatoire. Subsequently she taught, then in 1946 she began working with French radio as a producer and as assistant head of the sound-effects department. Her stage works include ballet and tableaux as well as operas; she also composed for orchestra, and chamber ensembles, and works for cinema and broadcasting.

Works

1938–39 *Cadet-Roussel*, opera-bouffe, Librettist: A. de la Tourasse and Jean Limozin
1947 *Les Deux Rendez-vous*, opera-comique, Librettist: Pierre Bertin, after G. de Nerval, commissioned by the French government
1953 *Le Chapeau à musique*, children's operetta
1953–55 *La princesse de Babylone*, opera-bouffe, Librettist: Pierre Dominique, after Voltaire
1958–63 *La Coquille à Planetes*, radio opera, Librettist: Pierre Schaeffer,
1958–63 *Cymbeline*, opera, Librettists: La Tournier and M. Jacquemont, after Shakespeare
1966 *Balthazar, ou Le mort vivant*, opera-bouffe, Librettist: P. Dominique
1970 *Un Clavier pour un autre*, opera, Librettist: J. Tardieu
(Source: Sadie and Samuel)

Germany

Phillippine Schick (February 9, 1893, Bonn–January 13, 1970, Munich) was a lecturer in music, theory, English language and literature at the

University of Munich. In addition to her opera and operetta she wrote pieces for orchestra, for chamber ensembles, piano, sacred music, much vocal music, and ballets.

Works

1906 *Der Blumenzwist*, operetta
1934–39 *Severina*, opera
(Source: Cohen)

Rosa van Embden Danziger 20th century

Works

1909 *Die Dorfkomtesse*, opera, Librettist: Erich Urban
1916 *Ulanenstreiche*, opera, Librettist: Magnus Hase
(Source: http://operadata.stanford.edu/)

Amalie Nikisch (1860, Brussels–1938) was married to the conductor Artur Nikisch.
Their son Mitja became a noted pianist.

Works

1911 *Meine Tante, deine Tante*, opera, Librettist: Ilse Friedlander, Amalie Nikisch
1914 *Daniel in der Löwengrube*, opera, Librettist: Ilse Friedlander based on Ernest von Wolzogen
1915 *Immer der Andere*, opera, Librettist: Ilse Friedlander, Amalie Nikisch
(Sources: http://operadata.stanford.edu/; Cohen)

Lena Stein-Schneider (January 3, 1874, Leipzig–June 17, 1958, Munich) was a writer and a composer. She toured the United States in 1923, 1924, 1925, and 1928.

Works

1909 *Der Luftikus*, operetta, Librettist: Lena Stein-Schneider
1912 *Konig Drosselbart*, operetta, Librettist: Wilhelm Ernst Asbeck
1919 *Lustige Liebe*, operetta, Librettist: Lena Stein-Schneider
1925 *Composer's Dream*, operetta
1928 *Ein Hundert Kusse*, operetta, Librettist: Lena Stein Schneider
(Source: Cohen)

Lily Reiff (June 21, 1866, Hamburg–1958) studied in Munich at the Music Academy. She left the academy in 1883 to study with Franz Liszt in Weimer for a year, after which she returned to Munich for further study. Her compositions include music for orchestra, chamber music and vocal music. Thomas Mann dedicated a chapter of *Dr. Faustus* to her.

Works

1920 *Pucks Liebeslied*, opera, Librettist: Rudolph Lothar
(Sources: Cohen; http://operadata.stanford.edu/)

Greece

Eleni Lambiri (1882 or 1883, Athens–March 30, 1960, Athens) is considered the first modern Greek woman composer to have had a full professional career. Her father was the composer Georgios Lambiris. She studied at the Athens Conservatory and was awarded a bronze medal on graduation. In 1908 she went to the Leipzig Conservatory, where she stayed for four years. She returned to Athens, and the following year her first operetta was performed, reputedly followed by *Isolma* two years later in Milan. Although a conductor in Milan for a number of years, by 1925 she had settled in Patras, where she was director of the Patras Conservatory until 1953 when she retired. She wrote a symphony, string quartet, and several melodramas, writing the music for performance with a spoken text.

Works

1913 *To apokriatiko oneiro* [A Dream in Carnival], operetta
1915 *Isolma*, operetta, Librettist: Eleni Lambiri, said to have been staged in Milan
(Source: Sadie and Samuel)

Ireland

Mary Dickenson-Auner (1880–1965) lived in Germany, Romania and Austria as well as in Ireland. While she was in Austria in the 1930s the Nazis wouldn't allow her to perform in public or teach there. Subsequently she focused on composing, for the next twenty-five years. In addition to her operas her compositions include five symphonies, two oratorios, numerous chamber music works and songs.

Works

1906 *Der Schmerz*, opera
1944/46 *Maureen*, folk opera
1948/49 *The Shadowy Waters*, opera
1948/49 *Die sieben Raben*, opera
1953 *Illusionen*, opera

Italy

Mimi Novelli (20th century)

Works

1900 *Il coscritto*, opera, Librettist: Casserta
(Source: http://operadata.stanford.edu/)

Eugenia Calosso (April 21, 1878, Turin–after 1914) was a conductor as well as a composer. She began her career as a conductor at San Remo, staying with them until 1914. Under her leadership the orchestra toured extensively in Italy and throughout Europe. In addition to her opera, she composed for orchestra, singers, and instrumental works for violin and piano, as well as solo piano.

Works

Vespero, opera, Librettist: Ernesto Ragazzoni
(Source: Sadie and Samuel)

Albina Busky-Benedetti (b. ca. 1869)

Works

Clara d'Arta, opera
(Source: Cohen)

Emilia Gubitosi (February 3, 1887, Naples–January 17, 1972, Naples) studied at the Naples conservatory, graduating in 1906. Two years later a lyrical sketch for her opera *Ave Maria* was performed in Naples, followed by her second opera performed in Pisoia. She taught at the Naples Conservatory for more than forty years; throughout, she was a concert pianist and performed in Italy and Europe. Emilia was very interested in early Italian choral music and was responsible for the revival of interest in the music, giving concerts she often conducted.

Her husband was the composer Franco Michele Napolitano. Together they founded the Association Alessandro Scarlatti, which eventually led to the first Neapolitan symphony orchestra. Her composing was diverse and included orchestral pieces, a piano concerto, works for voice, solo instruments, chamber ensembles and for solo piano. She also wrote several books on musical technique.

Works

1906 *Gardenia Rossa*, opera, Librettist: Antonio Menotti-Buja
1910 *Nada Delwig*, opera, Librettist: Federigo Verdinois, Antonio Menotti-Buja
(Sources: Sadie and Samuel; http://operadata.stanford.edu/)

Jole Gasparini (b. ca. March 4, 1882, Genoa)

Works

1905 *Lisia*, operetta, Librettist: Mimi Resasco
1908 *Ester*, operetta, Librettist: Aldo Martinelli
1912 *L'amore non è cielo*, operetta, Librettist: Ernesto Gellona
1914 *Come andò*[?], operetta
1917 *Cose d'America*, operetta, Librettist: Camillo Rondoletti
(Source: http://operadata.stanford.edu/)

Emanuela Gennai (b. ca. 1886)

Works

1908 *Berta alla siepe*, opera, Librettist: Carlo Zangarini
1910 *Cinerella*, opera, Librettist: Giuseppe Adami
(Source: http://operadata.stanford.edu/)

Maddalena Meini-Zanotti (20th century)

Works

1909 *La Principessa Iris*, operetta, Librettist: Maddalena Meini-Zanotti, Florence
(Source: http://operadata.stanford.edu/)

Vincenza Garelli della Morea, Countess de Cardenas (1859, Valeggio, Pavia—after 1924, Rome?) often used the pseudonym Centa della Morea. After her studies in Turin, she married the Count de Cardenas and lived in Milan. She moved to Rome in 1888. In addition to her operas she wrote songs.

Works

1915 *Incantesimo*, operetta, Librettist: Giovanni Drovetti Padua
1916 *Il viaggio dei Perrichon*, operetta, Librettist: Giovanni Drovetti after E. Labiche, Turin

1924 *Le nozze di Leporello*, commedia, Librettist: L. Almirante, Teatro Social, Brescia

(Source: Sadie and Samuel)

Lidia Testore (20th century, Milan)

Works

1915 *Il bagno di Venere*, operetta, Librettist: Arturo Franci
1917 *Baccante*, operetta, Librettist: Zimar Baldo
1920 *La perla dell'atelier*, operetta, Librettist: Carlo Bonapace

(Source: http://operadata.stanford.edu/)

Elisabetta Oddone Sulli-Rao (August 13, 1878, Milan–March 3, 1972, Milan) was particularly interested in Italian folksongs. In addition to her operas she composed chamber music.

Works

1903 *La montanina*, opera, Librettist: Luisa Anzoletti
1908 *Rosa di Macchia*, opera, Librettist: Carlo Zangarini
1916 *Petruccio e il cavallo Capriccio*, opera, Librettist: Hedda [Lucia Maggia]
1920 *Flemma e Furia*, opera, Librettist: Giuseppe Fanciulli
1920 *A gara con le rondini*, opera, Librettist: Carlo Linati

(Sources: http://operadata.stanford.edu/; Cohen)

Elsa Respighi (March 24, 1894, Rome–March 17, 1996) began studying at the Conservatorio di Musica Santa Cecilia in Rome in 1911, where her instructors included Ottorino Respighi, with whom she studied composition. They married in 1919. She began publishing her songs in 1916 and published regularly until 1921. At that point her husband's career was paramount; however, they worked together, touring extensively in Europe, North America and South America. They collaborated on the ballet version of *Gli uccelli* in 1927.

When Ottorino died in 1936 the score of his opera *Lucrezia* was nearly complete. Elsa, with assistance from Ennio Porrino, completed the score, and the opera was performed at la Scala in 1937. The next year, working with Claudio Guastalla, Ottorino's librettist, she prepared a ballet version of *Antiche arie e danze* ("Ancient Airs and Dances"). She also wrote articles about Ottorino's music and eventually a biography, published in Milan in 1954. Although she was closely involved with her husband's legacy and work, she composed significant music on her own including a sacred drama, operas, a cantata, orchestral suites and a symphonic poem.

Works

c1920 *Fior di neve*, fairy opera
1941 *Alcesti*, opera, Librettist: Claudio Guastella
1945 *Samurai*, opera, Librettist: Claudio Guastalla

Books by or about Elsa Respighi:

Respighi, Elsa. *Fifty Years of Life in Music, 1905–1955*. With Giovanni Fontecchio and Roger Johnson. Lewiston: Edwin Mellen Press.
_____. *Ottorino Respighi: His Life Story*. Translated by Gwyn Morris. London: Ricordi, 1962.

(Sources: Sadie and Samuel; http://operadata.stanford.edu/)

Giulia Recli (December 4, 1890, Milan–December 19, 1970, Milan) studied the humanities in addition to singing, piano and composition. She's considered the first Italian woman composer to enter the symphonic repertory, and throughout her career she received numerous awards and honors. She performed at such major institutions as la Scala, Milan, and the Metropolitan Opera, New York. She was also a music critic. A prolific composer in many areas, her particular interest was in songs for which she often used Spanish, Greek and Persian themes.

Works

Cento ducati e Belluccia, fairy opera, after Giulio Cesare Croce
(Source: Sadie and Samuel)

Mexico

Julia Alonso (b. ca. 1889, Oaxaca) was a successful composer by the age of twenty-five. She later taught organ, piano and composition at the National Conservatory. Her compositions include two symphonies and chamber music.

Works

Tonantzin, opera
(Source: Cohen)

Sofía Cancino de Cuevas (b. ca. July 29, 1898, Mexico City) studied at the National Autonomous University of Mexico from 1932 to 1938. She then founded an Academy of Opera, which performed in the Palacio de Bellas Artes. She composed music for orchestra and chamber ensembles, as well as vocal music.

Works

1937 *Gil González de Avil*, opera
1945 *Anette*, opera
1950 *Michoacana*, opera
1952 *Promessa d'artista e parole di re*, opera
(Sources: Cohen; Wikipedia)

María Grever (August 16, 1885, Guanajuato–December 15, 1951, New York) is said to have composed at a very early age. As a child she travelled extensively in Europe with her parents. She married Leo Augusto Grever, an American oil company executive, in 1907. Nine years later they moved to New York. Over a period of years she had four professional recitals in New York.

María was a prolific writer of songs and was said to have composed at least 850 of them, many of which were immensely popular in Latin America. When she died her bust was placed in the composers' gallery in Chapultepec Park in Mexico City.

Works

1939 *El cantarito*, miniature opera
(Source: Sadie and Samuel)

Netherlands

Cornélie van Oosterzee (August 16, 1863, Batavia (now Jakarta), Java–August 12, 1943, Berlin) first studied in The Hague. Subsequently she moved to Berlin, where she lived for the rest of her life. She maintained close contact with The Netherlands, conducting Dutch orchestras and working as a music correspondent for a Dutch newspaper. She wrote orchestral works (one of the first Dutch woman to do so), chamber music and vocal music.

Works

1910 *Das Gelöbnis*
(Source: Sadie and Samuel)

When **Dina Appeldoorn** (December 24, 1884, Rotterdam–December 4/5, 1938, The Hague) graduated from the Royal Conservatory of The Hague in 1910, twenty of her songs had already been published. Dina eventually taught piano at the conservatory. After graduating she was a piano accompanist for several choirs in The Hague, but she increasingly was drawn to a career in composing. Her symphonic poem *Pêcheurs d'Islande* was performed by the Utrecht City Orchestra in 1912. Nine years later the *Jubileum-lied* she composed for the 25th anniversary of Queen Wilhelmina received a prize from the Nederlandsche Volkszang-bond in Utrecht. Dina continued to write choral works, which were widely performed.

Works

1927 *Duinsprookje*, children's operetta

(Sources: Sadie and Samuel; Wikipedia)

Saar Bessem (b. ca. March 13, 1907, Tiel) studied at the conservatory in Rotterdam; later she became principal teacher there, also teaching at the Montessori Lyceum. She wrote her own texts.

Works

Floris en Blancefloer, opera
Assepoester, operetta for children
Doornroosje, operetta for children
De niewwe Kleren van de Keizer, opera
De Prinses op de Erwt, opera
Reinaard, opera
De Varkenshoeder, opera
Zwaan Kleef aan, opera

(Source: Cohen)

Johanna Harmina Gerdina Mulder (b. ca. September 28, 1912, Middelburg) had a significant career as a choir conductor, leading women's and children's choirs in Holland, Britain, the United States, and on radio. She received the golden Medal of Honor, and the Order of Orange-Nassau from Queen Juliana. She wrote her own texts.

Works

1936 *De verdwenen konigzoon*, operetta for children
1938 *Prins Rudi en de toverstaf*, operetta for children
1940 *Gelukskinderen*, operetta for children
1949 *Marjolijntje in Sprookjeslana*, dedicated to the four Dutch princesses, operetta for children
1958 *De toverspiegel*, operetta for children
1959 *Als herdus in de nacht*, Christmas operetta for children
1963 *De wonderstaf*, operetta for children
1971 *Circus del mondo*, operetta for children

(Source: Cohen)

Poland

Julia Dorabialska (May 22, 1895, Sosnowiec–July 20, 1944, Wolomin) was a musicologist, pianist and composer. She studied at the Warsaw

Conservatory and at the Moscow Conservatory. She was awarded her doctorate from the Jagelian University in Cracow in 1924. The following year she completed her course in composition at the Warsaw Conservatory. Subsequently she had an appointment as professor of harmony, musical form and history, and the piano, a position she held from 1929 to 1939.

Works

Dewaki, opera, Librettist: Schure
Hanusia, opera, Librettist or after G. Hauptmann
(Source: Cohen)

Anna Maria Klechniowska (April 15, 1888, Borowka, Ukraine–August 28, 1973, Warsaw) studied at the Conservatory of Warsaw and the Conservatory of Lemberg (now Lviv). She then studied at the Leipzig Conservatory from 1906 to 1908 and at the Kraków Music Institute until 1911. She graduated from the Vienna Music Academy in 1917. The following year she began teaching her own music courses in Warsaw, which she continued until 1939. She then studied with Nadia Boulanger in Paris. In 1947 she became professor of the piano in the Folk Institute in Lodz. She was awarded the Prime Minister's Prize for her children's compositions in 1951. Her elementary piano manual of 1916 was used for many decades. She composed orchestral music, chamber music, vocal music, two ballets, and music for piano.

Works

1930 *Bilitis*, opera, after Greek mythology
(Sources: Sadie and Samuel; Cohen)

Irene Poldowski (Lady Dean Paul) (May 16, 1880, Brussels–January 28, 1932, London) the daughter of Henryk Wieniawski, the Polish violinist, used Poldowski as a pseudonym. Her uncle was the pianist and composer George A. Osborne. Irene studied first at the Brussels Conservatory then in Paris. After her marriage to Sir Aubrey Dean Paul she lived in London and subsequently returned to Paris, where she studied at the Schola Cantorum under Vincent d'Indy. Her compositions include music for orchestra, chamber ensembles, piano and vocal music. Two of her songs, published in 1900, were under the name Wieniawska; otherwise her music was published under Poldowski.

Works

Laughter, operetta
(Sources: Sadie and Samuel; Cohen)

Pomerania

Else Streit (July 27, 1869, Pomerania–after 1920) was a pianist, violinist and lecturer in addition to her composing. She studied at the Karlsruhe Conservatory from 1893 to 1897 and at the Stern Conservatory in Berlin from 1898 to 1902. She then taught at several schools and conservatories. Her compositions include sacred music, vocal music, orchestral music, and music for chamber ensembles.

Works
1928 *St. Nikolaus und Seine Gehilfen*, Christmas opera
(Source: Cohen)

Romania

Berta Bock (March 15, 1857, Sibiu [Hermannstadt]–April 4, 1945, Sibiu) grew up in a family that had a strong tradition of music. As a child she studied piano, theory, and singing. She gave concerts and recitals in Austria, Germany and Transylvania. Her opera reflects her interest in Saxon folklore in Transylvania.

Works
1927 *Die Pfingstkrone*, Librettist: Anna Schuller, performed in Transylvania and subsequently in Cleveland in 1931.
(Source: Sadie and Samuel)

Russia

Yuliya Lazarevna Weissberg (often under Veysberg) (December 25/January 6, 1880, Orenburg, Russia–March 1 [or 4], 1942, Leningrad) entered the St. Petersburg Conservatory in 1903, where she studied piano with Rimsky-Korsakov and instrumentation with Alexander Glazunov. In 1905 she was dismissed for participating in a strike. Subsequently she went to Germany and studied with Engelbert Humperdinck and Max Reger. In 1912 she returned to St. Petersburg, took her examinations, and received her degree.

From 1921 to 1923 she was choral director at the Young Workers' Conservatory. She married Audrey Nikolayevich, the son of Rimsky-Korsakov. From 1915 to 1917 she was on the editorial board of the first Russian music magazine, *Muzïkal'nïy sovremennik*. She died in World War II during the siege of Leningrad. She composed music for orchestra, many vocal and choral pieces, and chamber music. Much of her music is for children and often reflects her interest in folklore.

Works

1923 *Rusalochka* [The Little Mermaid], opera, Librettist: S. Parnok after Hans Christian Andersen

1935 *Gyul'nara*, opera, Librettists: Weissberg and Parnok, excerpts published

1937 *Gusi-lebedi* [Geese-Swans], children's opera, Librettists: Weissberg and S. Marchak, Moscow

1937 *Myortvaya tsarevna* [The Dead Princess], radio opera, after A.S. Pushkin

1937 *Zaykin dom* [A Little Rabbit's House], children's opera, Librettist: W. Weltmann, Moscow

(Sources: Sadie and Samuel; http://operadata.stanford.edu/)

Spain

Ònia Farga i Pellicer (b. ca. November 25, 1882, Barcelona) studied at the Municipal School of Music. When she was fifteen she won every prize the school awarded, including the composition prize for *Grand March for Orchestra and Organ*, which was performed at the Palacio de Bellas Artes. She was a violinist and pianist, and she performed in Spain, France and Switzerland. In addition to her opera and the orchestral piece she composed chamber music, vocal music, and a requiem mass.

Works

La bella Lucinda, opera

(Source: Cohen)

After her studies at the Royal Conservatory of Madrid, **María Rodrigo** (1888, Madrid–1967, Puerto Rico) worked in popular musical theater. Subsequently she went to Munich for further studies. She taught at the Madrid Conservatory and was assistant conductor at the Royal Opera House. During the Spanish Civil War she and her brother, the psychologist Mercedes Rodrigo, went to Switzerland. In 1939 they moved to Bogota, Colombia, and in 1950 to Puerto Rico. María Rodrigo and Pablo Casals founded the Puerto Rico Conservatory of Music.

Works

1915 *Becqueriana*, opera, Librettists: J. Alvárez Quintero and S. Alvárez Qunitero, Madrid

1915 *Diana cazadora*, zarzuela, Librettists: J. Alvárez Quintero and S. Alvárez Qunitero, Madrid

1921 *La romería del Rocío*, zarzuela, Librettist: S. Valverde, Barcelona; *La flor de la vida*, zarzuela
1925 *Canción de amor*, zarzuela
El roble de la Jarosa, zarzuela
(Sources: Sadie and Samuel; Cohen)

United States

Mabel Wheeler Daniels (November 27, 1877, Swampscott, Massachusetts–March 10, 1971, Cambridge, Massachusetts) attended Radcliffe College, where she sang in the glee club and composed several operettas for the group. She received her BA in 1900. Subsequently she studied with George Chadwick at the New England Conservatory of Music. In 1902 she was the first woman in Thuille's score-reading class at the Munich Conservatory. She directed the Radcliffe Glee Club from 1911 to 1913, then was head of music at Simmons College in Boston from 1913 to 1918. At that point she turned her full attention to composing. She was a Fellow at the MacDowell Colony for twenty-four summers. The Schlesinger Library at Radcliffe College holds a collection of her papers, scores and press cuttings. Mabel composed orchestral works, music for chamber ensembles, for piano, two ballets, and a large number of vocal and sacred pieces.

Works
1900 *A Copper Complication*, operetta, Librettist: Rebecca Lane Hooper
1900 *The Court of Hearts*, operetta, Librettist: Rebecca Lane Hooper
1902 *Alice in Wonderland Continued*, incomplete?
1909 *The Legend of Marietta*, operetta

Books by or about Mabel Daniels:

Daniels, Mabel Wheeler. *An American Girl in Munich: Impressions of a Music Student*. Boston: Little, Brown, 1905.

(Source: Sadie and Samuel)

Anice Potter Terhune (October 27, 1873, Hampden, Massachusetts–November 9, 1964) studied at the Cleveland Conservatory, then went on to study in Rotterdam and New York. She utilized the pseudonym Morris Stockton to avoid confusion with her husband, who was the author of the Lassie books.

Works
1904 *Hero Nero*, opera
1911 *The Woodland Princess*, operetta

Books by or about Anice Terhune:

Terhune, Anice. *Across the Line* [autobiography]. New York, 1967.
_____. *The Bert Terhune I Knew.* New York: Harper, 1943.
(Source: Cohen)

Jane Van Etten (Mrs. Alfred Andrews) (early 20th century, born in St. Paul, Minnesota) studied in New York and Paris, then in London. She toured Europe as an opera singer. Her works were performed in the western part of the United States. She received the David Bispham medal from the American Opera Society of Chicago for *Guido Ferranti* in 1926.

Works

1914 *Guido Ferranti*, opera, Librettist; Elsie M. Wilbor, after Oscar Wilde: *The Duchess of Padua*
(Source: Cohen)

The parents of **Celeste de Longpré Heckscher** (February 23, 1860, Philadelphia–February 18, 1928, Philadelphia) objected to her studying music, but she persevered and had early training in piano and composition. She married in 1883. In the 1890s she studied composition and orchestration in Philadelphia and reputedly also studied in Europe. Her compositions include an orchestral suite, *Dances of the Pyrenees*, which also was staged as a ballet, chamber music and songs. She gave a concert of her own compositions in New York in 1913. She was president of the Philadelphia Operatic Society for many years. Her opera *Rose of Destiny* premiered in Philadelphia as a fund-raiser for the Red Cross.

Works

The Flight of Time, opera
1918 *Rose of Destiny*, opera, Librettist: Celeste de Longpre Heckscher
(Sources: Sadie and Samuel; Wikipedia)

Mana-Zucca (December 25, 1885, New York–March 8, 1981, Miami) was born Augusta Zuckermann but changed her name when in her teens. She claims to have performed with the New York Philharmonic at a very early age. Norton Grove states that this assertion, and many other aspects in her unpublished memoirs, hasn't been verified. Apparently she did perform in the United States and Europe early in the twentieth century. She began publishing her compositions in 1915 and claimed to have published about 1,100, about half of the total she composed. Among her compositions are orchestral works, music for chamber ensembles, piano, and vocal works. Her manuscripts and papers are at the University of Miami.

Works

c.1920 *Hypatia*, opera
c. 1920 *Queue of Ki-Lu*, opera
(Source: Sadie and Samuel)

Eleanor Everest Freer (May 14, 1864, Philadelphia, Pennsylvania–December 13, 1942, Chicago) grew up in a musical family, her father being the organist Cornelius Everest and her mother a singer. Eleanor was also an accomplished singer and sang in *HMS "Pinafore"* when she was in her teens. She also began composing at that time.

She studied singing in Paris from 1883 to 1886 and also composition, then she studied in Leipzig, where she sang for Verdi and Liszt. On her return to the United States she taught in Philadelphia and New York. In 1891 she married, and the family eventually settled in Chicago.

She actively promoted modern music and was deeply committed to opera being sung in the language of the country. She established the Opera in Our Language Foundation in 1921, and helped establish the David Bispham Memorial Fund (Bispham visited her home when she was growing up). In 1924 both organizations merged to become the American Opera Society of Chicago. She later said that her work with the foundation inspired her to write operas. In addition to her operas she composed chamber pieces, music for piano, and vocal music. The Newberry Library in Chicago has her papers and scrapbooks.

Works

1922 *The Legend of the Piper*, opera, after Josephine Preston Peabody: *The Piper*
1925 *Massimilliano, the Court Jester, or the Love of Caliban*, opera, Librettist: Elia. W. Peattie
1926 *The Chilkoot Maiden*, opera, Librettist: J.J. Underwood, after an Alaskan legend
1928 *A Christmas Tale*, opera, Librettist: Barrett H. Clark after M. Bouchor
1928 *The Masque of Pandora*, opera, Librettist: Freer after H.W. Longfellow
1928 *Preciosa, or The Spanish Student*, opera, Librettist: Freer after Longfellow
1929 *Frithiof*, opera, Librettist: Freer, after C. Shaw's translation of E. Tegner *Frithiof's Saga*
1929 *Joan of Arc*, opera, Librettist: Freer
1931 *A Legend of Spain*, opera, Librettist: Freer, after Washington Irving's *Tales of the Alhambra*
1934 *Little Women*, opera, Librettist: Freer after L.M. Alcott
1936 *The Brownings Go to Italy*, opera, Librettist: G.A. Hawkins-Ambler, about Robert Browning and Elizabeth Barrett Browning

Books by or about Eleanor Freer:

Freer, Eleanor Everest. *Recollections and Reflections of an American Composer.*

[S.l.: s.n.], c1929.

(Source: Sadie and Samuel)

Harriet Ware (August 26, 1877, Waupan, Wisconsin–1962) made her debut at age fifteen, playing with an orchestra in St. Paul. She studied in Paris and Berlin. A concert pianist, she toured in the United States, playing piano with symphony orchestras. She was married to Hugh Krumbhaar, and in some listings she is found under that last name.

Works

1923 *Undine*, opera
Priscilla, opera, after Longfellow
Sinner's Secret, opera
The Love Wagon, operetta
Waltz for Three, operetta

(Source: Cohen)

Lucile Crews (August 23, 1888–November 3, 1972, San Diego) earned her BMus in 1920 from Redlands University. Later, she studied in Berlin for a year, then spent a year in Paris studying orchestration under Nadia Boulanger. She returned to Germany, where she taught singing in Berlin and toured as an accompanist. She received a Pulitzer Traveling Scholarship in 1926, the first award of that scholarship made to a woman. She composed for orchestra, chamber music and vocal music.

Works

1923 *The Call of Jeanne d'Arc*, opera, adapted from Percy Mackaye's *Joan of Arc*
1926 *Eight Hundred Rubies*, opera, Librettist: John Neidhardt
1935 *Ariadne and Dionysius*, opera

(Sources: Cohen; http://operadata.stanford.edu/)

Kathleen Lockhart Manning (October 24, 1890, Hollywood, California–March 20, 1951, Los Angeles) was a singer and composer. In 1908 she studied in Paris, then toured France and England for about five years, also singing with the Hammerstein Opera Company in London during the 1911–1912 season. She composed several works for orchestra, and a string quartet. Her great strength was vocal music and she was particularly noted for her art songs.

Works

1925/26 *Operetta in Mozartian Style*, operetta

(Source: Sadie and Samuel)

Adeline Appleton (b. ca. November 29, 1886) began composing when she was twelve. She studied privately and at the Wisconsin College in Milwaukee. She composed chamber music and vocal pieces in addition to her opera.

Works

1926 *The Witches' Well*, opera, Librettists: Appleton with Percy Davis
(Sources: Cohen; http://operadata.stanford.edu/)

Gena Branscombe (November 4, 1881, Picton, Ontario–July 26, 1977, New York City) studied at the Chicago Musical College, having won a scholarship at the age of fifteen. She won the gold medal for composition in 1901 and 1902. After graduating she continued her studies in Chicago and taught. In 1907 she became head of the piano department at Whitman College in Walla Walla. She went to Berlin, studying composition and orchestration under Engelbert Humperdinck. Subsequently she studied conducting at New York University.

From 1921 to 1931 she conducted her own music. She is perhaps best known through her founding of the Branscombe Choral, a women's chorus that lasted from 1933 to 1954. She wrote, composed and arranged many works for them, and she commissioned works by other women composers. She was active in women's arts organizations and was a strong supporter of American music and of women composers. In 1928 the League of American Pen Women awarded her their prize for the best work produced by a woman composer, for *Pilgrims of Destiny*. She received an honorary Master of Arts degree from Whitman College in 1932.

She was a prolific composer with many orchestra pieces, works for chamber ensembles, piano pieces and vocal pieces. Her manuscripts are at the Music Division of the New York Public Library for the Performing Arts.

Works

C1928 *The Bells of Circumstance*
(Source: Sadie and Samuel)

Ruth Lynda Deyo (April 20, 1884, Poughkeepsie, New York–March 4, 1960, Cairo, Egypt) had a substantial performing career. She gave her first concert when she was nine, at the World Columbian Exposition in Chicago, in 1893. In 1904 she performed in Berlin, then she played with several orchestras in the United States and Europe. William Mason, Teresa Carreño and Edward MacDowell were among her teachers. She appeared in recitals with Fritz Kreisler and Pablo Casals. In 1925 she settled in Egypt and focused on her composing. Her opera, in which she attempted to reconstruct ancient

Egyptian music, was composed to be performed on the occasion of the marriage of King Farouk of Egypt. In 1931 the prelude was performed by Stokowski and the Philadelphia Orchestra.

Works

1930 *The Diadem of Stars*, opera
(Sources: http://american-music.org/publications/bullarchive/Sears231.htm; Cohen; Laurence)

When **Ione Pickhardt** (b. ca. May 27, 1900, Hampstead, New York) was twelve she won a scholarship to the National Conservatory of Music in New York and studied there for eight years. Her debut as a pianist was with the New York Philharmonic Orchestra, but her family disapproved of her having a career as a pianist. Later, she was assistant music critic for the *New York Evening Mail*, and it was at that time she began composing. Her compositions include two piano concertos for orchestra.

Works

1930 *Moira*, opera, dramatization of Irish Legends, Librettist: George Gibbs, Jr.
(Source: Cohen)

Clara Anna Korn (January 30, 1866, Berlin, Germany–July 14, 1940, New York) went to the United States when she was three. Eventually she began a career as a concert pianist and had some measure of success. But she received a letter from Tchaikovsky, who had seen manuscripts of some of her compositions when he was in New York, and he urged her to be a composer. At that point she turned her focus to composing. In 1891 she received a scholarship to the National Conservatory in New York, where Dvorak was among her instructors. After her studies she taught theory at the Conservatory.

She was active in several venues. She founded the National Federation of Music Clubs, the Women's Philharmonic Society, and the Manuscript Society of New York. She wrote for music journals. Clara was a strong believer that women should have access to more opportunities in music: "How can any woman produce a successful orchestral work under existing conditions? You write a song, and some accommodating singer will sing it for you and give you the chance to correct mistakes; the same with a solo piece, or any other solo composition. But where is the orchestra that will 'try' a manuscript orchestral selection, especially if it is not at all certain that it is worth trying?" (letter to the editor of *Musical Courier*, August 7, 1907, 26).

Her compositions include orchestral works, music for chamber ensembles, piano music and vocal music. Very little of her music was published.

Works

1932 *Their Last War*, opera, Librettist: Korn, Boston
(Source: Sadie and Samuel)

Amy Marcy Cheney Beach (September 5, 1867, Heniker, New Hampshire–December 27, 1944, New York City) was an outstandingly prolific and noted composer. She was a child prodigy, showing remarkable musical ability at a very early age. Her first teacher was her mother; at the age of seven she gave her first public recitals in which she played music by Beethoven, Chopin and Handel as well as her own pieces. Her family moved to Boston in 1875, and it was recommended that Amy attend a European conservatory, but her family was against this and engaged local musicians to teach her.

She was in Boston at a remarkable time, and her family friends included Henry Wadsworth Longfellow and Oliver Wendell Holmes. Also among that circle was Henry Harris Aubrey Beach, a physician who lectured on anatomy at Harvard. He and Amy married in 1885. Up until that time Amy performed with the Boston Symphony Orchestra and made other public appearances. Dr. Beach preferred that she curtail her performances, and Amy turned her focus to composing. She continued with some public performances and regularly performed in selected private venues.

Dr. Beach died in 1910. In 1911 Amy went to Europe, determined to establish herself as a performer and a composer and to promote the sale of her works. She came back to the United States at the outbreak of World War I and immediately began touring and giving concerts. In 1915 she moved to New York. Amy was active in several organizations, and was cofounder of the Society of American Women Composers. She was interested in helping further the careers of younger musicians. While she composed a remarkable amount of vocal music and sacred music, as well as music for piano, in the United States and Europe it was her large-scale works that established her as such a significant composer.

Works

1932 *Cabildo*, opera, Librettist: N.B. Stephens, performed 1945, Athens, Georgia

Books by or about Amy Beach:

Block, Adrienne F. *Amy Beach, Passionate Victorian: The Life and Work of an American Composer, 1867–1944*. New York: Oxford Univ. Press, 1998.
Jenkins, W.S. *The Remarkable Mrs. Beach, American Composer: A Biographical Account Based on Her Diaries, Letters, Newspaper Clippings, and Personal Reminiscences*. MI: Harmonie Park, 1994.
(Source: Sadie and Samuel)

Lily Strickland (January 28, 1887, Anderson, South Carolina–June 6, 1958, Hendersonville, North Carolina) began composing in her teens. From 1901 to 1904 she attended Converse College. The following year she received a scholarship to study at the Institute of Musical Art in New York. In 1920 she and her husband, J. Courtney Anderson, moved to India, where they lived for nine years. During that time Lily traveled in the Far East and Africa. In 1930 she and her husband returned to the United States.

Lily became very interested with non-Western music when she lived in India, and she wrote articles comparing Indian and European music idioms. Earlier she'd become interested in Native American music, and she incorporated some of the melodies in her pieces and in her operetta *Laughing Star of Zuni*. She wrote orchestra works, music for piano, several ballets, vocal and sacred music. Lily also painted watercolors, primarily while she lived abroad. The largest collection of her paintings can be found at the Anderson University Art Museum in Anderson, South Carolina, which also holds some of her music and publications.

Works

1933 *Jewel of the Desert*, operetta
1946 *Laughing Star of Zuni*, operetta
(Sources: Cohen; Sadie and Samuel; Wikipedia)

Dorothy James (December 1, 1901, Chicago–December 1, 1982, Florida) received her BM and MM at the American Conservatory of Music in Chicago, having previously studied at the Eastman School of Music and the University of Michigan. In 1927 she joined the faculty at Eastern Michigan University in Ypsilanti, remaining there until 1968. She received several prizes and awards, including four MacDowell Fellowships. On her retirement from Eastern Michigan University in 1971 she received an honorary doctorate of musical arts. Her compositions include orchestral works, chamber music, vocal and sacred music, pieces for piano, and organ music.

Works

1933 *Paola and Francesca*, opera, Librettist: S. Phillips
(Sources: Sadie and Samuel; Cohen)

Carrie Lewis (December 26, 1865, Boston–1951) studied in Germany from 1890 to 1892. She married Leo Rich Lewis, a composer and professor of music at Tufts College. In 1934 she received an honorary AM from Tufts College.

Works

1934 *The Rose and the Ring*, opera

Carnival of the Flowers, operetta
One Day's Fun, operetta
The Queen of the Garden, operetta, for children
(Sources: Cohen; http://composers-classical-music.com/b/BullardLewisCarrie.htm)

The musical education of **Pauline Alderman** (January 16, 1893, Lafayette, Oregon–June 22, 1983, Los Angeles) extended over decades. First there was a year at the University of California in Berkeley, from 1916 to 1917; from 1923 to 1924 at the Juilliard School of Music; the University of Washington in 1933; and the University of Strasbourg in 1939. In 1946 she received her PhD from the University of Southern California. Throughout those years she taught at various schools, conservatories and colleges. At the 2nd International Congress of Women in Music, April 1982, she was honored for her contributions to the field of music and women in musicology. Her operetta *Come On Over* won the ASCAP Award for 1940, the first time the prize was won by a woman.

Works

1936 *Bombastes Furioso*, opera, after a play by William Barnes Rhodes
1941 *Come On Over*, operetta
(Sources: Wikipedia; http://operadata.stanford.edu/)

Laura Lawton Reynolds (b. ca. June 23, 1886, Allendale, South Carolina) received her BM from the Virginia Woman's College, University of Richmond, in 1903. From 1906 to 1907 she was at the Atlanta Conservatory of Music in Georgia. Her compositions include several piano pieces.

Works

1936 *Historical Pageant*, operetta
1940 *Music Land*, operetta
1941 *Pageant of the Month*, operetta
Christmas operettas
(Source: Cohen)

Dorothy Gaynor Blake (November 21, 1893–October 10, 1967, St. Louis) was the daughter of Jessie L. Gaynor, who was her first teacher. She also studied in Berlin before World War I. In 1912 she married Robert Edwin Blake, a lawyer and Rhodes Scholar. Their three sons were also active in music. Dorothy, with Rudoph Ganz, organized and developed the first Children's Symphonies with the St. Louis Symphony Orchestra; other states adopted their program model. From 1929 to 1934 she was education director for the St. Louis Symphony. She was a judge for piano competitions and gave piano performances in the public schools, particularly schools in underprivileged areas.

She published widely: twenty-six instruction books for first and second grade children, instrumental and vocal sheet music, songs and operettas for older students. She had more than 800 published musical works to her credit. Dorothy, who also had artistic talent, often designed and illustrated covers for her works. Her music is still available today.

Works

The Blue Belt, operetta
A Get-Acquainted Party, operetta
(Sources: Cohen; http://www.womenscouncil.org/cd_web/Blake.html)

Radie Britain (March 17, 1903, Texas–May 23, 1994) received her BMus from the American Conservatory in 1921. She then went to Europe and studied in Munich, then in Berlin.

After her return to the United States she eventually attended the Chicago Conservatory and spent two seasons at the MacDowell Colony. In 1930 she joined the faculty of Girvin Institute of Music in Chicago, where she stayed for four years, then joined the faculty of the Chicago Conservatory and stayed there until 1939. From 1940 to 1960 she lived in Hollywood, where she taught piano and composition. Many of her compositions received national or international awards. The National League of American Pen Women awarded her *Rhapsodic Phantasy for Piano* and *Barcarola* their first national awards.

She composed a large amount of music for orchestra and for chamber ensembles, many piano pieces, vocal and choral music, three ballets, and sacred music.

Works

1937 *Ubiquity*, opera, Librettist: Lester Luther
1946 *Happyland*, operetta (for children?), Librettist A. Greenfield
1952 *Carillon*, opera, Librettist: R. Hughs
1953 *The Spider and the Butterfly*, children's operetta
1960 *Kuthara*, chamber opera, Librettist: Lester Luther
(Source: Sadie and Samuel)

Hazel Cobb (July 15, 1892, Groesbeck, Texas–September 8, 1973, Dallas) received her BMus in 1922 and her MMus in 1924 from the American Conservatory of Music. She composed piano pieces and vocal pieces in addition to her operettas.

Works

Daughter of Mohammed, operetta
Lamps Trimmed and Burning, operetta
(Source: Cohen)

Katherine Kennicott Davis (June 25, 1892, St. Joseph, Missouri–April 20, 1980, Concord, Massachusetts) received the Billings Prize for composition at Wellesley College in 1914. Subsequently she taught piano and theory at Wellesley. Stetson University in Florida awarded her an honorary doctorate. Nadia Boulanger was among her instructors. Katherine composed chamber music, a symphonic poem, and vocal and choral music.

Works

Cinderella, opera
The Unmusical Impresario, opera, Librettist: Heddie Root Kent
(Sources: Cohen; http://operadata.stanford.edu/)

Shirley Graham Du Bois (November 11, 1906, Indiana–March 27, 1977) (dates vary) was an author and playwright in addition to being a composer. She became well known for her activities in African-American causes. In 1921 she married Shadrach T. McCants, with whom she had two sons. Shirley moved to Paris to study composition at the Sorbonne in 1926. She and her husband divorced the following year. She earned her BA in 1934 and a year later completed her master's degree. In 1936 she was appointed director of the Chicago Negro Unit of the Federal Theater Project, which was part of the Works Progress Administration. Among her responsibilities was writing musical scores and directing.

In 1951 she married W.E.B. Du Bois. A decade later they emigrated and became citizens of Ghana, where he died in 1963. Politics in Ghana became increasingly unsettled, and Shirley was forced to leave. She then settled in Cairo, Egypt. In addition to her composing Shirley wrote in several genres, particularly biographies of African-American and world personages for young people.

Works

1932 *Tom Tom: An Epic of Music and the Negro* (1932), an opera
(Sources: Cohen; Wikipedia)

Florence Pauline Wickham (1860, Beaver, Pennsylvania–October 20, 1962, New York) graduated from Beaver College with a gold medal in music. She studied singing privately in Philadelphia, then went to Berlin to continue her studies. Her singing debut was at the Royal Court Theater in Wiesbaden, Germany, when she was twenty. This was the start of a very successful career. She sang at Covent Garden in London and in Munich. In 1909 the Metropolitan Opera in New York hired her. Although she was with the Metropolitan Opera for only three years, she sang twenty-two roles in 169 performances. She received the Medallion for Arts and Sciences, as well as the Title of Court Singer at a court concert in Berlin.

She married Eberhard Lueder in 1911. Two years later she retired from the opera to compose. The premier of *Rosalind*, which was sponsored by her friend Mrs. Franklin D. Roosevelt, took place at the Rockridge Theater (an open-air setting) in Carmel, New York. Although some sources say she was the first woman ever to write both music and lyrics of an opera, this isn't true. She was awarded the Women's Achievement Award of the National Conference of Christians and Jews in 1950. Florence also wrote choral pieces, songs, and several ballets.

Works

1938 *Rosalind*, operetta, based on Shakespeare: *As You Like It*
1957 *The Legend of Hex Mountain*, operetta
(Sources: Cohen; https://sites.google.com/site/pittsburghmusichistory/pittsburgh-music-story/classic/florence-wickham)

Julia Frances Smith (January 25, 1911, Denton, Texas–April 27, 1989, New York) graduated from North Texas State University in 1930, then received a scholarship to attend Juilliard Graduate School, where she stayed from 1932 to 1939. During that time she completed her MA at New York University. While there she studied under Marion Bauer. Also during the 1930s she was the pianist for the Orchestrette Classique [*sic*] of New York, a women's orchestra. She also toured, giving concerts in Europe, the United States, and Latin America. She taught at Hartt College from 1941 to 1946 and founded their department of music education. In 1952 she earned a PhD, also from New York University. Her compositions include music for orchestra, band, and for chamber ensembles, piano music, and vocal music.

Works

1938 *Cynthia Parker*, opera, Librettists: Julie Smith and J.I. Fortune, revised 1977
1943 *The Stranger of Manzano*, opera, Librettist: J.W. Rogers
1946 *The Gooseherd and the Goblin*, opera, Librettist: Josephine F. Boyle
1953 *Cockcrow*, opera, Librettist: C.D. Mackay, after Grimm
1953 *The Shepherdess and the Chimneysweep*, Christmas opera, Librettist: C. D'Arcy Mackay
1963 *Daisy*, opera, Librettist: Bertita Harding, about Juliette Gordon Low, founder of the Girl Scouts

Books by or about Julia Smith:

Smith, Julia Frances. *Aaron Copland: His Work and Contribution to American Music.* New York, Dutton, 1955.
_____. *Master Pianist: The Career and Teaching of C. Friedburg.* New York, 1963.
(Source: Sadie and Samuel)

Rebecca Dunn (b. ca. September 23, 1890, Guthrie, Oklahoma) was an author as well as a composer. She earned a degree from Washburn College in Topeka, Kansas, in 1912, then from Kansas State Agricultural College in Manhattan, Kansas, in 1913. She did revisions and arrangements for many songwriters in the United States, Canada and Italy; she also composed songs, often writing the text. *Sunny*, her first operetta, was awarded first prize in a national contest sponsored by Junior Plays, Inc., in Seattle. One of her songs, "Hallelujah Rain," a spiritual, was placed in the Scottish National Library in Glasgow as a representative work of American composition. Rebecca also wrote articles for national magazines and for the Kansas City newspaper. She was on the board of directors for several businesses and was included in the 1959 *Who's Who of American Women*.

Works

Purple on the Moon, operetta
Sunny, operetta, won a national prize
Several children's operettas
(Sources: Cohen; http://ochf.wordpress.com/2012/05/19/245/)

Marianne Genet (b. ca. 1876, Watertown, New York) was an organist and teacher. In addition to her operetta she composed vocal and sacred music.

Works

The Green Sybil, operetta
(Source: Cohen)

Eloise Klotz Heaton (b. ca. June 1, 1909, Balewinsville, New York) received her BMus from the University of Syracuse in 1933, then an MA in 1960. She also earned a certificate in choir teaching from the Royal Conservatory of the University of Toronto. In addition to her operetta she composed chamber music, vocal and sacred music, and teaching pieces. The Eloise K. Heaton Fellowship in Music Composition and Theory at the University of Syracuse is named for her. The university houses her papers.

Works

1938 *The Queen's Garden*, operetta
(Source: Cohen)

Frances McCollin (October 24, 1892, Philadelphia–February 25, 1960, Philadelphia) became blind when she was five. Her first music teacher was her father, who was a violinist, lawyer, and one of the founders of the Philadelphia Orchestra. She studied piano and compositions at the Pennsylvania Institute for Instruction for the Blind. She composed orchestral works, music for chamber group, organ music, much piano music, vocal music and sacred music. Her works were widely performed and also were broadcast on the radio. Frances won numerous awards for her music and used many pseudonyms. Her printed scores and manuscripts are in the music department and the Fleisher Collection of the Free Library of Philadelphia.

Works

King Christmas, operetta, for children
(Source: Cohen)

Mae Wheeler Nightingale (b. ca. December 30, 1898, Blencoe, Iowa) studied at several California universities and colleges. She first taught privately, then from 1926 to 1959 she taught at various schools and universities. The California Music Teachers' Association and the Kimber Foundation awarded her the Mancini Award for distinction in music education. She was an authority on the adolescent boy's voice. Her compositions include vocal music and choral and voice arrangements.

Works

Queen of the Sawdust, operetta for children, Librettist: Mae Nightingale
Ride 'Em Cowboy, operetta for children
(Source: Cohen)

Mildred Barnes Royse (February 9, 1896, Illinois–1986) received her teacher's diploma from the American Conservatory, Chicago, then went on to study at Columbia University, New York. Subsequently she studied with Walter Piston and Leo Sowerby. She composed two suites for orchestra, chamber music, vocal and sacred music.

Works

The Gingerbread Man, operetta for children
Naughty Ninky, operetta for children
(Source: Cohen)

Patty Stair (November 12, 1869, Cleveland–April 26, 1926, Cleveland) was an organist, pianist and choral conductor and lecturer. She attended the Cleveland School of Music, then in 1889 joined its faculty. In 1892 she also began teaching at the University School and taught at both schools until her death in 1926. She composed pieces for orchestra and chamber ensembles.

Works

The Fair Brigade, operetta
An Interrupted Serenade, operetta
Sweet Simplicity, operetta
(Sources: Sadie and Samuel; Cohen)

Mabel Wood (March 12, 1870, Brooklyn–March 1, 1954, Stamford, Connecticut) studied at Columbia University and Smith College. She first became known for her songs and vocal music then began composing in larger forms. In addition to her vocal music her compositions include music for orchestra and chamber ensembles, and two ballets.

Works

The Jolly Beggars, opera
(Source: Cohen)

Mary Hale Woolsey (March 21, 1899, Spanish Fork, Utah–1969) was an editor and writer as well as a composer. She studied at Brigham Young University in Utah and at Columbia University in New York. She composed primarily vocal music and songs. Her papers are at Brigham Young University.

Works

The Enchanged Attic, operetta
The Giant Garden, operetta
The Happy Hearts, operetta
Neighbors in the House, operetta
Starflower, operetta
(Source: Cohen)

USSR

Lyubov Lvovna Streicher (March 3, 1888–March 31, 1958, Moscow) graduated in composition from the St. Petersburg Conservatory. She taught at the Yekaterinodar Music School and also conducted their symphony orchestra. She held teaching positions at several schools and conservatories and composed chamber music, an orchestral piece, a ballet, chamber music, piano music, and vocal music. She made arrangements of folk songs of the USSR, Czechoslovakia, Hungary and Rumania.

Works

1932 *Chasi*, operetta for children

(Source: Cohen)

Varvara Andrianovna Gaigerova (October 4, 1903, Oryekhovo-Zuyevo–April 6, 1944, Moscow) began her career as a pianist and concertmistress in 1917 when she was fourteen and continued until 1923. Four years later she graduated from the Moscow Conservatory. She was concertmistress at the Bolshoi Theater from 1936 to 1944. She was interested in the musical folklore of the southeastern people of Soviet Russia and wrote orchestral music, and music for chamber ensembles, piano music and vocal music.

Works

1937–40 *Krepost u kamennogo broda*, opera, Librettist: Gaigerova, based on Lermontov and some Caucasian poets

(Source: Cohen)

Stefania Anatolyevna Zaranet (September 23, 1904, Kotelnich–January 17, 1972, Leningrad) graduated from the Leningrad Conservatory in 1926. For the next ten years she taught piano at the conservatory and the Worker's High School. She was artistic director of the Philharmonia in Gorky from 1942 to 1944. She composed for orchestra, chamber ensembles, vocal music, several ballets, music for over twenty plays, and film music.

Works

1937 *Chest mundira*, operetta, Librettist: E. Pavlov
1939 *Schastlivui put*, operetta, Librettist: E. Pavlov
1949 *Zolotoi fontan*, operetta, Librettists: K. Guzynin and A. Masiennikov
1954 *Taina morya*, operetta

(Source: Cohen)

Viktoria Sergeyevna Levitskaya (July 20, 1911, Kharbin–1988) graduated from the Moscow Conservatory in 1938. Three years later she completed postgraduate studies. After 1949 she was editor of opera and symphonic works for Murgiz, music publishers. She composed symphonic works, chamber works, music for piano and vocal works.

Works
1938 *Teni I zemlya dvizhetsya*, opera
1944 *Tarasova noch*, opera, Librettist: Y. Galitsky
(Source: Cohen)

1940–1970

The cataclysmic disruptions of World War II had a profound effect on music and opera, as they did on everything else. Eventually the economics of the arts revived, but much was different. Credentials came to matter somewhat differently than in the past, and many composers were earning advanced degrees and participating in higher education. There was a strong international thrust for many composers as well. The number of women who were conducting is intriguing.

Interest in indigenous, native, traditional and folk music continued to be strong, and undoubtedly there was a heightened awareness of their fragility. In Russia, Tatyana Chudova and Irina Elcheva took part in "folk song expeditions." Kikuko Kanai became director of the Japanese Association of Folklore Music. Eva Harvey, who was the first South African to write an opera and a member of the first South African symphony, sought out traditional music. In the United States Eusebia Hunkins became an authority on Appalachian music. Ivana Lang-Beck in Yugoslavia, Ruth Lomon in the United States, and Nina Vladimirovna Makarova and Natalia Nikolayevna Levi in the USSR also sought out, studied and utilized traditional music.

Getting an opera performed grew increasingly difficult. Many composers were writing operas more suited to smaller venues, operas that didn't require the complicated and expensive production of "grand opera" and the opera houses.

Argentina

María Isabel Curubeto Godoy (1904–August 25, 1959) was playing in concerts when she was eight; at twelve she composed a quartet and sonatas. She studied at the Conservatory of Cordoba, then in Europe on a scholarship, spending time in Rome and Vienna. She composed chamber music and music for piano and theater.

Works

1946 *Pablo y Virgínia*, opera, Librettist: Simoni
(Source: Cohen)

Ashkabad

Seda Grigorievna Babayeva (June 1, 1922, Ashkhabad–) graduated from the Tashkent Conservatory in 1950. Around 1964 she lectured at the conservatory. Subsequently she was a director of Uzbek radio and television. She composed chamber music and music for orchestra, piano, and stage works and spectacles.

Works

1968 *Zarena*, opera, based on *Bakhchisaraiski fontan* by Pushkin
(Source: Cohen)

Australia

When **Margaret Sutherland** (November 20, 1897, Adelaide–August 12, 1984, Melbourne) was nineteen she was invited by the director of the New South Wales State Conservatorium of Music to be a soloist with the NSW State Orchestra in public concerts. She had studied at the Marshall Hall (now Melba) Conservatorium and at the Melbourne University Conservatorium. During World War I she gave recitals and taught, which she continued to do until 1923. During that time she wrote teaching pieces for the piano. In 1923 she went to London, where she was a pupil of Arnold Bax, and to Vienna for further study. Two years later she returned to Melbourne. She composed little for the next ten years, but beginning in 1935 she composed, taught and performed. She was a strong advocate of Australian music.

Recognition of her music was limited for many years, but in the 1960s there was a surge of interest in Margaret and in Australian music in general. Her opera premiered at the Festival of Contemporary Opera and Music in Hobart in 1965. In 1969 she received an honorary DMus from the University of Melbourne; the following year she was made an OBE. She composed many orchestral works and works for chamber ensembles, music for piano, vocal and sacred music, two ballets and incidental music.

Works

1965 *The Young Kabbarli*, chamber opera, Librettist: M. Casey, Hobart

Margaret Sutherland wrote numerous books for young people and adults including:

The Fledgling. Auckland, Oxford: Oxford University Press, 1986.
Getting Through and Other Stories. London: Heinemann, 1977.
(Source: Sadie and Samuel)

Anne Boyd (April 10, 1946, Sydney–) grew up on a farm in the outback in Queensland. When she was eleven she moved to Canberra. She received her BA from the University of Sydney in 1969, winning the Frank Albert Prize. A Commonwealth Overseas Scholarship allowed her to study at York University in England, where she was awarded the DPhil in 1972. She then accepted a position as lecturer in music at the University of Sussex. Returning to Australia, she focused on composing for several years. She was appointed reader and head of the newly established music department at the University of Hong Kong, where she stayed for ten years. In 1991 she was appointed professor of music at the University of Sydney. She and Winsome Evans were featured in the award-winning documentary *Facing the Music.*

Works

1976 *The Little Mermaid,* opera
1980 *The Beginning of the Day,* opera
2012 *Daisy Bates at Ooldea*
(Sources: Sadie and Samuel; http://sydney.edu.au/news/84.html?newsstoryid=10328)

Alison Bauld (May 7, 1944, Sydney–) first studied drama at the National Institute of Dramatic Art and worked for a short time as an actress. She read English and music at Sydney University and received her BMus in 1968. The following year she received a Moss Travelling Scholarship to London, where she studied with Elisabeth Lutyens (see entry) and Hans Keller. In 1974 she received her PhD from York University. A year later she received a Gulbenkian Dance Award for composition. After serving for three years as musical director of the Laban Centre in London, she returned to Australia to assume the position of composer-in-residence at the New South Wales Conservatorium. She received a bursary from the Arts Council of Great Britain in 1980. Her works include music for chamber ensemble, piano, vocal music, and theater.

Works

1988 *Nell,* opera
(Source: Sadie and Samuel)

Belgium

Berthe di Vito-Delvaux (May 17, 1915, Angleur–April 2, 2005) grew up in a musical family; her father was an organist. She studied at the Royal Music Conservatory of Liege. In 1938 she began teaching at the Royal Conservatory. Five years later she won the Prix de Rome. Her many prizes and awards include the prize Marie from Liege, the Prix Modeste Grétry, medals from the Association des Arts, Sciences et Lettres of France and the Prix du Salon. Her many compositions include works for orchestra, chamber ensembles, piano, vocal and sacred works, and ballets.

Works

1944–46 *La Malibran*, opéra romantique, Librettist: N. de Sart
1949 *Les Amants de Sestos*, opera
1950–51 *Abigail*, opera, Librettist: J. de Sart
1952 *La Leçon*, operetta for children
1959 *Spoutnik, opera*
1967 *Maribel, comic opera*
1975–76 *Grétry*, comic opera, Librettist J. Schetter

(Sources: Sadie and Samuel; Cohen)

Bulgaria

Zhivka Klinkova (July 30, 1924, Samokov–2002) made her debut as a concert pianist in 1948. Three years later she graduated from the Sofia Academy of Music. That same year she began as a composer and conductor of the state-sponsored Philip Koutev Folksong and Dance Company, which she continued until 1960. For the next eight years she studied in Germany. Subsequently she worked as a freelance composer. She composed a significant number of orchestral works, music for chamber ensembles, at least two ballets, and vocal works.

Works

1956 *Petko Samohvalko* [Boastful Petko], children's opera, Librettist: N. Trendafilova, Berlin
1980 *The Most Improbable*, fairy-tale opera, Librettist: Klinkova
1981 *Cyril and Methodius*, opera, Librettists: V. Markovski and J. Gyermek
1992 *Vassil Levski*, opera, Librettist: Klinkova

(Sources: Sadie and Samuel; http://operadata.stanford.edu)

Canada

Barbara Lally Pentland (January 2, 1912, Winnipeg–February 5, 2000) was one of the composers who ran into parental opposition to her having a career in music, particularly composing. She began composing when she was nine. At age fifteen she attended a private boarding school, where she studied piano and theory with Frederick H. Blair, who encouraged her to pursue her interest in music. In 1929 she went to Paris where she studied composition with Cécile Gauthiez. The following year she returned to Winnipeg but continued her studies by correspondence.

She composed a considerable number of pieces between 1930 and 1936 and won several competitions, but she also was continuing her studies. A fellowship in composition from the Juilliard School enabled her to move to New York and further her studies. In 1939 she was again in Winnipeg, where she held a position at the University of Manitoba. She spent two summers at Tanglewood studying with Aaron Copland. She also spent two summers at the MacDowell, overlapping with Dika Newlin, who introduced her to many of Arnold Schoenberg's works. In 1949 she took a position at the University of British Columbia in Vancouver, where she stayed until 1963. At that time she turned all her attention to composing. She composed widely, with many works or orchestra and chamber ensembles, music for organ, many pieces for piano, a ballet incidental music and vocal music.

Works
1952 *The Lake*, chamber opera, Librettist: Dorothy Livesay
(Sources: Sadie and Samuel; http://operadata.stanford.edu)

Dorothy Forrest Cadzow (August 9, 1916, Edmonton, Alberta–2001) wrote, lectured arranged music, and composed. She received a BA and teacher's diploma from the University of Washington, Seattle. In 1942 she received a three year fellowship in composition to attend the Juilliard Graduate School. Following that she taught, did freelance arranging and wrote for *International Musician* until 1949, when she joined the music department at the University of Washington. She wrote pieces for orchestra, string quartet, piano, and vocal music.

Works
1958 *Undine*, opera
(Source: Cohen)

Jean Coulthard (February 10, 1908, Vancouver–2000) had her first music lessons from her mother, who was a pianist and organist. When Jean was twenty she won a scholarship from the Vancouver Woman's Music Club, which she used to study at the Royal College of Music in England. After she received her diploma she returned to Canada and became head of the music departments of St. Anthony's College and Queen's Hall School. She continued her studies intermittently in the 1940s and 1950s; during that time she received critiques from Arthur Benjamin, Darius Milhaud, Bela Bartok, Bernard Wagenaar, and Nadia Boulanger. From 1947 to 1973 she was with the department of music at the University of at the University of British Columbia. She received numerous awards and prizes and at least two honorary doctorates. Her many compositions include works for orchestra, chamber ensembles, vocal and sacred music, and piano music.

Works

The Return of the Native, opera, after Thomas Hardy, with Edna Baxter
(Source: Sadie and Samuel)

Margaret Drynan (December 10, 1915, Toronto–February 18, 1999, Oshawa, Ontario) had a varied career as organist, percussionist, choirmistress, singer, journalist and teacher. In 1943 she received a BMus from Toronto University. She was founder (and conductor for 15 years) of the Royal Canadian College of Organists and was a Fellow of that organization. Her interest in music education led to her being music consultant for the Durham Board of Education for twenty-one years; she also taught privately and was percussionist with the Oshawa Symphony orchestra. In 1983 the YWCA awarded her the title of Woman of Distinction of the Year in the Arts. A writer and journalist, she contributed articles to music periodicals and was the Canadian editor of *Diapason* magazine.

Works

The Canada Goose, operetta
(Sources: Cohen; http://www.thecanadianencyclopedia.ca/en/article/margaret-drynan-emc/)

Anne E. Eggleston (September 6, 1934, Ottawa–) studied in Ottawa then at the Royal Conservatory in Toronto, receiving her artist diploma in 1956. Two years later she was awarded an MMus from the Eastman School of Music. She received numerous awards in her career. Her compositions include music for orchestra, chamber music, vocal music, music for piano.

Works

1961 *The Wood Carver's Wife*, opera, Librettist: Pickthall
(Source: Cohen)

Cuba

Olga de Blanck (March 11, 1916, Havana–July 28, 1998) was the daughter of Hubert de Blanck, a composer and pianist who started the conservatory of music in Havana that became the National Conservatory. Olga first studied privately, then in 1938 she went to New York to continue her studies. From 1943 to 1944 she studied in Mexico, then in 1945 she returned to Cuba to be deputy director at the National Conservatory.

Her first works, collections of Cuban songs, were very popular. She and the writer M. Julia Casanova created modern music comedies that were performed on radio and in the theater. Subsequently she became the state advisor on music education. A prolific composer, she composed over three hundred works, including music for orchestra, chamber music, vocal music and a significant amount of music for theater.

Works

1958 *Un cuento de Navidad*, operetta
(Source: Cohen)

Czechoslovakia

Sláva Vorlová (March 15, 1894, Náchod, Czechoslovakia–August 24, 1973, Prague) studied privately and at the Vienna Conservatory. After passing her state examinations in 1918 she taught in Náchod. The following year she married and returned to Prague, where she often gave musical evenings. In 1945 she joined a master class in composition at the Prague Conservatory. She graduated in 1948, the first woman to receive a degree in composition there, which she dedicated to Jan Masaryk. Her compositions at times have a folklore element. Later in her composing she focused on different uses of instruments and contemporary techniques. She wrote songs and jazz compositions under the pseudonym Mira Kord. In addition, she composed many works for orchestra and for chamber ensembles, piano music, vocal and choral work, and incidental music.

Works

1949 *Zlaté ptáče* [The Golden Bird], fairy-tale opera, Librettist: V.H. Roklan
1952 *Rozmarýnka*, folk opera, Librettist: V.H. Roklan, after V. Hálek
1955 *Náchodská kasace* [Nachod Cassation], historical opera
1958 Dva světy [Two Worlds], opera, Librettist V.H. Roklan, after A. Jirásek
(Sources: Sadie and Samuel; Cohen)

East Germany

Ruth Zechlin (June 22, 1926, near Freiberg–August 4, 2007) was a harpsichordist and organist. From 1943 to 1949 she studied at the Leipzig Hochschule für Musik. After graduation she took a position at the Hanns Eisler Hochschule für Musik in East Berlin teaching composition. She was made a full professor in 1984, the first woman in Germany to have such an appointment. At the same time, she was a full member of East Germany's Akademie der Künste. She became vice-president of the Berlin Akademie der Künste in 1990. Her main focus in composing was orchestral music and music for chamber ensembles, but she also composed music for organ, piano and vocal music.

Works

1968 *Reineke Fuchs*, opera, Librettist: Gunther Deicke after von Goethe
1990 *Die Salamandrin und die Bildsäule*, opera, Librettist: F. Göhler, after C.M.
  Weiland

(Sources: Sadie and Samuel; http://operadata.stanford.edu)

England

Imogen Holst (April 12, 1907, Surrey–March 9, 1984, Aldeburgh) was the daughter of Gustav Holst. Her earlier works show his influence, but she soon developed her own style and explored other forms and tonalities. She studied at the Royal Academy of Music, where she won the Cobbett Prize in 1928 and was awarded the Octavia Travelling Scholarship two years later.

In 1952 Imogen became musical assistant to Benjamin Britten and moved to Aldeburgh. She became involved with organizing the annual Aldeburgh Festival and later she was joint artistic director of the festival, helping it gain a position of preeminence in British musical life. She did little composing during that period. In 1964 she gave up her work as Britten's assistant. She resumed her composing and also focused on securing her father's musical legacy. In addition to opera she wrote music for stage, orchestra, chamber ensembles, vocal music and instrumental works.

Works

1945 *Young Beichan*, opera, Librettist: Beryl de Zoete
1950 *Benedick and Beatrice*, opera, Dartington

Imogen also was the author of numerous books on music and composers, including:

Holst, Imogen. *Britten.* Series: The Great Composers. London: Faber, 1965.
_____. *Henry Purcell, 1659–1695: Essays on His Music.* London, New York: Oxford University Press, 1959.
_____. *Holst.* Series: The Great Composers. London : Faber and Faber, 1974.
_____. *Tune.* London: Faber & Faber, 1962.
Williams, Ralph Vaughan, Gustav Holst, Ursula Vaughan Williams, and Imogen Holst. *Heirs and Rebels: Letters Written to Each Other and Occasional Writings on Music.* London, New York: Oxford University Press, 1959.

(Sources: Sadie and Samuel; http://operadata.stanford.edu)

Patricia Ann Friedberg (May 4, 1934, London–) first studied journalism in London, then attended Marquette University from 1969 to 1971. She was also an author, and wrote for television and theater in Zimbabwe, South Africa, and America.

Works

Simcha 71, opera 1960s
Twenty-One Aldgate, opera
(Source: Cohen)

Elisabeth Lutyens (July 6, 1906, London–April 14, 1983, London) studied at the École Normale in Paris when she was sixteen. She continued her studies at the Royal College of Music. In 1932 her ballet *The Birthday of the Infanta* was produced, the first significant public performance of her music. Much of her early music, including the ballet, was withdrawn, as her style continued to evolve and develop. Her domestic life tended to be uneven, which often made it difficult to focus on the composing she wanted to do. Instead she composed for film and radio to support her family. She was a prolific composer with a substantial number of works for orchestra, chamber ensembles, organ piano vocal and sacred music, and incidental music.

Works

1954 *Infidelio*, opera, Librettist: E. Lutyens
1965–67 *The Numbered*, opera, Librettist: Volonakis, after E. Canetti: *Die Befristeten*
1973 *The Waiting Game*, opera, Librettist: E. Lutyens
1975 *The Goldfish Bowl*, opera, Librettist: E. Lutyens
1976 *Like a Window*, opera, after letters of V. Van Gogh

Books by or about Elisabeth Lutyens:

Lutyens, Elisabeth. *A Goldfish Bowl.* London, Cassell, 1972.
Mathias, Rhiannon. *Lutyens, Maconchy, Williams, and Twentieth-Century British Music: A Blest Trio of Sirens.* Farnham, Surrey, England: Ashgate, c2012.

(Sources: Sadie and Samuel; http://operadata.stanford.edu)

Elizabeth Maconchy (March 19, 1907, Hertfortshire–November 11, 1994) began composing at an early age. From 1923 to 1929 she attended the Royal College of Music, where her instructors included Charles Wood and Vaughan Williams. An Octavia Travelling Scholarship in 1929 allowed her to study in Prague. The following year her Piano Concertino was performed, the first public performance of her music. When she returned to London her music was played at a Promenade concert, which proved to be a turning point for her. In 1932 she contracted tuberculosis and had to leave London, never to live there again.

Elizabeth was active in several organizations. In 1977 she was made a CBE; a decade later she was made a DBE. She composed many works for orchestra, and for chamber ensembles, sacred and vocal music, works for piano, and several ballets. Her works were played throughout Europe, in Australia and in the United States. Her daughter Nicola LeFanu (see entry) is also a composer.

Works

1956/57 *The Sofa*, opera, Librettist: U. Vaughan Williams, London
1957/58 *The Three Strangers*, opera, Librettist: Maconchy, after Thomas Hardy
1960/61 *The Departure*, opera, Librettist: A. Ridler
1968 *The Birds*, opera, Librettist: Maconchy after Aristophanes, London
1969 *The Jesse Tree*, church opera, Librettist: Ridler
1969 *Johnny and the Mohawks*, children's opera, Librettist: Maconchy, London
1975 *The King of the Golden River*, children's opera, Librettist: Maconchy after John Ruskin, Oxford

Books by or about Elizabeth Maconchy:

Mathias, Rhiannon. *Lutyens, Maconchy, Williams, and Twentieth-Century British Music: A Blest Trio of Sirens.* Farnham, Surrey, England: Ashgate, 2012.

(Source: Sadie and Samuel)

Freda Swain (October 31, 1902, Portsmouth–January 29, 1985, Chinnor) studied at the Royal College of Music, receiving the Sullivan Prize for composition in 1917. One of her teachers was Arthur Alexander, whom she married in 1921. Three years later she was appointed professor at the Royal College of Music, a position she held until 1940. She was interested in new music and founded the British Music Movement, dedicated to the promotion of new music. At the beginning of World War II her husband was stranded in South Africa. Freda wrote a piano concerto for him, using very thin paper, and sent it by airmail in installments. The concerto, which Alexander performed, became known as the "Airmail Concerto." In 1940 Freda joined her husband, and they toured in South Africa giving recitals for two pianos. Subsequently they toured in Australia, returned to South Africa and then went home to

England, in 1943. After the war she established the NEMO concerts to promote new music. She composed music for orchestra, many pieces for chamber ensembles, music for piano, organ, vocal and sacred music.

Works

1959 *Second Chance*, opera, Librettists: Swain and M. Rodd
The Spell, opera, incomplete
The Shadowy Waters, "operatic setting," based on Yeats
(Source: Sadie and Samuel)

Melanie Ruth Daiken (July 27, 1945, London–) studied at the Royal Academy of Music, the University of Ghana, and the Paris Conservatoire. She taught at several venues before being appointed head of composition and contemporary music studies at the Royal Academy of Music in 1986. She has composed orchestral works, music for chamber ensembles, for solo instruments, and vocal music.

Works

1968 *Eusebius*, opera, Librettist: Daiken, Paris
1971 *Mayakovsky and the Sun*, opera, Librettist: V. Mayakovsky, Edinburgh
Playboy of the Western World, opera, Librettist: J.M. Synge
(Source: Sadie and Samuel)

Cohen lists **Bryony Phillips Jagger** (March 10, 1948, Salford, England) as a dual British and New Zealand national. She was awarded a BA with honors from Cambridge in 1971. She then studied Far Eastern music, literature and history, and returned to Cambridge where she received an MA with honors in 1974. She studied composition privately in Boston and subsequently studied electronic music and theater at the University of Auckland in New Zealand. In 1970 she founded—and was musical director of—New Hall Madrigal Group. She performed widely, playing the oboe in orchestras and chamber ensembles in England and New Zealand, as well as singing in choirs. Her works have been performed on radio and in concert in both New Zealand and England. In 1984 she was appointed a visiting scholar to New Hall, Cambridge.

An immensely prolific composer in many genres—orchestral, chamber, vocal—she also has composed for the theater, in addition to her opera and operetta.

Works

1978 *Release from Hell*, operetta, from Dr. Setsuko Ito
1980 *Chitra*
(Source: Cohen)

When **Madeleine Dring** (September 7, 1923, London–March 26, 1977, London) was ten she won a violin scholarship to the junior department of the Royal College of Music. She later won a scholarship to continue as a senior student. Theater was always a strong interest, and she studied drama and mime. Many of her compositions are for theater. She also composed orchestral music, works for chamber ensembles, and for theater, piano music and vocal music.

Works

Cupboard Love, opera
(Source: Sadie and Samuel)

Estonia

Lydia Auster (May 30, 1912, Northern Kazakhstan–April 3, 1993) graduated from the Omsk Technical School of Music in 1931. For the next four years she attended the Moscow Conservatory, graduating in 1936.She then became musical editor for Turkmen Radio. She was appointed music supervisor of the Estonian Television and Radio Committee in 1945, then became head of the Musical Foundation of the Union of Composers of the Estonian SSR. She received the title Merited Artist of the Estonian SSR in 1955. Her compositions include pieces for orchestra and chamber ensembles, piano four ballets, vocal music and incidental music for children's plays.

Works

1970 *Maiskoye utro*, opera
(Source: Cohen)

France

Yvonne Desportes (July 18, 1907, Coburg–December 29, 1993, Paris) studied at the Paris Conservatoire and won the Prix de Rome in 1932. Eleven years later she began teaching at the conservatoire. She became well known as a teacher and wrote works on music education. In addition to her operas she composed at least two ballets, music for orchestra, for chamber ensembles and vocal music.

Works

1939/1940 *Maître Cornelius*, opera, Librettist: Marcel V. Belvianes, after Honoré de Balzac

1943 *La Farce du carabinier*, opera comique
1952 *Mimi Pinson*, operetta
1965 *Le Forgeur de merveilles*, opera, Librettist: Desportes, after F.-J O'Brien

Books by or about Yvonne Desportes (according to Cohen):

Comment former l'oreille musicale, 1970.
L'Initiation au langage musical. 3 vols. Billaudot, 1981
(Source: Sadie and Samuel)

As a child, **Wally Karvéno** (b. ca. 1914, Germany) spent several years in Switzerland. Her mother was a brilliant violinist, her father a biologist. After his death the family went to France. Wally, although primarily interested in music, spent several years in film, where she met many celebrities. She soon returned to music, giving concerts. In addition to her opera she wrote piano, vocal and chamber music.

Works

1941 *La Fiancée du diable*, opera, Librettist: Pal Stoecklin
(Sources: Cohen; www.edilivre.com>Accueil>Auteurs>Karveno)

Marcelle de Manziarly (October 1 [October 1/13], 1899, Kharkiv–May 12, 1989, Ojai, California) divided her career between France and the United States. Her education included studying with Nadia Boulanger in Paris. A noted pianist and a conductor, she gave concerts and conducted in the United States; she also taught in Paris and New York. She composed for orchestra and chamber ensembles, for piano and for voice.

Works

1954 *La Femme en flèche*, chamber opera
(Source: Sadie and Samuel)

Henriette Roget (b. ca. January 9, 1910, Bastia, Corsica) had a successful career as an organist, pianist and professor. She studied at the Paris Conservatoire and won prizes in harmony, fugue and organ, the piano, history and accompaniment. In 1933 she was awarded second in the Prix de Rome. The next year she became organist at the Oratoire du Louvre St. Clotilde, then at the Great Synagogue from 1934 to 1952. In 1957 she became professor at the Paris Conservatoire, teaching accompaniment and score reading. She was singing mistress at the opera. She composed numerous pieces for orchestra, including at least one symphony, chamber music, music for organ and for piano, teaching pieces (piano) for children, vocal music, one ballet, and music for radio. Her "Hymnes à l'aviation" won a prize at the Paris Exhibition in 1937.

Works

1957 *Master of Song*, opera
(Source: Cohen)

Rolande Falcinelli (February 18, 1920, Paris–) gave her first concert when she was seven. At the Paris Conservatoire she won numerous first prizes; she also won the Grand Prix de Rome and was the first woman to win the Prix Rossini. In addition to her composing she was an organist, pianist and lecturer; she taught at the American Conservatory in Fontainebleau, at the École Normale de Musique, and then at the Paris Conservatoire. A prolific composer, her compositions include over fifty for orchestra, numerous pieces for chamber ensembles, music for piano, vocal music, sacred music including an oratorio and at least one mass, music for ballet, and three operas. She also published transcriptions for organ, an anthology of classical organ music, and a book on organ technique.

Works

Icare, opera
Louise de la Miséricorde, opera
Pygmalion délivré, opera

Books by or about Rolande Falinelli:

Falinelli, Rolande. "École de la Technique Moderne de l'Orgue" (unpublished)
_____. *Initiation à l'orgue*. Paris: Bornemann/Leduc, 1971.
(Source: Cohen)

Adrienne Clostre (October 9, 1921, Thomery–2006), who studied at the Paris Conservatoire, won the Prix de Rome in 1949 for her cantata *La Résurrection de Lazare*. She also won the Grand Prix Musical de la Ville de Paris in 1955, the Prix Florence Gould in 1976, and the Grand Prix de la Musique of the Société des Auteurs et Compositeurs Dramatiques in 1987. Her compositions include numerous works for stage, orchestra and various instruments, as well as many vocal works.

Works

1960 *Le Chant du cygnet*, chamber opera, Librettist: Adrienne Clostre, after Chekhov
1989 *Annapurna*, opera, Librettists: Adrienne Clostre, Maurice Herzog
Numerous chamber operas
(Sources: Sadie and Samuel; http://operadata.stanford.edu)

Like a number of other French women composers, **Lucie Robert** (October 3, 1936, Rennes–) was an organist, pianist, and lecturer as well as being a composer. She studied at the Paris Conservatoire and received numerous first prizes. In 1965 she won the Premier Grand Prix de Rome. Later, she taught at the conservatoire. She was prolific, composing symphonic music, concertos for oboe, flute, and piano, chamber music, piano music and vocal music.

Works

1963 *L'Épouse injustement soupçonnée*, opera, based on a text by Jean Cocteau
(Source: Cohen)

Jeanine Rueff (February 5, 1922, Paris–1999) studied at the Paris Conservatoire. In 1945 she won the Favareille-Chailley-Richez Prize for her piano quintet; three years later she won the second Grand Prix de Rome. She was an accompanist at the Paris Conservatoire in 1950. In 1959 she began teaching there. Her compositions include music for orchestra, chamber music, and a ballet.

Works

1954 *La Femme d'Énée*, chamber opera
(Sources: Cohen; Wikipedia)

Both the father and the sister of **Ida Rose Esther Gotkovsky** (August 26, 1933, Calais–) were noted violinists. Ida Rose studied at the Paris Conservatoire, where her instructors included Messiaen and Nadia Boulanger. She won numerous prizes.

Works

1964 *Le Rêve de Makar*, opera, Librettist: W. Korolenko
(Sources: Cohen; Wikipedia)

Monic [*sic*] **Cecconi-Botella** (September 30, 1936–) studied at the Paris Conservatoire. She won the First Grand Prix de Rome for composition in 1966. Later she became interested in the possibility of combining elements of music, sculpture, painting and architecture. She composed ballets, music for orchestra, chamber music, vocal music, music for piano and theater, electronic music, and multimedia.

Works

1969 *La Méprise*, chamber opera, Librettist: Pierre Gripari
1991 *Il signait…. Vincent!*, opera, Librettist: Jacques Unal
(Sources: Cohen; http://operadata.stanford.edu)

Germany

Alice Samter (June 11, 1908, Berlin–2004) studied in Berlin, but as her studies were interrupted by World War II, she didn't graduate from the Berlin Hochschule für Musik until 1946. She worked as an art and a music teacher in Berlin high schools until 1970. Much of her earlier music was destroyed in the war. She composed music for orchestra, a significant amount of chamber music, music for theater and incidental music, piano music, and a considerable amount of vocal music. Her papers are housed in the Berlin State Library.

Works
1957 *Der falsche Graf*, adapted from Gottfried Keller
(Sources: Sadie and Samuel; http://operadata.stanford.edu)

Hungary

Júlia Hajdú (September 8, 1915, Budapest–October 23, 1987, Budapest) graduated from the Budapest Academy of Music, having studied composition and instrumentation, as well as folk music, where her teacher was Zoltán Kodály. Her debut as a composer in 1948 was on Hungarian Radio. That same year one of her compositions won first prize in Radio Budapest's song festival. She also won an award from the Hungarian Folk Song Festival in 1950. Two years later she received a special prize of the Hungarian Republic. She was the first woman composer for theater in Hungary and had a special gift for the operetta-like tradition of Budapest. She was one of the most successful composers of songs and light music for over forty years, with compositions include at least fourteen operettas and musicals.
(Sources: Sadie and Samuel; Cohen)

Erzsébet Szőnyi (April 25, 1924, Budapest–) received her diploma in music teaching from the Budapest Academy of Music in 1945. Subsequently she earned diplomas in composition, conducting and the piano, in 1947. From 1945 to 1946 she stood in for Zoltán Kodály at the academy and taught his folk music classes. The next year she received a French State scholarship to study at the Paris Conservatoire; her teachers included Nadia Boulanger and Olivier Messiaen. She began teaching at the Franz Liszt Academy in Budapest; in 1960 she became director of the school's music faculty. She received numerous prizes and awards, including the Erkel Prize for Composition in 1959. She was involved with music education on many levels throughout her career, and wrote on teaching, particularly Kodály's teaching methods.

Her compositions include music for orchestra, chamber music, ballets, theater music, music for organ, for piano and vocal music.

Works

1953 *Dalma*, opera, after M. Jókai
1955 *A makrancos királylány* [The Stubborn Princess], children's opera, Librettist: E. Kováts, Budapest
1960 *Firenzei tragédie* [The Florentine Tragedy], opera, after Oscar Wilde, Meiningen
1974 *Az aranyszárnyú méhecske* [The Little Bee with Golden Wings], children's opera, Librettist: E. Orbán, Philadelphia
1980 *Vidám sirató*, Librettist: Sandor Weores
1987 *Elfrida*, Librettist: Laszlo Arany

(Sources: Sadie and Samuel; Cohen; http://operadata.stanford.edu)

Ireland

Joan Trimble (b. ca. June 18, 1915, Enniskillen) studied at the Royal Irish Academy of Music in Dublin as a scholarship student from 1930 to 1936. She earned her BA in 1936 and her MusB the following year from Trinity College in Dublin. Subsequently she was at the Royal College of Music in London, where her instructors included Ralph Vaughan Williams and Herbert Howells for composition. She received the Royal College of Music Cobbett Prize in 1940 for her Phantasy Trio and also received the RCM Sullivan Prize for composition.

In 1938 she and her sister Valerie, who had performed with her earlier, formed a piano duo. They performed in major venues and had long and successful careers. Many of Joan's works were written for their performances. Other composers wrote for them as well, and they performed a wide range of music. Joan taught piano at the Royal College of Music for many years. Her compositions include orchestral works, piano music, works for chamber ensembles, vocal music, arrangements, and film music. *Blind Raftery* was the first television opera written by a woman composer.

Works

1957 *Blind Raftery*, television opera, Librettist: Cedric Cliffe, after D. Byrne

(Sources: Sadie and Samuel; Wikipedia)

Ina Boyle (March 8, 1889, Enniskerry, County Wicklow–March 10, 1967, Enniskerry) lived most of her life in Ireland but periodically traveled to London to study with Ralph Vaughan Williams. She had great success with her orchestral and vocal work *Soldiers at Peace*, and her orchestral work *The*

Magic Harp received a Carnegie award. Hers was a quiet and isolated life, and there was little opportunity for her music being performed.

Works

1964 *Maudlin of Paplewick*, opera, after Ben Jonson's *The Sad Shepherd*

Books by or about Ina Boyle:

Maconchy, Elizabeth. *Ina Boyle: An Appreciation, with a Select List of Her Music.* Dublin, 1974.

(Source: Sadie and Samuel)

Israel

Sarah Feigin (July 1, 1928, Riga–April 24, 2011) studied at the Riga Music Academy from 1946 to 1950. In 1959 she received her MA in composition from the academy. After graduating she was composer and musical consultant at the Choreographical Institute and Opera in Riga for about thirteen years. In 1972 she settled in Israel. After teaching at the Conservatory of Kiron for one year she founded the Conservatory in Holon, for immigrant teachers, and was director for about ten years. She composed chamber music, vocal music, ballets, teaching pieces, and music for piano.

Works

1959 *The House of the Cat*, operetta for children

(Sources: Sadie and Samuel; Cohen)

Italy

Barbara Giuranna (November 18, 1899, Palermo, Italy–July 31, 1998) graduated from the conservatory in Naples in 1923 but continued her composition studies after graduation. In 1924 she married Mario Giuranna, a composer and conductor, and they went to the United States. In 1929 two of her compositions had their first performances in Chicago and were repeated at the Metropolitan. Barbara and her husband returned to Italy in 1933.

She was the first Italian woman composer at the Venice Biennale, in 1936. From 1937 to 1976 she taught at the Saint Cecilia Conservatory in Rome and became the music consultant to RAI, the public radio, in the 1950s. Here her work included making transcriptions and realizations of operas by Paisiello and Cimarosa. Her music was widely known; in 1990 the International Leonard Bernstein Academy organized a concert in Rome in her honor.

She composed a mass, music for orchestra, for chamber ensembles and solo instruments.

Works

1941 *Jamanto*, opera lirica, Librettist: Bergamo
1961 *Mayerling*, opera lirica, Librettist: A. Vioviani, Naples
1978 *Hosanna*, opera lirica, Librettist: Carlo Pinelli, Palermo
(Source: Sadie and Samuel)

Teresa Procaccini (March 23, 1934, Foggia–) began composing at a young age. She first studied piano at the Foggia Conservatory. After graduating she continued her studies in organ and composition, then attended the Rome Conservatory of Saint Cecilia, where she studied film music, and the Accademia Musicale Chigiana in Siena, where she studied composition. She returned to Foggia Conservatory, first to teach organ and composition, then she took the position of director for about a year. In 1979 she went to the Rome Conservatory of Saint Cecilia as a lecturer in composition. In addition to her operas she composed ballets, music for orchestra and chamber ensembles and vocal music. Throughout her career she won many prizes, including the International String Quartet Competition in 1981.

Works

1970 *La vendetta di Luzbel*, opera, Librettist; Proccacini, after F. Lopé de Vega
1973 *La prima notte*, comic opera, Librettist: Massaron
1975 *Piazza della musica*, operetta for children
1975 *Questione di fiducia*, comic opera, Librettist: Massaron
1984 *L'uomo del tamburo*, opera
(Sources: Sadie and Samuel; Cohen)

Japan

Kikuko Kanai (March 13, 1911, Okinawa–February 17, 1986) received a fine arts degree from the University of Tokyo in 1936. She became director of the Japan Association of Folklore Music and was a member of the Japan Federation of Composers. In 1968 the Okinawan government awarded her a prize for her opera, *Okinawa monogatari*.

Works

Okinawa monogatari, opera
(Sources: Cohen; Wikipedia)

The Netherlands

Johanna Bordewijk-Roepman (August 4, 1892, Rotterdam–October 8, 1971, The Hague), who began composing when she was twenty-five, was largely self-taught as a composer. (She did have lessons in orchestration with Eduard Flipse, principle conductor of the Rotterdam Philharmonic Orchestra, when she was in her forties.) Her first suite for orchestra, *The Garden of Allah*, was inspired by a visit to North Africa. In 1940 her orchestral work *Les Illuminations* was performed under Flipse. Her works were performed throughout the 1940s and 1950s, and she received numerous commissions.

Works
1943 *Rotonde*, opera, Librettist: F. Bordewijk

(Source: Sadie and Samuel)

Tera de Marez Oyens (August 5, 1932, Velsen–August 29, 1996) was a harpsichordist, pianist, violinist, conductor and lecturer. After graduating from the Amsterdam Conservatory in 1953 she studied composition and electronic composition at the Institute of Sonology of the University of Utrecht, where she earned her diploma in electronic music in 1965. For years she taught at the conservatory in Zwolle. She gave radio talks on musical education, electronic music, and women composers; in her television appearances she conducted orchestras and choirs. Her compositions include orchestral works, music for chamber ensembles, for piano, vocal and sacred music, ballets, music for theater, incidental music, and numerous pieces of electronic music.

Works
1960 *Dorp zonder muziek*, operetta for children
1966 *De Kapitein is jarig*, operetta for children
1962 *Liedje gezocht*, operetta for children
1966 *Van de vos Reynaerde*, operetta for children

(Sources: Sadie and Samuel; Cohen)

Poland

At the same time **Grażyna Bacewicz** (February 5, 1909, Lodz–January 17, 1969, Warsaw) attended the Warsaw Conservatory and studied philosophy at Warsaw University. After graduating in 1932 she went to Paris, where she studied with Nadia Boulanger and André Touret, the violinist. She then taught in Lodz, but after a year returned to Paris for further study. In 1936 she was made principle violinist of the Polish Radio Orchestra. She toured and quickly became known in many parts of Europe as a brilliant violinist and a promising composer (she also was a notable pianist). Two months before the outbreak of World War II she returned to Poland. After the war she resumed her performances as a concert violinist, performing until the mid–1950s, when she turned her full attention to composing.

She was already well known as a composer. Her compositions won top awards in many of the most prestigious competitions. Grażyna was also known for her short stories, novels and autobiographical anecdotes. Surely one of the more prolific composers, she has many orchestral works, chamber works, music for piano, violin, vocal and sacred music, ballets, and incidental music to her credit.

Works
1959 *Przygoda Króla Artura*, opera for radio, Librettist: Edward Fischer
(Source: Sadie and Samuel)

Bernadetta Matuszczak (March 10, 1937, Toruń–) graduated from the State Higher School of Music in Poznań in 1958. She went on to receive her MA in 1968 from the State Music College in Warsaw. Subsequently she studied with Nadia Boulanger in Paris. She had a particular interest in operas and oratorios, and often worked with Polish music theatres. Her works have been widely performed at music festivals and she's received numerous prizes in international competitions, as well as in Poland. Her compositions include music for orchestra and for chamber ensembles, vocal and sacred music.

Works
1967 *Julia i Romeo*, chamber opera, Librettist: Bernadetta Matusczak, after William Shakespeare
1974 *Misterium Heloizy*, opera
1978 *Pamiętnik wariata* [The Diary of a Madman], opera, Librettist: Bernadetta Matuszczak, after Nikolay Gogol
1979 *Apocalypsis*, opera, Librettist: Bernadetta Matuszcak
(Sources: Sadie and Samuel; http://operadata.stanford.edu)

Joanna Bruzdowicz (May 19, 1943, Warsaw–) began her studies at the Warsaw Lyceum of Music and continued at the Conservatory of Music, graduating with an MA in 1966. She toured in Europe as a pianist for about two years, then received a French government scholarship to study in Paris. Her teachers included Olivier Messiaen and Nadia Boulanger; she also studied electronic music with Pierre Schaeffer. For her doctorate at the Sorbonne she wrote a thesis on "Mathematics and Logic in Contemporary Music." After completing her studies in France, she and her husband, Horst-Jürgen Tittel, settled in Belgium. Her compositions include music for orchestra, chamber ensembles, piano, vocal music, film music and electronic music. Her manuscripts are at the University of Southern California.

Works

1968 *Kolonia karna* [The Penal Colony], opera, after Franz Kafka
1973 *Les Troyennes* [The Women of Troy], opera, after Euripides
1982 *Bramy raju* [The Gates of Paradise], opera, after Jerzy Andrzejewski
(Sources: Sadie and Samuel; http://operadata.stanford.edu)

Portugal

Maria de Lourdes Martins (Clara da Silva) (May 26, 1926, Lisbon–August 31, 2009) first studied at the Conservatório Nacional in Lisbon. Subsequently a Gulbenkian Foundation scholarship allowed her to study in Germany. She received a diploma from the Orff Institute at the Mozarteum in Salzberg in 1960. Returning to Portugal, she became director of the Orff-Schulwerk courses sponsored by the Gulbenkian Foundation in Lisbon. From 1971 to 1978 she taught at the Lisbon Conservatory; at the same time she served as director of the Portuguese branch of the International Society of Music Educators. Her works include orchestral pieces, works for chamber ensembles, for piano, choral and vocal music, and music for theater.

Works

1958 *Silêncio, onde estás tu?*, radio opera, Librettist: T. Maria Gersao
1984 *Três máscaras*
(Source: Sadie and Samuel)

Romania

Mansi Barberis (March 12, 1899, Iaşi, Romania–October 10, 1986, Bucharest) studied at Iaşi Conservatory from 1918 to 1922, then in Berlin for a year and Paris from 1926 to 1927 where her instructors included Vincent d'Indy. She taught singing at the Iaşi Conservatory from 1934 to 1950 and opera from 1941 to 1950. Subsequently she taught in Bucharest. A prolific composer, her compositions include music for orchestra, chamber ensembles, piano, vocal music, and music for theater. She often used folk-like melodies and themes in her operas.

Works

1946 *Prinţesă îndepărtată* [The Distant Princess], opera, Librettist: M. Codreanu, after E. Rostand, revised 1976, Iaşi
1958 *Apus de soare* [Sunset], opera, Librettist: G Teodorescu, after B. Stefanescu-Delavrancea, Bucharest
1963 *Kera Duduca*, television opera, revised 1970, Librettist: A. Ionescu-Arbore, after N. Filimon: *ciocoii vechi şi noi*, Bucharest
1980 *La Charette aux Paillaces*, opera, Librettist: A. Ionescu-Arbore
1982 *Căruţa cu paiaţe* [The Cart with Clowns], opera, Librettist: A. Ionescu-Arbore, after M. Stefanescu, Iaşi

Books by or about Mansi Barberis:

Barberis, Mansi. *From Dawn to Dusk.* Translation of *Din zori până în amurg* (A Volume of Her Recollections). Bucharest, 1989.

(Sources: Sadie and Samuel; Cohen)

Russia

Lyudmila Alexseyevna Lyadova [Lyadova] (March 29, 1925, Sverdlovsk) graduated from the Sverdlovsk Conservatory in 1948. During the 1940s she and N. Panteleyeva performed vocal duets; she also gave concert tours performing her own songs, both as pianist and singer. She composed music for orchestral, choral music, and approximately five hundred songs.

Works

1960 *Pod chyornoy maskoy* [Behind a Black Mask], operetta, Librettist: Y. Lelgant
1984 *Shakhtyorskiye nevesti* [Miners' Brides], opera, Librettist: Petrova
1986 *Dva tsveta vremeni* [Two Colors of the Time], opera, Librettists: E. Kushakov and A. Snitsarenko

(Source: Sadie and Samuel)

The mother of **Irina Mikhaylovna Elcheva** (November 28, 1926, St. Petersburg–) was Hadezhda Bogolyubova, a pianist, composer and music theorist. During World War II she studied at the Mussorgsky College in Leningrad; subsequently she studied at the Leningrad Conservatory, graduating in 1950 in piano and in 1958 in composition. She was part of folk song expeditions in 1953 and 1956; then she began collecting folk songs independently, publishing an edition of collected folk songs in 1968. In addition to her opera she composed a symphony in memory of those who died in the blockade of Leningrad.

Works

1962 *Spartak*, opera

(Source: Sadie and Samuel)

Maria Semyonovna Zavalishina (b. ca. December 26, 1903, St. Petersburg) graduated in 1929 from the Leningrad Musical College. She then headed the music department of the Northern Siberian Dramatic Theater from 1929 to 1934 and was an instructor in the Odessa Art Department from 1938 to 1941. For the next three years she was headmistress of the Music School in Sovetsk, Kirov region, which she founded. She also lectured at the Music School in Kirov. At that time she composed for theater. Subsequently she was on the Artistic Committee of the Moldavian SSR and lectured at the Odessa Conservatory. After 1951 she was a deputy of the artistic director of the Philharmonia. Her compositions include music for orchestra, chamber music, music for piano, incidental music for more than eighty plays and films, and vocal music. She composed for children and adults.

Works

1966 *Esli druzya*, opera
1978 *Kol i druzie*, children's operetta
(Source: Cohen)

Tatyana Alexeyevna Chudova (June 16, 1944–) first studied at the Central Music School in Moscow, then at the Moscow Conservatory. Her strong interest in folk culture and music resulted in her participating in folk expeditions. Her music, particularly the symphonic suites and operas, strongly reflect that interest. She has composed music for orchestra, ballet, choral music and music for a variety of instruments.

Works

1966–67 *O myorvoy tsaverne i semi bojatiryakh* [The Dead Princess and the Seven Heroes], fairy-tale opera, Librettist Chudova after Pushkin
1978 *Na derevnyu dedushke* [To the Village, to Grandfather], opera, Librettists: V. Schuldzik and I. Maznina, after Chekhov: *Van'ka*
(Source: Sadie and Samuel)

Scotland

Isobel Dunlop (pseud. Violet Skelton) (March 4, 1901, Edinburgh–May 12, 1975, Edinburgh) organized concerts for the Scottish Arts Council from 1943 to 1948. The following year she became music secretary of the Saltire Society. She and Hans Oppenheim founded the Saltire Singers, a vocal quartet that became internationally known. She composed cantatas, music for chamber ensembles, a ballet, music for piano and for voice. The National Library of Scotland holds some papers and materials relating to her.

Works

The Silhouette, opera
The Scarecrow, operetta, for children
(Source: Cohen)

Thea Musgrave (May 27, 1928, Midlothian–) first studied at the University of Edinburgh; then, after an interval of private study she studied with Nadia Boulanger in Paris from 1950 to 1954. During that time she received her first commission, from the Scottish Festival at Braemar. In 1954 she received a commission from the BBC, for which she composed *Cantata for a Summer's Day*.

In the early 1960s she was a lecturer for the extramural department of London University, and a visiting professor at the University of California in Santa Barbara. Subsequently she lectured frequently at colleges and universities in the United Kingdom and the United States, and served as a member of the central music advisory panel for the BBC. Her compositions have been performed by major orchestras in Europe and the United States, often with her conducting.

Thea received many awards, including the Donald Francis Tovey Prize and the Lili Boulanger Memorial Prize while she was a student, the Koussevitzky Award, several Guggenheim fellowships, and numerous honorary doctoral degrees. Her compositions include orchestral works, music for chamber ensembles, for piano, vocal and sacred music, several ballets, and electronic music. Most of her works were commissioned.

Works

1955 *The Abbot of Drimock*, comic opera, Librettist: Maurice Lindsay, London
1963 *Marko the Miser*, children's opera, Librettists: Musgrave and F. Samson, after A.N. Afanas'yev, England
1964/65 *The Decision*, opera, Libettist: Maurice Lindsay, London
1973 *The Voice of Ariadne*, chamber opera, Librettist: Amalia Elguera, after Henry James *The Last of the Valerii*, England
1977 *Mary Queen of Scots*, opera, Librettist: Musgrave, after Elguera *Moray*, England
1979 *A Christmas Carol*, opera, Librettist: Musgrave, after Charles Dickens
1981 *An Occurrence at Owl Creek Bridge*, radio opera, Librettist: Musgrave after Ambrose Bierce
1984 *Harriet, the Woman Called Moses*, opera, Librettist: Musgrave
1992 *Simón Bolívar*, opera, Librettist: Musgrave
(Source: Sadie and Samuel)

South Africa

Maria Van der Mark (b. ca. August 12, 1912, Rotterdam) was a librettist and composer. She began studying music in Rotterdam when she was six. In

1935 she immigrated to South Africa, where she studied at the University of the Witwatersrand in Johannesburg. She was particularly interested in songs and often wrote the words as well as the music. Many of her songs were used for music therapy with epileptic patients.

Works

1959 *Diepwater se hoek*, operetta
1967 *Hanepoot en Muskadel*, operetta
1968 *Volund*, opera
(Source: Cohen)

Eva Noel Harvey (October 30, 1900–December 12, 1984, Johannesburg) was the first South African to write an opera—and it was grand opera. At the Johannesburg Conservatory she studied piano and violin then focused primarily on the violin. She was a member of the first symphony orchestra in Johannesburg. One of her strong interests was encouraging any South African who showed musical promise. Many of her songs reflect an interest in music of other traditions. She wrote over 400 songs as well as a ballet, music for piano, and music for chamber orchestra. Her music was performed in Europe and the United States as well as in South Africa. Eva also wrote poetry, sang and painted.

Works

1965 *Esther*, opera
1966 *Ruth and Naomi*, opera
1966 *Yugao*, miniature opera
(Source: Cohen)

Spain

Elena Romero (November 7, 1923, Madrid–1996) began her concert career when she was twelve. She studied piano in Barcelona, then studied composition and conducting in Madrid. Subsequently she studied in Freiburg, Breslau (Wrocław), Heidelberg, and Paris. For several years she toured in Europe. She conducted her own orchestral compositions. She composed music for orchestra, chamber ensembles, choral music, instrumental music, and a ballet.

Works

1957 *Marcela*, chamber opera
(Source: Sadie and Samuel)

United States

Dika Newlin (November 22, 1923, Portland, Oregon–July 22, 2006) received her BA in 1939 from Michigan State University in East Lansing, Michigan, and her MA in 1941 from the University of California, Los Angeles. In 1945 Columbia University awarded her their first PhD in musicology. Subsequently she taught at several colleges and universities. She was one of the last students of Arnold Schoenberg. In 1980 her book *Schoenberg Remembered: Diaries and Recollections, 1938–1976* was published. She wrote music for orchestra and for chamber ensembles, vocal and sacred music.

Works
1942 *Feathertop*, opera
1945 *The Scarlet Letter*, opera
Smile Right to the Bone, opera

Books by or about Dika Newlin:

Newlin, Dika. *Bruckner, Mahler, Schoenberg.* New York: King's Crown, 1947.
_____. *Schoenberg Remembered: Diaries and Recollections, 1938–76.* New York: Pendragon, 1980.
(Source: Sadie and Samuel)

Eda Rapoport (December 9, 1886, Daugaupils, Latvia–May 9, 1968, New York) came to the United States in 1908. She was awarded a scholarship to study at the Peabody Institute in Baltimore. Among her teachers in composition were Walter Piston, Aaron Copland, and Arnold Schoenberg. Her husband was Boris Rapoport, a noted anesthetist and the Department of Music at Columbia University sponsors the Boris and Eda Rapoport Prize in Composition (some listings for this often refer to her as "Edna"). She reputedly composed hundreds of works, in particular works for orchestra, chamber ensembles, music for piano, and vocal music. Her papers are held by Columbia University.

Works
1945 *The Fisherman and His Wife*, opera-fantasy, libretto after Grimm
1945 *G.I. Joe*, opera
(Sources: Cohen; Wikipedia)

Lora Aborn (1907–August 25, 2005) had her first public performance when she was ten, playing her own compositions. She studied organ at the Oberlin Conservatory and the American Conservatory of Music in Chicago. She graduated with honors and was awarded the gold medal for composition.

Lora was organist and music director at Frank Lloyd Wright's Unity Temple in Oak Park, Illinois, for over forty years. She often composed songs and choral pieces for the services. The Chicago Grand Opera Ballet commissioned her to compose the music for the ballet *American Women*. She composed orchestra pieces, music for organ, for piano, numerous choral works, at least fourteen ballets, and music for chamber ensembles.

Works

Gift of the Magi, opera
Mitty, opera
(Source: Cohen)

One of the first compositions of **Evelyn LaRue Pittman** (January 6, 1910, McAlester, Oklahoma–December 1992) was music for a Greek play, which she composed when she was very young. The play was produced by the Morehouse-Spelman Players at Spelman College. Evelyn attended Spelman and after graduation went to Langston University. She located in Oklahoma City, where she taught, organized an orchestra and chorus, had a weekly radio show, and founded a professional choir, the Evelyn Pittman Choir. The group performed on radio and represented Oklahoma and Texas at the 1938 World's Fair. She attended the Juilliard School of Music in New York and eventually studied at the University of Oklahoma, where she received her MM. In 1956 she went to Paris and studied under Nadia Boulanger.

Works

1948 *Against the River*, opera, Librettist: Helen Schuyler
1954 *Cousin Esther*, folk opera, Librettist: Evelyn Pittman
1970 *Freedom Child*, opera, about Martin Luther King, Jr.
(Source: Cohen)

Julia Amanda Perry (March 25, 1924, Kentucky–April 24, 1979, Akron, Ohio) first studied violin but changed her focus to piano. She attended Westminster Choir College in Princeton, New Jersey, where she received her bachelor's degree and in 1948 her MMus. Subsequently she studied at the Juilliard School of Music, spending summers at the Berkshire Music center in Tanglewood, Massachusetts. She received two Guggenheim fellowships, which led to her studying in Florence and Paris, where she studied with Nadia Boulanger.

After her return to the United States in 1959 she held teaching positions at Florida A & M College and at Atlanta University. Her works increasingly were performed by major orchestras; she received several awards, including the Boulanger Grand Prix and the National Institute of Arts and Letters. She suffered a stroke—the first of two—in 1971 that led to her being hospitalized. However, she taught herself to write with her left hand and continued to compose. Her compositions include symphonies and other works for orchestra, music for chamber ensembles, piano music, vocal and music, and an opera ballet.

Works

1953 *The Cask of Amontillado*, opera, Librettist: Perry, after Edgar Allan Poe
Three Warnings, opera
(Sources: Cohen; Sadie and Samuel; http://operadata.stanford.edu)

Elizabeth Gyring (1886, Vienna–1970, New York) studied in Vienna, where her pieces were performed in concert and on the radio by members of the Vienna Philharmonic Orchestra and the Berlin Philharmonic Orchestra. She went to the United States in 1939. Her compositions include many orchestral works, music for chamber ensembles, piano, organ, vocal and choral music. Her manuscripts are at Washington State University and the American Music Center.

Works

1954 *Night at Sea and Day in Court*, opera
(Sources: Sadie and Samuel; Cohen)

Eusebia Simpson Hunkins (June 29, 1902, Troy, Ohio–September 9, 1980) studied at the Juilliard School of Music, several other American venues and Salzburg. She taught at Cornell College in Iowa. From 1972 to 1974 she was project director of Musical World of Ohio Broadcasts. An authority on Appalachian folk music, some of her operas reflect that interest. Her sacred music includes *Appalachian Mass*. She also wrote a ballet, chamber music, and music for voice.

Works

1954 *Smoky Mountain*, folk opera
1956 *Maniian*, opera
1956 *Young Lincoln*, folk opera
1956 *Spirit Owl*, operetta
1956 *Mice in Council*, opera
1956 *Reluctant Hero*, opera
1958 *Young Lincoln II*, folk opera
1958 *Child of Promise*, children's dance opera
1958 *Forest Voices*, operetta
1973 *What Have You Done to My Mountain?*, folk opera
1974 *The Magic Laurel Trees*, children's opera

1975 *Happy Land*, operetta
(Source: Cohen)

Lois Albright (20th century)

Works

1955 *Hopitu*, opera, Librettist: Milo William Billingsley
(Source: http://operadata.stanford.edu)

Mary Elizabeth Glockler Caldwell (August 1, 1909, Tacoma, Washington–2003) was awarded a BA in music from the University of California, Berkley. She studied composition in Munich and New York, and piano and organ in San Francisco. Beginning in 1933 she was an organist and choir conductor. She wrote sacred music including cantatas; *Carol of the Little King*, for choir and organ, sold 700,000 copies. Her opera *Gift of Song* has had over 200 performances in the United States, England and Canada.

Works

1955 *Pepito's Golden Flower*, opera, Librettist: Caldwell
1961 *A Gift of Song*, Christmas opera, Librettist: Caldwell
1965 *The Night of the Star*, opera, Librettist: Caldwell
1978 *In the Fullness of Time*, opera, Librettist: Caldwell
(Sources: Cohen; http://operadata.stanford.edu)

Judith Dvorkin (1930, New York–July 24, 1995) earned her BA at Barnard College in New York and her MA at Columbia University in New York. She also attended seminars at the University of California at Berkeley. Her compositions include music for chamber ensembles and vocal music.

Works

1964 *Cyrano*, chamber opera, Librettist: Judith Dvorkin
1983 *Blue Star*, opera, Librettist: Judith Dvorkin
1988 *Humpty Dumpty and Alice*, chamber opera, Librettist: Judith Dvorkin
1993 *The Frog Prince*, opera, Librettist: Judith Dvorkin
(Source: Sadie and Samuel)

Netty Simons (October 26, 1913, New York–April 1, 1994, New York) started teaching when she was thirteen. In 1931 she began studying at New York University School of Performing Arts with Percy Grainger. She then received a scholarship to study for a year at the Juilliard School of Music. Subsequently she returned to New York University; Percy Grainger and Marion

Bauer, also a composer, were among her teachers. In 1960–1961 she produced and coordinated composers' concerts at Carnegie Recital Hall. From 1966 to 1971 she was one of ten contemporary women composers in an American exhibition of the music division of the New York Public Library. She composed widely: music for orchestra, band, chamber ensembles, piano, vocal music and multimedia productions. Her works have been performed in a variety of venues all over the world. Her musical materials are at the New York Public Library, Lincoln Center.

Works

1956–58 *Bell Witch of Tennessee*, opera, from an American folktale, Librettist: Joan Simons

(Sources: Cohen; Sadie and Samuel)

Miriam Gideon (October 23, 1906, Greeley, Colorado–June 18, 1996) first studied in Boston with her uncle who was an organist and choral director. She received her BA in music at Boston University in 1926. Twenty years later she received an MA in musicology from Columbia University, then in 1970 a DSM in composition at the Jewish Theological Seminary of America. She held teaching positions at a number of colleges and institutions, primarily in New York. In 1975 she was elected to the National Institute of Arts and Letters, the second woman to receive that honor. Her music was performed in the United States, Europe and the Far East. Her compositions include works for orchestra, for chamber ensembles, piano music, and vocal and choral music.

Works

1958 *Fortunato*, opera, Librettist: Gideon, after S. Qunitero and J. Quintero

(Source: Sadie and Samuel)

Among the teachers of **Beatrice Laufer** (April 27, 1923, New York–) at the Juilliard School of Music was Marion Bauer, a notable composer herself. Beatrice's first symphony was performed in Germany and Japan in 1948 under the auspices of the U.S. State Department. The American Association of the United Nations commissioned her to write a work, which resulted in *Song of the Fountain*, performed in 1952 by an interracial chorus. The state of Connecticut commissioned her to write a choral work to commemorate the 1976 bicentennial. Many of her works were for orchestra; she also composed some chamber music, and a significant amount of vocal music, as well as a ballet. Her papers are at the New York Public Library.

Works

1958 *Ile*, opera, after Eugene O'Neill: *The Long Voyage Home*, opera
1968 *My Brother's Keeper*, opera

(Sources: Cohen; http://operadata.stanford.edu)

Nancy Hayes Van de Vate (pseuds. Helen and William Huntley) (December 30, 1930, Plainfield, New Jersey–) received her doctorate in composition from Florida State University in 1968. During the 1960s and 1970s she held teaching positions at several universities and colleges. She later moved to Europe and became a resident of Vienna in 1985. Her works include orchestra music, a significant amount of chamber music, music for theater, electronic music, piano music, and vocal music.

Works

1960 *The Death of the Hired Man*, chamber opera, after Robert Frost, revised in 1998.
1995 *Nemo: Jenseits von Vulkania*, opera, Librettists: Allen Cortes and Nancy Van de Vate, also in English
1995 *Der Herrscher und das Mädchen*, children's opera, Librettists: Allen Cortes and Nancy Van de Vate
1999 *All Quiet on the Western Front*, opera, after the novel by Erich Maria Remarque, rewritten in German and performed in 2002
2002 *Im Westen nichts Neues*, opera, after the novel by Erich Maria Remarque
2003 *Where the Cross Is Made*, opera, from the play by Eugene O'Neill
2009 *Hamlet*, opera in five acts, after Shakespeare

(Sources: Sadie and Samuel; Wikipedia)

Louise Talma (October 31, 1906, France–August 13, 1996, Saratoga Springs, New York) had her first music lessons with her mother, who was an opera singer. Louise then studied at the Institute of Musical Art (Juilliard School of Music) in New York from 1922 to 1930. In the summers of 1926 to 1939 she attended the Fontainebleau School of Music in France, where she studied with Nadia Boulanger. She also was there several summers after World War II. She received her BMus from New York University in 1931; two years later she received her MA from Columbia University.

Louise was awarded two Guggenheim fellowships, one in 1946, the other in 1947, the first woman to win the award twice. She also won the Isaac Newton Seligman prize for composition at the Institute of Musical Art in 1927, 1928, and 1929; the Pleyel Prize for Piano at Fontainebleau in 1927; the senior Fulbright research grant, which allowed her to spend ten months in Rome to compose her opera *The Alcestiad*; and the French Government Prix d'Excellence de Composition in 1951. She was the first American teacher at

Fontainebleau, teaching solfège for several summers. She was also the first woman to be awarded the Sibelius Medal for composition from the Harriet Cohen International Music Awards in London (1963). *The Alcestiad* was performed in Frankfurt in 1962, the first opera composed by an American woman to be performed in a major European opera house.

She was also the author of two textbooks. In addition to her operas she composed music for orchestra, chamber ensembles, piano, vocal music, and choral and sacred music. The Library of Congress is the principle holder of her papers and manuscripts. Materials may also be found in Yale University's Beinecke Rare Book and Manuscript Library, the Nadia Boulanger Collection at Harvard University's Isham Memorial Library, and the Conservatoire Américain in Fontainebleau, France.

Works

1962 *The Alcestiad*, opera, Librettist: Thornton Wilder
1976 *Have You Heard, Do You Know?*, opera, Librettist: Louise Talma
(Sources: Sadie and Samuel; American National Biography online)

Gloria Coates (October 10, 1934, Wausau, Wisconsin–) earned her BA and her BMus from Columbia University in theater and ballet, both in 1963, and her MMus from Louisiana State University in 1965. After moving to Munich in 1969 she worked more with large-scale ensembles. She remained in Germany, where she has been professionally active, holding numerous positions and receiving appointments as well as being actively involved with various organizations. Her compositions include orchestral works, music for chamber ensembles, vocal and choral music, a ballet, and music for theater.

Works

1962 *Fall of the House of Usher*, opera, Librettist: Gloria Coates after Poe
(Source: Sadie and Samuel)

Ruth Lomon (November 7, 1930, Montreal–) earned her performance diploma from the Quebec Conservatory in 1947 and her licentiate in 1950 from McGill University in Montreal, then continued her studies at the New England Conservatory of Music. She also studied at the Darmstadt summer course. She has taught composition and piano, and chamber music, often focusing on works written by women composers both contemporary and historic. Among her awards, many of which were for composition, she received a Yaddo Fellowship, a MacDowell Norlin Fellowship, Meet the Composer grants, and a National League of Penwomen scholarship for mature women. Her compositions include music for chamber ensembles, piano music, vocal and choral music. Some of her music reflects her interest in Native American ceremonials and themes.

Works

1963 *The Fisherman and His Soul*, chamber opera, from Oscar Wilde
(Sources: Cohen; Sadie and Samuel)

Wendy Carlos (November 14, 1939, Pawtucket–) received her AB from Brown University in 1962, then her MA from Columbia University in 1965. She was involved with electronic music early on, working as an advisor to Robert Moog on the Moog synthesizer. She worked also on creating electronic versions of orchestral sounds. In addition to electronic music she composed music for orchestra and chamber ensembles. Some of her works were composed under the name Walter Carlos, the name she was known as until 1979.

Works

1964/1965 *Noah*, opera
(Source: Sadie and Samuel)

Gloria Agnes Wilson Swisher (March 12, 1935, Seattle–) graduated with a BA summa cum laude from the University of Washington. She went on to get her MA at Mills College, studying under Darius Milhaud, then her PhD from Eastman School of Music in 1960. She taught at several institutions. Gloria received a Woodrow Wilson National Foundation Fellowship from 1956 to 1957. In 1981 she won a contest sponsored by the Thalia Symphony Orchestra. Her works include music for orchestra, band, chamber ensembles, piano and voice. She has also written a musical, and incidental music for theater. She is a founding member of Ars Nova Press, Inc., a nonprofit corporation that promotes and reprints the work of quality composers.

Works

1983 *The Artist and the Other*, chamber opera, Librettist: Willy Clark
(Sources: Cohen; Wikipedia)

Joyce Barthelson (May 18, 1908, Yakima, Washington–December 1, 1986) received first prize from ASCAP and the National Federation of Music for one of her operas. She had a long and varied career in music. After studying at the University of California, Berkeley, she worked for the National Broadcasting Company in San Francisco and the Arian Trio as an ensemble coach and pianist, making concert tours and lecture tours to universities throughout the United States. In 1935 she began working as assistant conductor for the New York Women's Symphony Orchestra, a position she held for five years. From 1942 to 1944 she was composer-in-residence at Western Maryland College. In 1944 she and Virginia Hoff founded a music school in Scarsdale, New York, and served as codirectors. The school continues as Hoff-Barthelson Music School. Subsequently she was a choral conductor in New York City and Westchester County, until 1960. She composed music for orchestra, chamber music, and vocal music.

Works

1967 *Chanticleer*, comic fantasy, literary source: Chaucer
1969 *Greenwich Village, 1910*, opera, Librettist: Joyce Barthelson
1973 *The King's Breakfast*, opera, Librettist: Joyce Barthelson, after Maurice Baring-Gould
1977 *Devil's Disciple*, opera, Librettist: Joyce Barthelson after Shaw
1981 *Lysistrata*, opera, Librettist: Joyce Barthelson
(Sources: Cohen; http://operadata.stanford.edu)

Carolyn Parkhurst Lloyd (April 12, 1924, Uniontown, Alabama–1980) received her BM at the University of New Mexico then continued her studies at the Eastman School of Music and at Columbia University. She taught privately for many years, some of that time in Caracas, Venezuela, where she was musical activities director at the Centro Venezolano Americano, from 1955 to 1968. *Doña Barbara* was composed to commemorate the 400th anniversary of Caracas.

Works

1967 *Doña Barbara*, opera, Librettist: Isaac Chocrón, based on the novel by Rómulo Gallegos
(Sources: Cohen; http://operadata.stanford.edu)

Margaret Garwood (March 22, 1927, New Jersey–) earned her MS from Philadelphia Music Academy. From 1965 to 1968 she held a Whiteside Foundation grant; from 1973 to 1977 she had a National Endowment for the Arts grant. She taught piano in several schools and academies. From 1965 to 1970 she was resident composer at the MacDowell Colony. She composed chamber music and song cycles; her ballet *Aesop's Fables* was commissioned by Young Audiences, Inc., in 1970.

Works

1967 *The Trojan Women*, opera, Librettist: Howard Wiley
1973 *The Nightingale and the Rose*, opera, Librettist: Margaret Garwood, based on Oscar Wilde

1983 *Rappaccini's Daughter*, opera, Librettist: Margaret Garwood, after Nathaniel Hawthorne
1987 *Joringel and the Songflowers*, opera, Librettist: Margaret Garwood after Jakob and Wilhelm Grimm
(Sources: Cohen; http://operadata.stanford.edu)

Patsy Rogers (January 5, 1938, New York–) studied at Bennington College, where one of her teachers was Vivian Fine (see entry). In 1960 she received her BA, followed by her MA in 1962. She has taught guitar, piano, the recorder and composition at several colleges and universities. She was composer-in-residence at the Chamber Music Conference and Composers' Forum of the East in 1979. Her compositions include works for orchestra, chamber ensembles, vocal works, a ballet, incidental music and music for theater.

Works

1968 *Woman Alive: Conversation Against Death*, chamber opera, using poems by Eve Merriam
(Source: Cohen; http://www.patsyrogers.org/compositions.htm#opera)

Jean Reynolds Davis (November 1, 1927, Cumberland, Maryland–February 25, 2015) received her Bachelor of Music degree from the University of Pennsylvania. She won several medals and awards. Her compositions include two symphonies, music for woodwind quintet, vocal music and a ballet for children.

Works

The Elevator, opera
The Mirror, opera
(Source: Cohen)

Lucia Dlugoszewski (June 16, 1934, Detroit–April 11, 2000) showed musical talent at an early age and studied at the Detroit Conservatory. At Wayne State University she was a premedical student and took physics courses. When her plans to go to medical school didn't work out she moved to New York City, where she studied music privately and began composing. She formed close ties with the artistic and poetic community in New York, more so than with the musical community. Subsequently she published articles on aesthetics and modern dance and a book of poetry. She also taught choreography. From 1953 to 1964 she was composer-in-residence for the Erick Hawkins Dance Company. In addition to being a prolific composer she invented more than one hundred percussion instruments. She received numerous commissions, and her music was widely performed in the United States, Europe and Canada, often with Lucia performing.

Among her awards was a Guggenheim fellowship and grants from the National Education Association as well as a Tompkins Award for poetry. She was the first woman to win the Koussevitzky International Recording Award. Her compositions include many dance scores, works for orchestra and for chamber ensembles, works for percussion and works featuring percussion, piano music, and music for theater.

Works

1970 *The Heidi Songs*, opera, Librettist: John Ashbery
(Sources: Cohen; Sadie and Samuel)

Olga Gorelli (June 14, 1920, Bologna–February 18, 2006) first composed when she was a child in Italy. She came to the United States with her family and became an American citizen in 1945. She studied at the Curtis Institute, Yale University, and Smith College; her instructors included Gian Carlo Menotti, Paul Hindemith, and Darius Milhaud. From 1948 to 1950 she was a teaching fellow at Smith College, then a lecturer at Hollins College, and from 1954 to 1957 she was a faculty member at Trenton State College. She has composed works for orchestra, chamber pieces, songs, dance dramas and incidental music for theater, and teaching pieces.

Works

1972 *Between the Shadow and the Dream*, opera
Dona Petra, opera
(Sources: Cohen; Wikipedia)

Vera Nicolaevna Preobrajenska (April 27, 1926, San Francisco–) was a writer and editor in addition to her composing. Her MA in 1953 was from San Francisco State University; she went on to receive an MA and a PhD from Bernadean University, Las Vegas. Darius Milhaud, Alexander Tcherepnin and Dmitri Shostakovich were among her teachers.

From 1956 to 1961 she was concert manager for Musical Artists of America. She lectured at the University of California, Berkeley from 1965 to 1968. Her articles appeared in various musical publications. For many years, commencing in 1949, she was a writer, arranger and orchestrator for commercial song writing. The National League of American Pen Women awarded her two composition prizes. She was very prolific, with many compositions for orchestra, chamber ensembles, piano, as well as music for organ and for voice. She also wrote dance scores and choral music.

Works

The Money Lender, chamber opera, after Dostoevsky
(Source: Cohen)

USSR

Natalia Nikolaevna Levi (September 10, 1901, St. Petersburg–January 3, 1972, Leningrad) was an actress and translator as well as a composer. She graduated from the Russian Drama School in 1924, became an actress, and for seven years was head of the Mobile Theater. In 1936 she graduated from the Leningrad Conservatory. She then moved to Petrozavodsk and began collecting folk songs of northern peoples of the Soviet Union. During World War II she was in Leningrad working as a translator and composer of war songs at the front. She received two medals for her songs that hailed the defense of Leningrad. Her vocal music includes many pieces of music for choir and orchestra of folk instruments as well as songs and arrangements of folk music. She also wrote incidental music for plays and films.

Works

1940 *Karelskaya skaska*, opera, Librettist: V. Chekhov or after(?)

Books by or about Natalia Nikolayevna Levi:

Levi, Natalia Nikolayevna. *Songs of the Peoples of the Karelo-Finnish Republic.* With unidentified coauthor
(Source: Cohen)

Klara Abramovna Katzman (b. ca. May 31, 1916, Surazh) studied at the Leningrad Conservatory, graduating in 1941. She wrote much incidental music for theater and film, orchestra music, a ballet, and vocal music.

Works

1943–44 *Nepoferennye*, operetta, Librettist: B. Pevzner
1955 *Mark Beregovik*, operetta, Librettist: A. Geveksman
1957 *Lyubov buvaet raznaya*, operetta
1962 *Polovodie*, opera
1967 *Lyubava*, opera
1969 *Malchish-Kibalchish*, opera, Librettist: I. Keller
1973 *Rytsarskaya ballada*, opera
(Source: Cohen)

From an early age **Nina Vladimirovna Makarova** (July 30, 1908, Nizhni-Novgorod–January 15, 1976, Moscow) was interested in Russian and Mari folk songs. She began studying at the Music School in Gorki when she was fifteen, then two years later entered the Moscow Conservatory, graduating in 1927. She did postgraduate work, which she completed in 1938. She traveled widely outside Russia. Her husband was the composer Aram Khachaturian. Her compositions include orchestral works, chamber music, vocal music, including cantatas, incidental music, and music for piano.

Works

1947 *Muzhestvo*, opera, dedicated to builders of Komsomolsk
1956 *Zoya*, opera
(Source: Cohen)

Lyubov Borisovna Nikolskaya (b. ca. May 17, 1909, Vani, Georgia) was a lecturer and writer in addition to being a composer. In 1945 she graduated with distinction from the Leningrad Conservatory, where she had studied historical theory and composition. She taught in the school and became head of the department of theory and composition, then went on to teach at the Sverdlovsk Conservatory and lecture at the Uralsk Conservatory. She wrote for Russian musical journals. In addition to her operettas she composed orchestral music, chamber music, a ballet for children, vocal music and piano music.

Works

1952 *Devushka-semidelushka*, operetta for children
1954 *Petukh i Lisa*, operetta for children
1956 *Ugomon*, operetta for children
1958 *Alenkly tsvetochek*, operetta for children
1959 *Serebryanoye kopitse*, operetta for children
1975 *Olino kolechko*, operetta for children, Librettist: S. Marchak
(Source: Cohen)

Sonia Pinkhasova Abramova (June 2, 1930, Tashkent–) graduated from the Tashkent Conservatory in 1954. She composed music for orchestra, chamber music, vocal music, incidental music for theater, and music for piano.

Works

1954 *Tamara*, opera
(Source: Cohen)

Zhanetta Alexandrovna Kuznetsova (pseudo Eugenia Strella) (July 26, 1937, Irkutsk–) graduated from the Moscow Conservatory in 1967.

Works

1959 *Posle bala,* opera, after Tolstoy
1971 *Don Juan v Egipte,* opera
1978 *Khleb ty moi,* opera
(Source: Cohen)

Elga Avgustovna Igenberga (February 10, 1921–2003) graduated from the Azerbaijanian Conservatory in 1964. She was musical consultant at the Galgava Theatre and also served as concertmistress of the Latvian Philharmonia from 1945 to 1959. In addition, she was musical director of vocal ensembles. She composed music for piano and vocal music.

Works

1964 *Annele,* operetta
1972 *Tretya lyubov,* operetta
(Source: Cohen)

Meri Shalvovna Davitashvili (March 13, 1924, Tbilisi–) graduated from the Kutais Music School in 1941. Subsequently she entered the Tbilisi Conservatory, graduating in 1946. For the next two years she was concertmistress at the conservatory. She became a member of the board of the Union of Soviet Composers in the Georgian SSR in 1956. Her compositions include music for orchestra, chamber ensembles, piano music, a ballet, incidental music for theater, and vocal music.

Works

1966 *Kadzhana,* children's opera
1972 *Natsarkekia,* children's opera
(Source: Cohen)

Zlata Moiseyevna Tkach (May 16, 1928, Moldava–January 1, 2006) graduated from the Kishinev Conservatory. She wrote music for orchestra, chamber ensembles, cantatas and other vocal music, and a ballet.

Works

1974 *Golubi i kosuyu linei ku*
(Source: Cohen)

Tatiana Ivanovna Vasilieva (February 27, 1943, Irkutsk–) graduated from the Moscow Conservatory in 1968. She was a lecturer at the Krasnodarsk Institute of Culture.

Works

1966 *Aleshi i chernaya kurtsa*, operetta for children
(Source: Cohen)

Vera Petrovna Gerchik (b. ca. December 6, 1911, Yekaterinoslav, Dnepropetrovsk) graduated from the Moscow Conservatory in 1937. She was then musical director of the Moscow Radio for a year, subsequently going on to teach. She also became editor for the Central Music Publishing Company. She composed pieces for piano, a symphony, chamber music, and choral pieces and vocal music.

Works

1967 *Lesniye chudessa*, operetta
(Source: Cohen)

Lia Robitashvili (October 26, 1930, Tbilisi–) graduated from the Tbilisi Conservatory in 1955. She was a lecturer at music schools in Tbilisi. Her compositions include choral music and other vocal pieces, music for piano, and a piano concerto for children with orchestra.

Works

1967 *Imeniny Fiaki-Malshki*, children's operetta
(Source: Cohen)

Lili Mikhailovna Iashvili (May 10, 1920, Tiflis–) wrote musical reviews for newspapers in addition to her composing and teaching. She graduated from the Tbilisi Conservatory in 1953, then went on to be a lecturer, first at a music school then at a theater school. She was awarded the title of Honored Art Worker of the Georgian Soviet Socialist Republic in 1966. Her compositions include music for orchestra, vocal music, and chamber music.

Works

1968 *Bashmaki Babadzhany*, children's opera
1971 *Irmisa*, children's opera
(Source: Cohen)

Zinaida Petrovna Ziberova (b. ca. December 1, 1909, Darmstadt, Germany) moved to Rostov-on-the-Don after 1925, attended the music school there and graduated in 1928. She worked as a pianist in clubs from 1925 to 1929, then became conductor and artistic director of amateur productions and events in Rostov. She also was active in local government. She wrote music for orchestra, chamber ensembles, vocal music—some with orchestral accompaniment, a ballet, and many pieces for theater.

Works

Kot v sapogakh, operetta
(Source: Cohen)

Venezuela

María Luisa Escobar (December 5, 1908, Venezuela–May 15, 1987) played the piano and composed at an early age. She studied at the Colegio de Welgelegen in Curaçao and continued her studies in Paris. Maria was particularly interested in indigenous tribal music and folklore of Venezuela. She became artistic director of Radio Caracas in 1931; she was founder of the Ateneo de Caracas and, until 1942, president. The next year she founded the Venezuelan Society of Authors and Composers and was its president until 1972. She received many honors, medals, and awards, and she often represented Venezuela at international music conferences. Her compositions include music for orchestra, for piano, vocal music, several ballets, and arrangements of Venezuelan traditional native music.

Works

Bianca Nieves, opera
Cuento Musical, opera
El Rey Guaicaipuro, opera
La Princesa Girasol, operetta
(Source: Cohen)

Wales

Grace Mary Williams (February 19, 1906, Barry–February 10, 1977, Barry) was a scriptwriter and teacher as well as a composer. She received her BMus in 1926 from the University of Wales in Cardiff. For the next four years she studied at the Royal College of Music in London, where her teachers included Vaughan Williams. Among her classmates there were Dorothy Gow, Imogen Holst and Elizabeth Maconchy, a remarkable group of women composers. They maintained contact with each other in later years. A traveling scholarship from the Royal College of Music allowed her to study with Egon Wellesz in Vienna from 1930 to 1931. She later taught in London, then in 1946 she returned to Glamorganshire. She worked on educational programs, primarily writing educational scripts, for the BBC. At that time she was making a name for herself as a composer. Her compositions include orchestral works, music for piano, vocal music, sacred choral music, and incidental music.

Works

1966 *The Parlour*, opera, Librettist: Williams, after Guy de Maupassant: *En Famille*
(Sources: Sadie and Samuel; http://operadata.stanford.edu)

Yugoslavia

Ivana Lang-Beck (November 15, 1912, Zagreb–January 1982) studied at the Music Academy of Zagreb. After completing her studies she was assistant to a professor, then later was made a professor herself. She taught at the teachers' college in Zagreb from 1940 to 1943, then at the Vatroslav Lisinski Music Academy, also in Zagreb. She attended lectures in Salzburg at the Mozarteum. Some of her compositions were performed there as well as in Straasburg, Italy, the Soviet Union, and on Yugoslav radio and television. Ivana had strong interest in Istrian folk music and often utilized elements of it in her own compositions. She wrote for orchestra, chamber ensembles, harp, much music for piano, choral and vocal music, often with orchestra, ballets, and incidental music for theater, including puppet theater.

Works

1955 *Kastavski kapetan*, opera
(Source: Cohen)

1970 to Present

Change. Experimentation. Evolution. Questioning.

All are hallmarks of twentieth century opera ... but something happened. Throughout opera's history reasonable proportions of older operas and new operas were performed, and seemingly there was always room for new operas. But as the twentieth century progressed, fewer new operas were commissioned and performed. In the second half of the century the repertory became quite fixed—calcified some might say. To keep the opera experience fresh, traditional operas were reinterpreted, had new staging (sometimes radically so) or were "transferred" to a different time period. At times the result was reminiscent of the demand for spectacle in opera's earlier days.

But where were the new operas? Where were the "older" operas written by composers other than the select "mainstream" composers? And even those operas were limited to the standard repertory. Someone who attended opera could go through life thinking that many of these composers composed only one or two operas. A few new operas were produced by major opera houses and were well received, but few, if any, fully entered the repertory. "Traditional" operas and a sprinkling of twentieth century operas—all written by men—dominate opera seasons.

Opera is thriving, however. The amount of opera available—the number of opera festivals, particularly in Europe—is astounding. In the United States the bright note is the increase in productions by smaller, regional or local opera companies, colleges, universities, and what might be called "chamber" productions.

Composers continue to write smaller operas, chamber operas, and miniature operas. They use different terminology, but the point is that these operas provide a significant and immensely less expensive and less complicated alternative to the traditional operas in traditional opera house settings. A few operas by women composers are being produced in significant venues. There are indications of interest in historic "forgotten" or "lost" operas, often by "forgotten" composers—male and female.

Opera may be looking ahead to change—and to relearning its own history.

Argentina

Irma Urteaga (March 7, 1929, Argentina–) studied at the National Conservatory in Buenos Aires and at the Instituto del Teatro Colón. She was director of the opera studio and house répétiteur at the Teatro Colón from 1974 to 1978. During 1986–1988 she held similar positions at the Ecuador Opera. She wrote orchestra works, choral and vocal works, and music for chamber ensembles. Norton Grove describes *La Maldolida* as a "humorous and affectionate operatic parody."

Works
1987 *La Maldolida*, chamber opera, Librettist: Alberto Dimant
(Sources: Sadie and Samuel; http://operadata.stanford.edu/)

Australia

Winsome Evans (October 26, 1941–) earned a bachelor of music degree with honors in composition from the University of Sydney. She is a professional harpsichordist and an arranger. She also has been the director of the Renaissance Players, an early music ensemble, and an associate professor of music at the University of Sydney. Being interested in the history of the harpsichord, she "recomposed" Johann Sebastian Bach's works for solo violin and for the clavicembalo, a relative of the harpsichord known since 1323. She received the British Empire Medal in the Queen's Birthday Honours List in 1980. Six years later she received the Medal of the Order of Australia for services to music. The award-winning documentary *Facing the Music* (2001) featured Winsome Evans and her colleague Anne Boyd.

Works

1972 *Son of Getron*, 12–13th century liturgical drama
1974 *L'Amfiparnaso*, opera
1974 *The Play of Herod*, 12–13th century liturgical drama
1974 *Slaughter of the Innocents*, 12–13th century liturgical drama

(Sources: Cohen; Wikipedia)

When **Betty Beath** November 19, 1932, Queensland–) was in her teens she was a finalist in the Australian Broadcasting Commission's concerts and vocal competitions. In 1950 she received a Queensland University music scholarship and entered the Sydney Conservatory of Music. She married David Cox, a writer and illustrator, and the two of them spent time in Indonesia during the 1970s. She became very interested in the cultures of Bali and Java, an interest that is reflected in some of her music. At the third International Congress on Women in Music in Mexico City in 1984 she represented women composers of Australia. She served several terms on the board of the International League of Women Composers. Betty was resident composer at North Adams State College in Massachusetts in 1987.

Works

1973 *The Strange Adventures of Marco Polo*, opera, commissioned by Queensland Opera Company, Librettist: David Cox
1974 *Francis*, opera, based on St. Francis of Assisi, Librettist: David Cox

Books by or about Betty Beath:

Beath, Betty. Articles on school operas. In *Innovations in Australian Secondary Education*. McGraw-Hill, 1977.
_____. *Reflections from Bali*. With David Cox. Allison-Wesley Publishers, Sydney, Australia, 1981.
_____. *Spice and Magic*. With David Cox. Boolarong Publications, 1981.

(Sources: Cohen; Sadie and Samuel; http://operadata.stanford.edu/)

Austria

Luna Alcalay (October 21, 1928, Zagreb, Yugoslavia–October 9, 2012) was born in Croatia but studied and lived in Vienna. From 1951 to 1957 she studied at the Musikhochschule in Vienna, where she graduated with a prize. The next year the Austrian Academy of Sciences gave her a scholarship to ROM, the Austrian Cultural Institute. She was a prolific composer; her compositions include music for orchestra, a large amount of music for chamber groups, music for piano, a ballet, and vocal music.

Works
1958 *Antigone modell*, opera
1989 *Jan Palach*, opera
(Sources: Cohen; womeninmusic.com)

Johanna Doderer (September 18, 1969, Bregenz, Austria–) studied composition in Graz; later she studied film and media composition in Vienna. She has received numerous prizes and commissions, and is a prolific composer. Her compositions include orchestral works, chamber music and instrumental works.

Works
2000/01 *Die Fremde*, opera, Librettist: Johanna Doderer, after Euripides' *Medea*
2002–06 *Strom*, opera, Librettist: Johanna Doderer after Euripides' *The Bacchae*
2009–2010 *Der leuchtende Fluss* [A Kind of Yellow], Librettist: Wolfgang Hermann
(Source: Wikipedia)

Azerbaijan

Sevda Mirza Kyzy Ibragimova (November 28, 1939–) graduated from the Azerbaijanian Conservatory in 1964, having studied piano and composition. Subsequently she was a lecturer in composition.

Works
1970 *Koltso spravedlivovsti*, opera
(Source: Cohen)

Shafiga Gulam Akhundova (January 21, 1924–July 26, 2013) studied Azerbaijanian music and composition at the Baku conservatory, graduating in 1953. She composed music for orchestra, chamber groups, vocal music, and incidental music for theater.

Works

1972 *Galin gayasi,* opera

(Sources: Cohen; Wikipedia)

Franghiz Ali-Zadeh (May 29, 1947–) studied at the Baku Conservatory in the early 1970s. After her postgraduate work she taught at the conservatory. She was awarded the prize of the Azerbaijan Composers' Union in 1980. In 2007 she was elected chair of that Union. Her works combine the tradition of Azerbaijan music with twentieth century Western music.

Works

Legenda o belom vsadnike

(Source: Sadie and Samuel)

Bulgaria

Dora Draganova (January 29, 1946, Sofia–) graduated from the Sofia State Academy of Music in 1972. After graduation she began her teaching career at the academy. From 1971 to 1991 she edited *Native Song,* the choral literature magazine. In 1999 her musical play *Pippi Long-Stocking,* after Astrid Lindgren's book, won first prize in Dobrich. She also received an award from the Union of Bulgarian Composers for her piano collection *Children's Corner.*

Works

1972 *Car Koshnichar,* comic opera, Librettists: Nikolaj Hajtov and Ivan Genov

(Sources: Sadie and Samuel; Wikipedia)

Elena Petrová (May 15, 1929, Sliven–2002) is one of the earliest Bulgarian woman composers we have much information about. She graduated from the Sofia Academy of Music in 1945 and also studied at Charles University in Prague for several terms. Subsequently she studied at the Academy of Arts and Music in Bratislava, and at the Janáček Academy of Arts and Music in Brno, graduating in 1970. After she completed her studies she began music theory at Charles University. She married Hanus Krupka, who was head of the Smetana Library in Prague. Her compositions include ballets, works for Orchestra, instrumental pieces, and vocal music.

Works

1982/83 *If the Sun Were Not to Return*, opera, Librettist: Petrová, after F.C. Ramuz
(Sources: Sadie and Samuel; Cohen)

Canada

Violet Archer (April 24, 1913, Montreal–February 21, 2000, Ottawa) grew up in Italy but returned to Canada to study at McGill Conservatory and McGill University, where she earned a BMus in 1936. She received a BMus in 1948 from Yale, followed by a MMus in 1949. From 1940 to 1947 she played percussion in the Montreal Women's Symphony Orchestra. Her orchestral piece *Britannia: A Joyful Overture* was selected by Sir Adrian Boult for broadcast by the BBC in 1942 and relayed to the troops in Europe. She had an active teaching career, teaching at several venues. In 1971 she was awarded an honorary DMus by McGill University; subsequently the University of Windsor awarded her an honorary DMus, in 1986, and the University of Calgary the LLD in 1989. She was the recipient of numerous awards and honors.

Works

1973 *Sganarelle*, opera, after Molière
1985 *The Meal*, opera, Librettist: Rowland Holt Wilson
(Sources: Sadie and Samuel; http://operadata.stanford.edu/)

Kristi Allik (February 6, 1952–) earned her BMus at Toronto University in 1975, her MFA at Princeton in 1977, and her DMA from the University of Southern California in 1982. She taught at several Canadian universities in the 1980s. In 1988 she cofounded with David Keane the computer laboratory for Applications in Music at Queen's University in Kingston. She has composed multimedia works, music for orchestra, chamber music incidental music, electronic music, and instrumental and choral music.

Works

1975 *Loom, Sword, River*, opera, based on Estonian mythology, Librettist: P. Such
(Sources: Cohen; Sadie and Samuel)

Elizabeth Raum (January 13, 1945, New Hampshire–) graduated from the Eastman School of Music with a BMus in oboe in 1966. In 1968 she became principal oboist in the Atlantic Symphony Orchestra. She moved to Canada in the mid–1970s and became principal oboist with the Regina Symphony Orchestra. In Regina she was a founding member of the Contemporary

Directions Ensemble. She received her MMus in composition from the University of Regina in 1983. The next year she composed *The Garden of Alice*, which firmly established her as an opera composer. Her opera *Eos: The Dream of Nicholas Flood Davin* focuses on the struggles of the Canadian politician who brought culture to western Canada. Her compositions include orchestral works, choral works, an oratorio and ballets.

Works

1981 *The Final Bid*, opera, Librettist: Raum
1985 *The Garden of Alice*, opera, Librettist Raum, after Lewis Carroll, *Alice in Wonderland*
1991 *Eos: The Dream of Nicholas Flood Davin*, opera, Librettist: Raum
(Source: Sadie and Samuel)

Micheline Saint-Marcoux (August 9, 1938–February 2, 1985) studied at the École Vincent-d'Indy in Montreal, then at the Montreal Conservatory (CMM), winning a first prize for her orchestral piece *Modulaire* in 1967. The next year she went to Paris, where she stayed for about two years. While there she and five other people founded the Groupe International de Musicque Electro-Acoustique, based in Paris. The group gave concerts in Europe, Canada and South America for several years. She taught at the CMM on her return to Quebec and also cofounded the Ensemble Polycousmie. Her compositions include incidental music for a dramatic work, orchestral music and music for various combinations of instruments, vocal music, and electronic music.

Works

1984 *Transit*, opera, Librettist: F. Théoret
(Source: Sadie and Samuel)

Costa Rica

Lola Castegnaro (Lolita) (May 16, 1900, Costa Rica–September 1979, Mexico City) first studied music with her father, Alvise Castegnaro, who was an Italian-born composer. Subsequently she studied singing and piano at the Milan Conservatory, then moved to Paris to compose. In 1941 she returned to Costa Rica, where she gave radio broadcasts and conducted opera for several seasons. She was also guest conductor of the National Symphony Orchestra. Her short biography of her father was published in Costa Rica in 1944. In 1945 she moved to Mexico. She successfully established herself as a composer, pianist and singing teacher, and she worked as a journalist. Her compositions include light music in popular Latin-American genres, as well an orchestral suite and her operetta.

Works

Mirka, operetta
(Source: Sadie and Samuel)

Denmark

Else Marie Pade (December 2, 1924, Arhus–) was very active in the Resistance during World War II; the account of her exploits reads like a novel or movie script. From 1945 to 1950 she studied at the Royal Danish Conservatory in Copenhagen. In the 1950s she increasingly focused on electronic music and twelve tone music. She was with Danish Radio from 1964 to 1973, then with the National Hospital in Copenhagen, where she participated in a research project studying the effect of "music concrete" (electro-acoustic) on the imaginations of mentally handicapped children.

She composed instrumental music and vocal music in addition to her electronic music.

Works

1974 *Far, mor og børn* [Father, Mother and Children], children's opera
(Sources: Sadie and Samuel; Cohen)

England

Nicola Frances LeFanu (April 28, 1947, Essex–) is the daughter of the composer Elizabeth Maconchy (see entry). Nicola first studied at St. Hilda's College at Oxford, where she received her honors degree in music in 1968. She also studied at the Royal College of Music in 1968 and 1969. Four years later she won the Mendelssohn Scholarship and a Harkness Award, which allowed her to spend a year in the United States. In 1988 she earned her doctorate in music from the University of London. She also holds honorary doctorates from the Universities of Durham and Aberdeen and from the Open University. In 1979 she married the composer David Lumsdaine; subsequently they were joint composers-in-residence at the New South Wales Conservatorium in Sydney, Australia. Nicola accepted a position as professor of music at York University in 1994. In 2008 she retired from teaching.

Works

1977 *Dawnpath*, chamber opera, Librettist: LeFanu, London

1990 *The Green Children*, children's opera, Librettist: Crossley-Holland
1992 *Blood Wedding*, opera, Librettist: Debra Levy, after F. García Lorca, London
(Sources: Cohen; Sadie and Samuel)

Betty Eileen Roe (July 30, 1930, London–) began piano lessons at age six. In her teens she was composing and arranging music while she assisted with choirs at her local church. She began studying at the Royal Academy of Music but left in 1947 to earn money; two years later she returned the RAM. In the 1950s she became involved with a drama group and began writing for musicals. From 1968 to 1978 she was director of music at the London Academy of Music and Dramatic Art. In 1970 she and her husband, John Bishop, founded Thames Publishing, which became a division of William Elkin Music Services after Bishop's death in 2000. She and her librettist, Marina Lines, have produced six operas, twelve musicals, a pantomime, and choral works. She has also composed a substantial amount of vocal music.

Works
1977 *The Legend of Gallant Bevis of Southampton*, opera. Librettist: Marina Lines
1986 *Canterbury Morning*, chamber opera, Librettist: Marina Lines
1992 *A Flight of Pilgrims*, chamber opera, Librettist: Marina Lines
2002 *Lunch at the Cooked Goose*, opera, Librettist: Marina Lines
2003 *Welcome to Purgatory*, opera, Librettist: Marina Lines
2006 *Brunel: The Little Man in the Tall Hat*, opera, Librettist: Marina Lines
2012 *Swindon: The Opera*, opera
(Sources: Cohen; Sadie and Samuel; Wikipedia)

Ilona Sekacz (April 6, 1948, Blackpool–) began studying music at Birmingham University, then changed to study drama and theater arts. She served as resident composer for the Unicorn Theatre for Children in London for three years writing scores. In 1982 she wrote the music for the Royal Shakespeare Company productions of *King Lear* and Edward Bond's *Lear*. She continued to work with the company as a freelance composer, writing music for many of their plays. She also has composed music for television. Her compositions include choral pieces, vocal works and instrumental works.

Works
1989 *A Small Green Space*, opera, Librettist: Fay Weldon
(Source: Sadie and Samuel)

A violist, **Sally Beamish** (August 26, 1956, London–) first studied at the Royal Northern College of Music focusing on performance, then later studied viola in Germany. Her focus gradually changed to composing, particularly after she moved to Scotland. She was awarded the Paul Hamlyn Foundation Award for outstanding achievement in composition in 1993. Subsequently she cohosted the Scottish Chamber Orchestra composers' course. Three years later she was composer-in-residence with the Swedish Chamber Orchestra and the Scottish Chamber Orchestra. The Scottish Arts Council awarded her a "Creative Scotland Award." A prolific composer, her orchestral music includes two symphonies and several concertos; she's composed chamber music, instrumental music, film scores, and theater music.

Works

1996 *Monster*, opera, based on the life of Mary Shelley, Librettist: Janice Galloway
2013 *Hagar in the Wilderness*, to a libretto by Clara Glynn
(Sources: Sadie and Samuel; Wikipedia; Opera; Scotland)

Diana Burrell (October 25, 1948, Norwich–) received her BA in music from Cambridge University in 1971, then taught in high school and freelanced as a viola player. In 1980 her *Missa Sancte Endeliente* attracted critical attention. She has received numerous commissions from orchestras, music groups and composers; she also has composed music for dance and television. Her many compositions include a ballet, music for orchestra, much vocal music, instrumental music, and music for chamber groups.

Works

1997 *The Albatross*, opera, after Susan Hill, Librettist: Burrell.
(Source: Sadie and Samuel)

Elena Langer (December 8, 1974, Moscow–) studied at the Gnessin School and at the Moscow Conservatory. She moved to London in 1999 and studied at the Royal College of Music, then at the Royal Academy of Music. Her first two operas, *Ariadne* and *The Girl of Sand*, were written while she was the first Jerwood Composer in Association at the Almeida Theatre in London. *Four Sisters* was commissioned by Dawn Upshaw to be performed at Bard College in New York. In addition to operas her compositions include contemporary classical music.

Works

2002 *Ariadne*
2003 *The Girl of Sand*, opera
2010 *The Lion's Face*, opera
2012 *Four Sisters*, opera
(Source: Wikipedia)

France

The parents of **Betsy Jolas** (August 5, 1926, Paris–) were part of the remarkable literary and artistic setting in Paris in the 1920s and 30s that included James Joyce, Ernest Hemingway, Henri Matisse and Sylvia Beach. In 1940 Betsy's family moved to New York. She attended the Lycée Français and Bennington College, from which she graduated in 1946. She then returned to Paris and continued her studies; later she taught at several colleges and universities. Her awards include a Koussevitzky Foundation Award, the Grand Prix de la Ville de Paris, and the Prix International Maurice Ravel. She composed for orchestra and chamber groups, and for piano.

Works

1975 *Le Pavillon au bord de la rivière*, chamber opera, Librettist: M. Raoul-Davis, after Huan Han Chin, Avignon
1986 *Le Cyclope*, opera, after Euripides' *Cyclops*, Avignon
1987 *Schliemann*, opera, Librettists: B. Bayen and B. Jolas, after Bayen, concert performance, Paris

(Sources: Sadie and Samuel; http://operadata.stanford.edu/)

Isabelle Aboulker (October 23, 1938, Paris–) began composing professionally for theater, film and television while she was studying at the Conservatoire National Superieur de Musique in Paris. Subsequently she was the chief accompanist and voice teacher at the conservatoire.

Works

1979 *La Lacune*, chamber opera, Librettist: E. Ionesco
1981 *Les Surprises de l'enfer*, opera
1980 *Jean de La Fontaine parmi nous*, opera for children

(Sources: Cohen; Wikipedia)

Michèle Reverdy (December 12, 1943, Egypt–) is a musicologist in addition to being a composer. She studied at the Paris Conservatoire and won several first prizes. She also was awarded a degree in literature from the Sorbonne. Her compositions include music for stage, orchestra, choral music and music for various instruments. She also wrote two books on the music of Olivier Messiaen.

Works

1985 *La Nuit qui suivit notre dernier dîner*, opera, Librettist: Jean-Claude Buchard
1990 *Le Précepteur*, opera, Librettist: Hans-Ulrich Treichel
1990 *Vincent*, opera, Librettist: Michel Siret-Gille
1991 *Un Signe dans l'espace*, opera, Librrettist/Source Italo Calvino

Books by or about Michèle Reverdy:

Reverdy, Michèle. *L'Oeuvre pour orchestra d'Olivier Messiaen*. Paris, 1988.
_____. *L'Oeuvre pour piano d'Olivier Messiaen*. Paris, 1978.
(Sources: Sadie and Samuel; http://operadata.stanford.edu/)

Georgia

Natela Damianovna Svanidze (September 4, 1926, Ahalzih–) graduated from the Tbilisi Conservatory in 1951 then continued her studies at the Moscow Conservatory. She joined the Georgian Drama Institute in 1956 and was appointed professor. Her music often reflects her strong interest in the music of Georgia, particularly folk part-singing and folk polyphony. Her compositions include vocal music, orchestral pieces and chamber music.

Works
1987 *Gaul-Gavkhe*, opera, Librettist: N. Svanidze, after T. Maglaperidze, unperformed
(Source: Sadie and Samuel)

Germany

A school trip to Manchester, England, in 1972 inspired **Susanne Erding** (November 16, 1955, Schwäbisch Hall–) to study English language and literature at Stuttgart University. From 1974 to 1979 she studied school music at the Stuttgart Musikhochschule; in 1979 she began teaching at the Musikhochschule. She studied composition at several international venues. Her works include orchestral music, chamber music, music for chamber ensembles and for solo instruments, and vocal music.

Works
1983 *Joy*, chamber opera, Librettist: R. Kift
1990 *Der Schneemann*, opera, Librettist: W. Jens
(Source: Sadie and Samuel)

Eva Schorr (September 28, 1927, Württemberg–) first studied with her father, who was an organist and music teacher. At age eight she was performing her own compositions, and as a teenager she won prizes for composition and organ. She studied at the State Music Academy in Stuttgart from 1947 to 1952 and later attended the Darmstadt summer school. She received an award at the GEDOK competitions in Mannheim and was awarded the gold medal at the 4th International Competition in Buenos Aires. Her compositions include music for orchestra, chamber ensembles, organ, piano, vocal and sacred music. She is also a skilled artist, and her graphic artworks have been shown in numerous exhibitions.

Works

1989 *Die Katze des Königs*, opera, Librettists Bilder, B. Frank
(Source: Sadie and Samuel)

Greece

Marielli Sfakianaki (January 12, 1945, Athens–) was the daughter of Kostas Sfanianakis, a composer, musicologist and pianist. In 1963 she entered the Athens Conservatory, where she studied singing until 1971 then studied composition until 1984. Her particular interest is vocal music, particularly choral music. Her novel *Echoes* received an award from the Society of Greek Writers.

Works

1988 *The Pagic Muper*, opera, Librettist: Sfakianaki
1988–93 *Minos*, opera, Librettist: Sfakianaki
(Sources: Sadie and Samuel; Wikipedia)

Israel

When she was two, **Rivka Elkoshi** (July 17, 1949, Radautz-Bokovina, Romania–) and her family left Romania and went to Israel. She received her BMus in piano performance from the Rubin Music Academy in 1973 and her MA in music education from New York University. She received several awards that allowed her to study in Israel and the United States. In 1976 she studied musicology at Hebrew University in Jerusalem. She received a PhD in music education and composition from the University of California, Los Angeles. In addition to her opera she composed vocal music, sacred music, and works for chamber groups.

Works

1980 *Intervals and Intrigues*, opera
(Source: Cohen)

Shulamit Ran (October 21, 1949, Tel-Aviv–) was setting poetry to music when she was seven. Two years later she was studying composition and piano with some of Israel's most noted musicians. Already an accomplished composer by 1962, she received scholarships from the American-Israel Cultural Foundation and Mannes College to study in the United States. She graduated from Mannes in 1967 and toured extensively in the United States and Europe for the next five years. In 1973 she was pianist for the performance of her orchestral piece *Capriccio* by the New York Philharmonic Orchestra under Leonard Bernstein. She was artist-in-residence at St. Mary's University in Halifax, Nova Scotia, in 1972 and 1973. Subsequently she joined the faculty of the University of Chicago, where she is professor of composition.

Shulamit's numerous awards and fellowships include Guggenheim fellowships and commissions from the Ford Foundation. In 1991 she won the Pulitzer Prize for music. She has received several honorary doctorates. Among her many appointments she was composer-in-residence with the Lyric Opera of Chicago. Her compositions include orchestral pieces, instrumental pieces, vocal music, music for ensembles and for keyboard.

Works

1997 *Between Two Worlds* (The Dybbuk), opera, *Chicago*
(Sources: Sadie and Samuel; http://music.uchicago.edu/page/shulamit-ran)

Italy

Teresa Procaccini (March 23, 1934, Foggia–) began composing at a young age and first studied piano at the Foggia Conservatory. After graduating she continued her studies in organ and composition at the Rome Conservatory of Saint Cecilia, where she focused on film music, and at the Accademia Musicale Chigiana in Siena, where she studied composition. She returned to Foggia Conservatory to teach organ and composition and was also director of the conservatory for about a year. In 1979 she went to the Rome Conservatory of Saint Cecilia as a lecturer in composition. In addition to her operas she composed ballets, music for orchestra, for chamber groups and vocal music. Throughout her career she won many prizes, including the International String Quartet Competition in 1981.

Works

1970 *La vendetta di Luzbel*, opera, Librettist; Proccacini, after F. Lopé de Vega
1973 *La prima notte*, comic opera, Librettist: Sergio Massaron
1975 *Questione di fiducia*, comic opera, Librettist: Sergio Massaron
1984 *L'uomo del tamburo*, opera
(Sources: Sadie and Samuel; women-in-music.com)

When **Irma Ravinale** (October 1, 1937, Naples–April 7, 2013) was at the Rome Conservatory of Saint Cecilia she studied composition, choral music and choral conducting. She also conducted literary research, which may account for her interesting choice of source for her opera. Following her studies at the conservatory she studied with Nadia Boulanger. In 1966 Irma returned to the conservatory as a teacher. Then she was director of San Pietro a Majella Conservatory in Naples until 1998, when she returned to the Conservatory of Santa Cecilia as director for a year. Throughout her career she continued composing for voice and a wide variety of instruments. Teresa Procaccini and Irma Ravinale, so closely contemporary, certainly must have known each other.

Works

1975 *Il ritratto di Dorian Gray*, opera, after Oscar Wilde, Turin

(Sources: Sadie and Samuel; Wikipedia)

Japan

Kazuko Hara (February 10, 1935, Tokyo–) graduated from the Tokyo National University of Fine Arts and Music in 1957. Five years later she went to France, where she studied first at the École Normale in Paris then studied composition at L'Academie International d'Ete in Nice. She also studied voice at the Bernedetto Mercello Music Academy in Venice. When she returned to Japan she studied Gregorian chant. In 1968 she became a professor at the Faculty of Music at Osaka University of Arts. She has received numerous prizes and awards. Her compositions include orchestra works and music for chamber ensembles, vocal works and music for piano.

Works

1981 *The Case Book of Sherlock Holmes: The Confession*, opera, Librettist: J. Maeda, after Arthur Conan Doyle
1982/1983 *On the Merry Night*, opera, Librettist: Hara, after I. Kikumura
1984 *Chieko-sho*, opera, Librettist: Maeda
1985 *Sute-hime*, opera, Librettist: Hara, after S. Muro
1986 *Sonezaki-shinju*, opera, Librettist: M. Chikmatsu
1987 *Beyond Brain Death*, opera, Librettist: Hara, after S. Fuimura
1988 *The History of Yosakoi-bushi*, opera, Librettist: Hara, after F. Tosa
1990 *Iwanaga-hime*, opera, Librettist: B. Yoshida, after Chikamatsu
1991 *Petro Kibe*, opera, Librettist: Hara, after G. Matsunaga
1991 *Nasu-no Yoichi*, opera, Librettist: I. Narushima

(Sources: Cohen; Sadie and Samuel; http://operadata.stanford.edu/)

Mayako Kubo (December 5, 1947–) studied at the Osaka College of Music from 1966 to 1970 then was a pianist in Tokyo. She went to the Vienna Musikhochschule in 1972. Five years later she attended the Darmstadt summer courses in contemporary music, then studied musicology at Vienna University. She has received numerous awards and fellowships. Her compositions include music for orchestra and chamber ensembles, vocal music and electronic music.

Works
1996 *Rashomon*, opera (Japanese version 2002)
2003/2004 *Osan—Secret of Love*, opera
2010 *Der Spinnfaden* [The Spinning Thread], opera
(Sources: Cohen; Wikipedia)

Kazakhstan

Gaziza Akhemetovna Zhubanova (December 2, 1927, Kazakhstan–December 13, 1993) grew up in a musical family; her father, Akhmet Zhubanov, was a composer and scholar as well as the organizer and conductor of the Kazakh Instruments Orchestra. Gaziza graduated from the Moscow Conservatory in 1954 but continued postgraduate work for the next three years. She was chairwoman of the Kazakh Composers' Union from 1962 to 1968. In 1967 she began teaching composition at the Alma-Ata Conservatory and was director of the conservatory from 1975 to 1987. Many of her compositions incorporate Kazakh classical music. She composed orchestral works, music for chamber ensembles, several ballets, and vocal and choral music.

Works
1975 *Enlik-Kebek*, opera, Librettis: S. Zhiyenbayev, after M. Auezov
1981 *Dvadtsat' vosem'* [Twenty-Eight], opera, Librettist: Mambetov
1987 *Kurmangazi*, opera, Librettist: H. Yergaliyev, completion of A. Zhubanov's opera
(Source: Sadie and Samuel)

Korea

Sook-Ja Oh (May 28, 1941, Seoul–) studied at Kyung Hee University, where she received her BA in 1971 and her MA in 1973. She continued her studies at the Peabody Conservatory in Baltimore studying electronic music in 1975 and 1976. During the summer of 1979 she participated in the conductors' summer course at the Salzburg Mozarteum. During some of this time she was teaching at Kyung Hee University. One of her pieces for chamber ensembles was selected for the Women Composers' Festival in Rome. She has also composed orchestral pieces and vocal music. Her interest in Korean musical traditions and shamanism are reflected in her compositions and also in her written pieces, which have been published in Korea.

Works

1990 *Won-Sul-Lang* [Wonsulling: The Son of a Knight], opera
(Sources: Sadie and Samuel; women-in-music.com)

Mexico

After graduating from the Conservatorio Nacional de Música, **Alicia Urreta** (October 12, 1933, Veracruz–December 20, 1987, Mexico City) studied with Alfred Brendel and Alicia de Larrocha. She also studied electronic music and acoustics at the Schola Cantorum in Paris. Returning to Mexico she was titular pianist of the Orquesta Sinfónica Nacional and at the same time instructor in acoustics at the Instituto Politécnico. Also at that time she was the performer in the premieres of all works that included piano composed by Stockhausen, Cage, Gilbert Amy, Manuel Enríquez and Halffter. She founded the Camerata de México, made numerous recordings and was the recipient of many awards. Her compositions include incidental music for plays, music for orchestra and electronic music.

Works

1972 *Romance de Doña Balada*, chamber opera, Librettist: Urreta
(Sources: Sadie and Samuel; Cohen)

Hilda Paredes (1959, Tehuacan, Puebla–) relocated to London in 1979. She graduated from the Guildhall School of Music, earned a master of arts at City University in London and a PhD at Manchester University. Her career is an international one, and she has received significant awards from the United States, Great Britain and Mexico. She participated in the Garden Venture Opera Project in Dartington and subsequently wrote her first chamber opera, *The Seventh Seed*. She has also taught at the University in Mexico City. Her awards include a Guggenheim fellowship, several awards from Fellowship for Creative Artists, Mexico, and a Music for Dance Award from the Arts Council of Great Britain.

Works

La séptima semilla [The Seventh Seed], chamber opera
El palacio imaginado, chamber opera
(Sources: Sadie and Samuel; hildaparedes.com)

New Zealand

Gillian Bibby (August 31, 1945–) earned a degree in English, and a BMus from the University of Otago in 1968, and an MA in musicology in 1969. She continued her studies at Victoria University in Wellington studying electronic music, receiving her diploma in 1970. From 1971 to 1975 she was studying in Berlin and Cologne. In 1974 she was awarded the Kranichstein Prize in new music and in 1975 the Boswil Artistic Residency in Switzerland. The next year she returned to New Zealand as a Mozart Fellow. Her professional activities include teaching, recording, giving concert performances, writing for New Zealand publications, and composing. She composes for stage, instrument and tape, choral groups and chamber ensembles.

Works

Sanctuary of Spirits, opera, Librettist: Alistair Campbell
(Source: Sadie and Samuel)

Jenny (Jennifer) Helen McLeod (November 12, 1941, Wellington–) was active musically from an early age, accompanying singers, violinists and choirs. She also learned about Maori poetry and legends from friends she made at that time. When she was sixteen she received an American Field Service scholarship to travel to the United States. When she returned to New Zealand she participated in a Cambridge (New Zealand) summer school program. She received her BMus from Victoria University, Wellington in 1964. She had become interested in Olivier Messiaen's music, and an Arts Council bursary allowed her to attend his classes at the Paris Conservatoire. While she was in Europe she also studied in Cologne.

In 1967 she was given a position as lecturer in music at Victoria University. Four years later she was made professor and stayed at the university until 1976. At that time she undertook to work for the Divine Light Mission in the United States. Five years later she returned to New Zealand and resumed her composing. She received the New Zealand Order of Merit for services to music in 1997. She composed music for orchestra, chamber ensembles, piano music, vocal music and incidental music.

Works

1971 *Under the Sun*, opera
Earth and Sky, opera
(Source: Sadie and Samuel)

Dorothy Quita Buchanan (September 28, 1945, Christchurch–) grew up in a family of musicians: both parents were pianists and she and her five sisters were all singers and instrumentalists. She received her BMus from Canterbury University in 1967. Six years later she founded the Christchurch Music Workshops. In 1976 she earned a teaching diploma from the Christchurch Teachers' College. She was appointed by the government to be the first New Zealand "composer-in-schools" in 1977, the same year she received a Queen Elizabeth II Arts' Council Grant. In 2001 she received the Officer of the New Zealand Order of Merit.

Works

Clio Legacy, opera after Witi Ihimaera
Woman at the Store, opera after Katherine Mansfield
The Mansfield Stories, opera after Katherine Mansfield

(Sources: Sadie and Samuel; Wikipedia)

Gillian Whitehead (April 23, 1941–) is one-eighth Maori, and as a child she responded strongly to natural settings and their Maori associations. She attended the University of Auckland from 1959 to 1962, then continued her studies at Victoria University, Wellington, where she received her BMus in 1964. She received her MMus from the University of Sydney in 1966. Having heard Peter Maxwell Davies lecture on composition and analysis in Adelaide she moved to London to study with him. From 1978 to 1980 she was composer-in-residence at Northern Arts, Newcastle upon Tyne. In 1981 she joined the faculty at the Sydney Conservatorium of Music and eventually became head of composition. She has composed music for orchestra and chamber ensembles, piano music, sacred and vocal music. Several pieces reflect Maori themes. In 2008 she was appointed a Distinguished Companion of the New Zealand Order of Merit for services to music and became Dame Gillian Whitehead.

Works

1975 *Tristan and Iseult*, chamber opera, Librettists: Malcolm Crowthers and Michael Hill
1979 *The Tinker's Curse*, children's opera, Librettist: J. Aiken
1984 *The King of the Other Country*, chamber opera, Librettist, Fleur Adcock
1986 *The Pirate Moon*, chamber opera, Librettist: Anna Maria Dell-Oso
1988 *Bride of Fortune*, chamber opera, Librettist: Anna Maria Dell-Oso
1995 *The Art of Pizza*, opera, Librettist: Anna Maria Dell'oso
1999 *Outrageous Fortune*, opera

(Sources: Sadie and Samuel; http://operadata.stanford.edu/)

Philippines

Alice Doria-Gamilla (September 20, 1931, Philippines–) began teaching piano in schools when she was twenty. In 1965 she received her BS in education magna cum laude from National University. Subsequently she studied music at the University of Santo Tomas Conservatory, majoring in piano. She composed music for orchestra, piano, vocal and sacred music, and music for theater.

Works

1974 *Sa Lahat ng Oras*, operetta
1974–75 *Zarauelas*, on family planning, 5 sequels, commissioned by the Asian Foundation and Zarzuela Foundation of the Philippines
1975 *Pasko'y Pag-Ibig*, operetta
1975 *Sumpaan ng Puso*, zarzuela
(Sources: Cohen; Wikipedia)

Lucrecia R. Kasilag (August 31, 1918, La Union–August 16, 2008) received her BA in 1936 from the Philippine Women's University and her BMus in 1949. She continued her studies at St. Scholastica College then attended the Eastman School where she received her MMus in 1950. In 1953 she was appointed dean of the College of Music and Fine Arts of the Philippine Women's University, a position she held until 1977. She became president and artistic director of the Cultural Centre of the Philippines in 1976 and remained so for ten years. She was consistently active in musical societies and received many national and international honors, including study grants from the Fulbright Scholar Commission, the J.D. Rockefeller 3rd Fund, the Asia Foundation and a cultural grant from the Federal Republic of Germany. Her interest in Asian music generated articles and essays and is reflected in various compositions using occidental and oriental instruments. Her compositions include orchestral works, music for chamber ensembles, for organ, for piano, vocal and choral music, dance scores and numerous pieces of incidental music.

Works

1976 *Jose, aking anak*, operetta

Books by or about Lucrecia Kasilag:

Franquelli, Angelica Rosario. *Lucrecia R. Kasilag: The Western and Oriental Influences in Her Compositions.* 1979.
(Sources: Cohen; Sadie and Samuel)

Poland

Marta Ptaszyńska (July 29, 1943, Warsaw–) studied in Warsaw at the Music School and in Poznan. In 1968 she received her MA from the Warsaw

Conservatory, graduating with distinctions in percussion, composition and music theory. A grant from the French government allowed her to study with Nadia Boulanger in Paris from 1969 to 1970. While in Paris she also attended a course in electronic music at the Groupe des Recherches Musicales of the French radio.

In 1972 she received a grant from the Kosciuszko Foundation that allowed her to study at the Cleveland Institute of Music for two years. The United States then became her permanent home. She frequently lectured on Polish music, and she performed in the United States, often including her own works in her concerts. During the 1970s and 1980s she held academic positions at several institutions. Her prizes and awards include a Simon J. Guggenheim Foundation Fellowship, the award at the International Rostrum of Composers at UNESCO in Paris, and the "Officer Cross of the Order of (Merit)" from the Republic of Poland. In 1998 she was appointed Professor of Music and the Humanities at the University of Chicago. She has composed orchestral pieces, music for chamber ensembles, piano music, vocal music, and music for theater.

Works
1971 *Oskar z Alwy* [Oscar from Alva], opera, Librettist: Z. Kopalko, after Byron
(Sources: Cohen; Sadie and Samuel; Wikipedia)

Elżbieta Sikora (October 20, 1943, Lwów–) first studied sound engineering at the State Higher School of Music in Warsaw, where she received her MA in 1968. After studying in Paris she returned to the school and studied theory, composition and conducting, receiving another MA in 1977. She moved to France in 1981 for further study; one of her instructors was Betty Jolas (see entry). Eight years later she became professor of electronic music at the conservatory in Angoulême. She has composed music for orchestra, chamber ensembles, vocal music, at least one ballet, and electronic music.

Works
1977 *Ariadna*, chamber opera, Librettist: Stanislaw Kasprzysiak
1983 *Derrière son double*, radio opera, Librettist: Jean-Pierre Dupre
1984–86 *L'Arrache-coeur*, radio opera, Librettist: Boris Vian
(Sources: Cohen; Sadie and Samuel; http://operadata.stanford.edu/)

Hanna Kulenty (March 18, 1961, Białystok, Poland–) composes contemporary classical music. She studied composition at the Chopin Music Academy in Warsaw from 1980 to 1986; the next two years she studied composition at the Royal Conservatory of Music in The Hague. She participated in several summer courses in Kazimierz and in Darmstadt, where she focused on contemporary music composition. A freelance composer, she has won numerous scholarships and commissions. Her compositions include music for orchestra, chamber ensembles, solo instruments, television plays and film music.

Works

1985 *Przypowieść o ziarnie* [Parable on Grain], chamber opera
1995 *The Mother of the Black-Winged Dreams*, chamber opera
2003 *Hoffmanniana*, opera
(Source: http://www.hannakulenty.com/05.1_biography.html?)

Romania

Liana Alexandra (May 27, 1947–January 10, 2011) first studied composition from 1965 to 1971 at the Ciprian Porumbescu Academy in Bucharest, receiving the Ciprian Porumbescu scholarship. She spent a year in Weimar studying in 1973 and took part in three sessions of summer composition courses in Darmstadt between 1974 and 1980. She was the first recipient of the Carl Maria von Weber Prize in 1979; she was a three-time recipient of the prize of the Union of Rumanian composers and twice won the Gaudeamus Foundation Prize. In 1983 she received a scholarship to study in the United States. She composed several symphonies and other orchestral music, works for chamber ensembles, music for organ, and vocal music.

Works

1978 *The Snow Queen*, children's opera, after Hans Christian Andersen
1980 *Crăiasa zăpezii*, opera
1987 *În labirint* [The Maze], chamber opera
1995 *Chant d'amour de la Dame à la Licorne*, chamber opera, using verses by Etienne de Sadeleer
(Sources: Cohen; Sadie and Samuel)

Carmen Petra-Basacopol (September 5, 1926, Sibiu–) studied at the Bucharest Conservatory from 1949 to 1956 and for four years also studied in philosophy. She was an assistant in the department of musical form at the conservatory from 1962 to 1966, at which time she became head of the department. Among her prizes and awards she received a diploma of honor at the international competition at Mannheim-Ludwigshafen in 1961 and the George Enescu Composition Prize of the Academy of Socialist Republic of Romania in 1980. She frequently wrote articles on music for the Romanian Press. Her compositions include works for orchestra and chamber ensembles, music for piano, vocal and instrumental music, and at least two ballets. A harpist, she specializes in writing for the harp.

Works

1983 *Coeur d'enfant*, opera, after Edoardo De Amicis
1989 *Apostol Bologa*, opera, after Rebreanu
(Sources: Cohen; Sadie and Samuel; http://operadata.stanford.edu/)

Violeta Dinescu (July 13, 1953, Bucharest–) first studied in Bucharest at the George Enescu School of Music then at the Bucharest Conservatory from 1973 to 1978. She then taught at the Enescu School. During the 1970s she also worked on Romanian folk music, which has had an influence on her music. She moved to Germany, where she lectured at the Hochschule für Kirchenmusik from 1987 to 1990 and also in Frankfurt at the Bayreuth International Youth Festival in 1990. From 1990 on she lectured at the Hochschule für Kirchenmusik in Bayreuth. She has traveled widely as a guest lecturer; her venues include South Africa and the United States. Among her awards and honors are prizes from the Union of Romanian Composers, second prize in the Mannheim International composition, and third prize in the Women and the Arts Festival in the United States. She has composed for orchestra, chamber ensembles, for piano, vocal music, and at least one ballet.

Works

1986 *Hunger und Durst*, chamber opera, after E. Ionesco, *Setea și foamea*, Freiburg
1986 *Der 35 Mai*, children's opera, after E. Kästner, Dresden
1991 *Eréndira*, chamber opera, after G. G. Marquez, Stuttgart
(Sources: Cohen; Sadie and Samuel; http://operadata.stanford.edu/)

Adriana Hölszky (June 30, 1953, Bucharest–) is the daughter of scientists. She began studying piano at the Bucharest music school when she was six. Two years later she began composing. From 1972 to 1975 she studied composition at the Bucharest Conservatory. She received her doctorate in musicology from the Sorbonne in Paris in 1976. That year the family moved to Germany, where she continued her studies. In 1980 she began teaching at the Stuttgart Musikhochschule and remained there for nine years. In the early 1990s she took composition seminars in Tokyo and Kyoto and at the IRCAM in Paris. From 1997 to 2000 she was professor of composition at the Rostock University of Music and Theatre. Subsequently she was professor of composition at the Mozarteum University of Salzburg. She has won significant prizes for composition, including the Valentino Bucchi, Rome, in 1979, and the Gaudeamus in 1981.

Works

1987 *Bremer Freiheit*, opera, Librettist: Thomas Körner, after R.W. Fassbinder
(Sources: Sadie and Samuel; Wikipedia)

Russia

The parents of **Elena Firsova** (March 21, 1950, Leningrad–) were both physicists. Elena began composing when she was twelve. In 1966 she attended music college in Moscow, then entered the Moscow Conservatory in 1970. During that time she wrote three orchestral works and her first chamber opera. Her music was first performed abroad in 1979. Five years later she had a commission from the BBC, her first foreign commission. With the international changes that occurred, travel barriers were removed, and Elena and her husband, the composer Dmitry Smirnov, moved to London in April 1991. They wrote music for commission to survive and received short-term residency invitations from Cambridge University and Dartington College of Arts. In 1993 they began a long-term affiliation with the music department at the University of Keele.

Works

1972 *Pir vo vremya chumï* [Feast in Plague Time], chamber opera, Librettist:
Firsova after A. Pushkin
1994 *Solovey i roza* [The Nightingale and the Rose], chamber opera, after Christine
Rossetti and Oscar Wilde, London
(Source: Sadie and Samuel)

Scotland

Judith Weir (May 11, 1954, Cambridge–) studied with John Tavener during her earlier years. Her parents, who were Scottish, instilled in her a deep appreciation and love for the folk music of Scotland. She spent a semester at Massachusetts Institute of Technology, where she worked on computer music. Following that she studied composition at King's College at Cambridge. Her first published work was a wind quintet, *Out of the Air*, which she wrote at Tanglewood in the summer of 1975. She was Southern Arts Composer-in-Residence from 1976 to 1979 then taught at Glasgow University for two years. She spent two years at Cambridge on a creative arts fellowship. From 1988 to 1991 she was Guinness Composer-in-Residence at the Royal Scottish Academy of Music and Drama. The following year she moved to London. She uses a variety of themes in her works, including the Bayeux tapestry, Chinese Yuan dramas, Serbian folksongs, and an early Icelandic saga. Her compositions include orchestral works, music for chamber ensembles, and vocal music. In addition to her operas she wrote stage works.

Works

1979 *King Harald's Saga*, opera, Librettist: Weir
1984 *The Black Spider*, children's opera, Librettist: Weir, after J. Gotthelf
1985 *The Consolations of Scholarship*, opera, Librettist: Weir
1987 *A Night at the Chinese Opera*, Librettist: Weir, after Chi Chun-hsiang
1989 *Heaven Ablaze in His Breast*, opera, Librettist: Weir, after E.T.A. Hoffman
1990 *The Vanishing Bridegroom*, Librettist: Weir after *Popular Tales of the West Highlands*, Glasgow
1994 *The Story of Blond Eckbert*, Librettist: Weir after J.L. Tieck, London

(Sources: Sadie and Samuel; http://operadata.stanford.edu/)

South Africa

Jeanne Zaidel-Rudolph (July 9, 1948, Pretoria–) received her BMus cum laude from Pretoria University Conservatory in 1969, and her MMus in 1971. A scholarship allowed her to do advanced postgraduate work at the Royal College of Music, London, in 1973 and 1974. She also worked in the Royal College of Music electronic studio. After further study at several venues, she earned a PhD in composition at the University of Pretoria, the first South African woman to be awarded a doctorate in composition. Her compositions include music for orchestra, chamber music, piano music, a ballet and vocal music.

Works

1978 *Animal Farm*, opera
(Source: Cohen)

Spain

María Teresa Pelegrí (March 4, 1907, Barcelona–1995) didn't compose seriously until later in life, more than twenty years after her marriage. She composed music for orchestra and chamber ensembles, vocal music, piano music and music for organ.

Works

1979/1983 *Herodes und Mariamne* [sic], opera, Librettist: F. Hebbel
(Source: Sadie and Samuel)

Sweden

Inger Wikström (December 11, 1939, Stockholm–) studied piano in Stockholm and London. In 1959 she made such successful debuts as a pianist in both cities that she was named artist of the year. She then pursued a career as a pianist, touring throughout the world. She founded the Nordic Music Conservatory at Österskär and was principal and senior piano teacher. In the late 1970s she also began composing and conducting.

Works
1982 *Junker Nils av Eka* [Junker Nils of Eka], family opera, Librettist: A Lindgren
1985 *Den fredlöse* [The Outlawed], opera, after A. Strindberg
1993 *Den brottsliga modern* [The Guilty Mother], after P.-A Beaumarchais
1992 *Näktergalen* [Nightingale], after Hans Christian Andersen
(Source: Sadie and Samuel)

Switzerland

Erika Radermacher (April 16, 1936, Eschweiler, West Germany–) studied piano in Cologne and Vienna and singing in Berne and Zurich. She moved to Switzerland after her marriage to the Swiss composer Urs Peter Schneider and was appointed professor of piano at the Berne Conservatory. She joined the Ensemble Neue Horizonte, a contemporary music group in Berne and continues her singing. Her composing began in the 1970s, and she has received numerous prizes in piano, as well as the Bernese music prize, which she and her husband jointly won in 1983. Her works include chamber music, vocal music, music for piano and electronic music.

Works
1990 *Das Tanzlegendchen*, opera, after G. Keller
(Sources: Cohen; Sadie and Samuel)

United States

Alice Shields (February 18, 1943–) received her BS in music in 1965, her MA in composition in 1967, and her DMA in music in 1975, all from Columbia University, where her focus was electronic music. From 1978 to 1982 she was associate director of the Columbia-Princeton Electronic Music Center. In 1994 she took a position as associate director for the development of the Columbia University Computer Music Center.

Early on she wanted to write for voice and took singing lessons when she was in graduate school. This led to her being the first AGMA Apprentice Opera Composer-in-Residence in the United States at the Lake George Opera Festival, for three years, serving as both composer and singer and also conducting and producing her opera *Odyssey* and scenes from her other early operas. This led to her singing—often challenging leading roles—with the New York City Opera, the Metropolitan Opera Studio, Washington National Opera, Wolf Trap Opera and other companies in the U.S. and Europe.

She has a strong interest and background in psychology; as assistant professor of psychology at New York University she has taught the psychology of music. She has also lectured on the same subject at a variety of institutions including the Santa Fe Opera, CUNY Center for Developmental Neuroscience, the American Psychological Association, and the National Association for the Advancement of Psychoanalysis. She has composed vocal and sacred music, incidental music for dance and for theater, and electronic music. Her operas are eclectic and cross-cultural.

Works

1968 *The Odyssey of Ulysses the Palmiped (Odyssey 1)*, opera, choreographed in Noh theater style, Librettist: Shields, based on *The Egyptian Book of the Dead* and Gilbert-LeConte's *The Odyssey of Ulysses the Palmiped*

1970 *Odyssey 2*, opera, choreographed in Noh theater style, Librettist: Shields, based on *The Egyptian Book of the Dead* and Roger Gilbert-LeConte's Dada play *The Odyssey of Ulysses the Palmiped*

1975 *Odyssey*, opera, choreographed in Noh theater dance style, Librettist: Shields, based on Homer's *The Odyssey*

1978 *Shaman*, opera, Librettist: Shields, using elements of Native American shamanism

1989 *Wraecca*, opera, Librettist: Shields (1989), using language from two Anglo-Saxon Poems, based on Gregorian chant

1992 *Mass for the Dead* 1992, opera, Librettist: Shields, using text from Bharata Natyam dance-drama and theatrical techniques from Greek drama, American Chamber Opera Company

1993 *Shivatanz*, mini-opera, Librettist: Shields, based on a traditional South Indian poem and dance, Akademie der Künste, Berlin

1994 *Apocalypse*, opera, Librettist: Shields; opera uses musical and theatrical techniques from Bharata Natyam dance-drama

2000/2011 *Komachi at Sekidera*, chamber opera, Librettist: Shields, based on a Noh play

2010 *Criseyde*, opera, Librettist: Shields; libretto is a new Middle English resetting of Chaucer's *Troilus and Criseyde*

2013 *Zhaojun: A Woman of Peace*, opera, Librettist: Shields; focuses on the position of women in ancient China

(Sources: Cohen; http://www.aliceshields.com/bio.html)

Dawn Constance Crawford (b. ca. December 19, 1919, Ellington Field, Texas) received a BA from Rice University in Houston in 1939 and a BM from Houston Conservatory. In 1942 she took a position as assistant director at the Houston Conservatory, a position she held for seven years. She went on the study composition at the Eastman School of Music. In 1964 she received an MA and a PhD from Columbia University. That same year she was on the faculty of the Dominican College music department. She lectured frequently on aspects of Brahms' Intermezzi, on songs by contemporary American composer, and on Italian art songs. Her compositions include orchestra pieces, music for chamber ensembles, and vocal and sacred music.

Works
1971 *The Pearl*, chamber opera, Librettist: Crawford, after John Steinbeck
(Sources: Cohen; http://operadata.stanford.edu/)

Kathleen St. John (May 28, 1942, Long Beach, California–) studied at San Diego State College as a music major from 1962 to 1966. She continued her studies at the Juilliard School of Music, earning her BM in 1968. Subsequently she studied at the Columbia-Princeton Electronic Music Center, where Alice Shields was one of her instructors. Her awards include the Juilliard award in composition and outstanding work for music theater, the Irvine Foundation scholarship in composition, five residency fellowships from the MacDowell Colony and the Virginia Center for the Creative Arts. Her compositions include works for orchestra, band, numerous works for chamber ensembles, vocal and sacred music, ballets, and multimedia works.

Works
1971 *The Clouds*, opera, after Aristophanes
(Source: Cohen)

Meredith Monk (November 30, 1943, Peru–) came from a musical family. Her mother, who was a pop and show singer, was on tour in Peru when Meredith was born. Meredith earned her BA in performing arts in 1964 at Sarah Lawrence College. *Juice*, her first theater piece, premiered at the Guggenheim Museum in New York in 1969. Throughout her career she has been interested in filmmaking, choreography, directing and theater—and has been involved in all of them. She has received many awards, including a MacArthur "Genius" Award, two Guggenheim Fellowships, and three "Obies" (off-Broadway theater awards). She has received honorary doctor of arts degrees from Bard College, the University of the Arts, the Juilliard School, the San Francisco Art Institute and the Boston Conservatory.

Works

1971 *Vessel*, opera
1972–73 *Education of the Girlchild*, opera
1976 *Quarry*, opera
1991 *Atlas*, opera, commissioned by the Houston Grand Opera
(Sources: Sadie and Samuel; Wikipedia)

Alice Parker (December 16, 1925, Boston–) always said that she sang before she spoke. When she was five she was composing, and she wrote her first orchestral score in high school. She studied at Smith College and earned a BA in 1947 and her MS in 1949 at the Juilliard School of Music. She was principal arranger for the Robert Shaw Chorale from 1948 to 1967. She is best known for her church music and her settings of American folk songs, hymns and spirituals. Her compositions also include music for chamber ensembles and piano music. She is also well known as a conductor. Her honors include the Smith College Medal, grants from ASCAP, the National Endowment for the Arts, and the American Music Center. She has been awarded four honorary doctorates.

Works

1971 *The Martyrs' Mirror*, opera, Librettist: John L. Ruth
1975 *The Family Reunion*, opera, Librettist: Alice Parker
1978 *Singers Glen*, opera
1982 *The Ponder Heart*, opera, Librettist: Alice Parker, after Eudora Welty
(Sources: Sadie and Samuel; https://www.giamusic.com/bios/alice-parker)

Alison Nowak (April 7, 1948, Syracuse, New York–) studied at Bennington College, where Vivian Fine (see entry) was one of her teachers, and earned her BA in 1970. She continued her studies at Columbia University, receiving her MA in 1972 and a DMA She has composed music for orchestra and chamber ensembles as well piano music.

Works

1973 *Diversion and Division*, chamber opera
(Sources: Cohen; http://composers.com/alison-nowak)

Elizabeth "Libby" Larsen (December 24, 1950, Wilmington Delaware–) received a BA in 1971, an MM in 1975 and a PhD in 1978 from the University of Minnesota. She was a resident composer with the Minnesota Orchestra from the 1983 season to 1987. Subsequently she was first organizer and then artistic director of the Hot Notes Series, focusing on the modern keyboard—reflecting her strong interest in integrating electronic instruments and synthesized sound. She receives numerous commissions and accepts many requests for speaking engagements and serving as a guest teacher. She is a particularly strong advocate of music education, American music and women composers. A prolific composer, her compositions include orchestral works, music for chamber ensembles, vocal and sacred music, multimedia, and music for harp.

Works

1973 *Some Pig*, opera
1977 *The Words Upon the Windowpane*, opera, after Yeats
1979 *The Silver Fox*, children's opera, Librettist: J. Olive, St. Paul, Minnesota
1979 *The Emperor's New Clothes*, opera, Librettist, Timothy Mason
1980 *Tumbledown Dick*, opera, Librettist: Vern Sutton, after H. Fielding, St. Paul, Minnesota
1982 *Psyke and the Pskyskraper*, chamber opera
1984 *Clair de Lune*, opera, Librettist: Patricia Hampl
1985 *Holy Ghosts*, opera, after Linney
1985 *A Wrinkle in Time*, opera, Librettist: W. Green
1987 *Frankenstein: The Modern Prometheus*, opera, Librettist: Elizabeth Larsen, after Mary Shelley
1988 *Christina Romana*, opera, Librettist Vern Sutton
1989 *Beauty and the Beast*, opera
1993 *Mrs. Dalloway*, opera, Librettist: B. Grice after Virginia Woolf, Cleveland
    Woman of Letters, opera

(Sources: Sadie and Samuel; http://operadata.stanford.edu/)

Beth Anderson, (January 3, 1950, Lexington, Kentucky–) received her BA in 1971 from the University of California, Davis, her MFA in 1973 from Mills College in Oakland, California, and an MA the following year, also from Mills College. In 1975 she moved to New York, where she founded *Ear* magazine; she was coeditor and a principle contributor of *Ear* from 1973 to 1979. Subsequently she taught and was the accompanist for dancers in several prominent dance companies. Her compositions include music for orchestra, chamber ensembles, piano, dance scores, vocal music, electronic music, and multimedia.

Works

1973 *Queen Christina*, opera, after Hans Christian Andersen
(Source: Sadie and Samuel)

Janice Giteck (June 27, 1946, Brooklyn–) received her BA in 1968 and her MA in 1969 from Mills College, California, where Darius Milhaud was one of her instructors. The next year she was at the Paris Conservatoire, where she studied with Olivier Messiaen. Returning to the United States she was at the Aspen School in Colorado, where Milhaud again was one of her instructors. Subsequently she held teaching positions at several universities in California, then in 1979 she joined the faculty of the Cornish College of the Arts in Seattle, where she taught both composition and women's studies. In 1986 she received a second MA, this one in psychology, from Antioch University in Ohio. She was a founding member of the Port Costa Players, and was music director of the Oakland Museum and KPFA Radio. She has received several awards and commissions. Her compositions include music for chamber ensembles, vocal music, incidental music, and music for theater.

Works

1976 *A'agita*, opera, Librettist: R. Giteck, after Pima and Papgo texts
(Source: Sadie and Samuel)

The parents of **Edith Borroff** (August 2, 1925, New York–) were both musical; her mother Marie Bergersen was a composer and pianist and her father a tenor. Edith first studied at Oberlin College Conservatory. She earned her BMus in 1946 and her MM in composition in 1948 from the American Conservatory in Chicago. In 1958 she received her PhD in musicology from the University of Michigan. She was at Hillsdale College in Michigan, as professor and associate dean, from 1958 to 1962, then at Eastern Michigan University from 1962 to 1966. In 1973 she was appointed professor of music at the State University at Binghamton, New York, where she stayed until 1992. She has composed music for orchestra, chamber ensembles, organ, piano, vocal and sacred music, and incidental music. Her papers are at the Newberry Library in Chicago, Illinois.

Works

1977 *The Sun and the Wind*, opera, Librettist: Borroff

Books by or about Edith Borroff:

Borroff, Edith. *American Operas: A Checklist*. Edited by J. Bunker Clark. Warren, MI: Harmonie Park, 1992.
_____. *The Fairbank Collection*. Binghamton, NY: College Music Society.
_____. *The Instrumental Works of Jean Joseph Casanea de Mondonville*. Ann Arbor, 1959.
_____. *An Introduction to Elisabeth-Claude Jacquet de la Guerre*. Brooklyn: Institute of Mediaeval Music, 1966.
_____. *Music in Europe and the United States: A History*. New York: Ardsley House, 1990.

_____. *Music in Perspective*. With Marjory Irvin. New York: Harcourt Brace
Jovanovich, 1976.
_____*Music Melting Round: A History of Music in the United States*. New York: Ard-
sley, 1995.
_____. *The Music of the Baroque*. New York: Da Capo, 1978.
_____. *Notations and Editions: A Book in Honor of Louise Cuyler*. Edited by Edith
Borroff. New York: Da Capo, 1977.
_____. *Three American Composers*. Lanham, MD: University Press of America,
c1986.
(Source: Sadie and Samuel)

Ivana Marburger Themmen (April 7, 1935, New York–) studied at the
New England Conservatory in the early 1950s and subsequently at the Eastman School in Rochester, New York, and the Berkshire Music Center. She
lived in Europe in the mid–1960s studying chamber music and giving concerts
as a pianist. After her return to New York she studied orchestration. Her
commissions and awards include a grant from the New Jersey Arts Council
in 1978 for completion of an opera. Her compositions include orchestral
works, music for chamber ensembles, vocal and instrumental works, and a
ballet.

Works

1977 *Lucian*, opera, Librettist: Norman Simon
(Sources: Cohen; http://operadata.stanford.edu/)

Carol Sams (1945–) received her MA in Music from Mills College and
her doctor of music arts from the University of Washington. *Salome, Daughter
of Herodias* had its premiere at the National Opera Association Convention
in Seattle.

Works

1977 *Salome, Daughter of Herodias*, opera, Librettist: Ivan Janer
1982 *Benjamin Ballou*, opera, Librettist: Ralph Rosenblum
1983 *The Beauty and the Beast*, opera, Librettist: Carol Sams, after the fairy tale
(Sources: Wikipedia; http://operadata.stanford.edu/)

Beverly Pinsky Grigsby (January 11, 1928, Chicago–) began her college
education in premedical studies at the University of Southern California then
decided to study composition with Ernst Krenek. She received her BA in 1961
and her MA in 1963 from California State University in Northridge. In 1986
she earned a DMA at the University of Southern California. Krenek had
introduced her to electronic music, and she went on to study computer music

at Stanford University. Subsequently she studied at Carnegie Mellon University in Pittsburgh, where she was appointed a fellow. She shifted her musical (and geographical) focus to study medieval music at Solesmes in France and at the Royal College of Music in London. In 1993 she returned to California State University to teach and also to found the school's computer music studio. She retired in 1992. She composed music for chamber ensembles, sacred music, vocal music, and film music. Her operas and dramatic cantatas have been produced in the United States, Europe and Brazil.

Works

1977 *Moses*, opera
1984 *The Mask of Eleanor*
(Source: Sadie and Samuel)

Jeanne Ellison Shaffer (May 25, 1925, Knoxville, Tennessee–2009) was singing on the radio when she was four. At eleven she began touring with the Paul Whiteman Orchestra. She received an AA in music in 1944 from Stephens College at Columbia, Missouri, a BMus from Samford University in Birmingham, Alabama, an MMus from Birmingham Southern College in 1958, and a PhD in 1970 from George Peabody College in Nashville. In the late 1950s and the 1960s she was a lecturer at several colleges, then taught in school districts and metropolitan areas in Illinois and Tennessee. She went on to teach at several colleges and universities, including Peabody College. In 1973 she became professor and chairperson of the division of fine arts at Judson College in Marion, Georgia.

Works

1977 *The Ghost of Susan B. Anthony*, chamber opera
1980 *The Heart of Dixie*, opera, Librettist: Robert S. Barmettler
1986 *The End of the Line*, opera, Librettist: Robert S. Barmettler
(Source: Cohen)

Vivian Fine (September 28, 1913, Chicago–March 20, 2000) received a scholarship from the Chicago Musical College to study piano when she was five years old. She stayed at the college until 1922. After studying privately for several years she entered the American Conservatory in Chicago, where Ruth Crawford Seeger was one of her teachers. Vivian was then thirteen. In 1931 she moved to New York and began her career as a pianist while continuing to study privately until about 1945. That year she began her extensive teaching career, first at New York University, then at the Juilliard School of Music. From 1964 to 1988 she was at Bennington College. She was also a composer and accompanist for modern dance groups. Among her honors and awards are a Ford Foundation grant, a Guggenheim Fellowship, and the Dollard Award. Her orchestral work *Drama* was nominated for a Pulitzer Prize. She was a prolific composer, with many orchestral works and pieces for chamber ensembles, music for piano, vocal music, several ballets, and sacred music. Her manuscripts are at the Library of Congress.

Works

1978 *The Women in the Garden*, chamber opera, Librettist: Fine

Books by or about Vivian Fine:

Cody, Judith. *Vivian Fine: A Bio-Bibliography*. Greenwood, 2002.
Von Gunden, Heidi. *The Music of Vivian Fine*. Scarecrow, 1999.
(Sources: Grove; Sadie and Samuel)

Kim Sherman (August 6, 1954, Elgin, Illinois–) received her BMus in piano from the Conservatory of Lawrence University in Wisconsin. She was a pupil of Thea Musgrave (see entry) in California in 1976 and 1977, studying composition, orchestration and opera. Kim then became composer in residence with the Illusion Theater Company in Minneapolis, where she composed scores, performed and toured with the company. She received an NEA Individual Artist grant for her chamber music and two Kudos Awards for theater scores. Joseph Papp commissioned her to compose a musical for the Public Theater in New York City in 1983. She has written incidental music for numerous productions; one of her best known collaborations is "O Pioneers" adapted from Willa Cather's book. Many of her scores have won awards. Her oratorio *Service for the Dead in Bosnia-Herzegovina*, in collaboration with playwright Erik Ehn, has been performed internationally. Her compositions include chamber music, vocal music, and music for theater.

Works

1979 *Claire*, opera
1987 *A Long Island Dreamer*, opera, Librettist: Paul Selig
1989 *Red Tide*, opera, Librettist: Paul Selig
(Sources: Cohen; http://kdsherman.com/Bio.htm)

Dorothy Rudd Moore (June 4, 1940, Delaware–) graduated from Howard University in Washington, D.C., in 1963 with a bachelor's degree in music. In the summer of 1963 she studied with Nadia Boulanger at the American Conservatory at Fontainebleau. She taught at the Harlem School of the Arts, at New York University 1965 to 1966, at New York University in 1969, and at Bronx Community College in 1971. She was one of the founders of the Society of Black Composers in 1968. She has received numerous commissions.

Her compositions include music for orchestra, for chamber ensembles, and vocal music.

Works

1979–85 *Frederick Douglass*, opera, New York
(Sources: Sadie and Samuel; http://operadata.stanford.edu/)

Ruth Schonthal (June 27, 1924, Hamburg–2006) began her studies at the Stern Conservatory in Berlin in 1929 when she was five years of age and continued there until 1934, when her parents emigrated to Sweden. From 1937 to 1940 she studied at the Royal Academy in Stockholm. The following year her family went east, crossed the USSR, and traveled to Mexico City, where they settled. Ruth continued her studies in piano and composition in Mexico City and gave a very successful concert of her music when she was nineteen. Paul Hindemith was in the audience, and he arranged for her to get a scholarship to attend Yale University and study composition. She received her AB in 1950. That same year she married Paul Seckel, a painter, and they settled in New York City. She began teaching in 1954, privately and holding part-time teaching positions. In 1979 she gave a concert in London; in the early 1980s she was playing in Germany. Her concerts were always successful, her music received with acclaim. She taught at New York University for years, only retiring because of health reasons. One of her students, Stephanie Germanotta, achieved fame in pop music as Lady Gaga.

The City of Heidelberg awarded her Internationaler Künstlerinnen Preis and honored her with an exhibition of her life and works at the Prinz Carl am Kommarkt Museum. She also received Meet the Composer grants, a certificate of merit from Yale for outstanding service to music, and an outstanding musician award from New York University. She was a finalist in the New York City Opera competition with her opera *The Courtship of Camilla*. Her compositions include orchestra works, music for chamber ensembles, piano music, vocal music and ballets.

Works

1979–80 *The Courtship of Camilla*, opera, after A.A. Milne
1988 *Princess Maleen*, opera for children, Librettist: Wallis Wood, after Grimm
(Sources: Sadie and Samuel; Wikipedia)

Jean Eichelberger Ivey (July 3, 1923, Washington–May 2, 2010) studied first at Trinity College, where she received her BA in 1944. Two years later she received an MM in piano from the Peabody Conservatory. She then taught at Trinity College for several years. In 1956 she received an MM in composition from the Eastman School, then in 1972 a DMUS in composition from the University of Toronto. For several years she was coordinator of the composition department at the Peabody Conservatory at Johns Hopkins University in Baltimore. In 1967 she founded Peabody Conservatory Electronic Music Studio and served as director. She toured widely as a concert pianist in Europe, the United States and Mexico. Her awards include a composer grant from the National Endowment for the Arts, the Distinguished Achievement Citation of the National League of American Pen Women

Works

1980–82 *The Birthmark*, opera, Librettist: Ivey, after Nathaniel Hawthorne
(Source: Sadie and Samuel)

Royce Dembo (March 19, 1933, Troy, New York–) studied at the Eastman School of Music, at Syracuse University and at Ithaca College. She married in 1953; she and her husband then lived for two years in Taiwan, where she taught music at Chinese and American schools. Returning to the United States she studied composition at UCLA and earned an MM in composition from the University of Wisconsin. Her compositions include chamber music, works for piano, vocal and sacred music; her music has been performed in Taiwan, Indonesia, Scotland, and the United States.

Works

1981 *The Audience*, chamber opera, Librettist: Glenn Miller
1979 *Beowulf*, drama for children, commissioned by the Wisconsin Art Board
(Sources: Cohen; http://operadata.stanford.edu/)

Judith Shatin (Shatin Allen) (November 21 1949, Boston–) received her AB from Douglas College in 1971, her MM from the Juilliard School in 1974, and her PhD from Princeton University in 1979. Many of her compositions are for combined electronic and acoustic media. Her music also includes orchestra works, music for various combinations of instruments, and vocal music. She has received commissions from many organizations, including the McKim Fund of the Library of Congress, the National Endowment for the Arts, and the Lila Wallace-Readers Digest Arts Partners Program. Her music is often featured at festivals throughout the world. She has held residencies at several venues in Europe and at MacDowell, the Virginia Center for the Creative Arts and Yaddo in the United States. She has served on boards for several national music organizations. She joined the faculty of the University of Virginia in 1979 and subsequently became director of the Virginia Center for Computer Music. Currently she is the William R. Kenan Jr. Professor at the University of Virginia.

Works

1981–82 *Follies and Fancies*, chamber opera, Librettists: Judith Shatin and Gloria Russo, after Molière: *Les précieuses ridicules*
(Sources: Sadie and Samuel; http://judithshatin.com/short-biography/)

Kay Gardner (February 8, 1941, Freeport, New York–2002) was a conductor, lecturer and flautist in addition to her composing. From 1958 to 1961 she studied conducting at the University of Michigan. Seven years later she founded the Norfolk [Virginia] Chamber Consort, which focused on avant-guard and contemporary music, and was its flautist. By 1972 she was in New York at the State University of Stony Brook studying flute. In 1974 she received her MMus. Three years later she was in Denver studying conducting. Her conducting debut was at the National Women's Music Festival in Champaign, Illinois, in 1978. That year she also founded the New England Women's Symphony in Boston. She also had a strong interest in the potential role of music in healing for healing purposes and presented to medical schools and health workers. Her compositions include music for orchestra and for band, a substantial amount of chamber music and vocal music.

Works

1981 *Ladies Voices: A Short Opera*, opera, Librettist: Gertrude Stein
(Sources: Cohen; Sadie and Samuel; http://operadata.stanford.edu/)

Natalia Raigorodsky (20th century, Tulsa, Oklahoma–) graduated from the American University in Washington, D.C., in 1963 with an MA in composition and music history. She went on to study privately at Yale and at the Juilliard School of Music. Subsequently she lectured, taught music theory and piano, programmed classical music for a radio station, and wrote as a music critic. Her compositions include orchestral music, works for chamber ensembles and sacred and choral music.

Works

1982 *The Promise of Peace*, opera
(Sources: Cohen; http://operadata.stanford.edu/)

Mira Spektor (20th century) graduated from Sarah Lawrence College then did postgraduate work at Mannes School of Music and the Juilliard School of Music. She was the founder and for six years the director of the Atlantic Opera Singers. She also founded the Aviva Players. Her compositions include vocal and sacred music, a cantata, and music for theater.

Works

1982 *Lady of the Castle*, opera, Librettists: Mira Spektor and Andrea Balis, after Lea Goldberg

1993 *Mary Shelley: Scenes from Her Life*, opera, Librettist: Colette Inez

Books by or about Mira Spektor:

Spektor, Mira. *From Seaside Houses: Poems*. Johnstown, OH: Pudding House, 1993.

_____. *The Road to November: New and Selected Poems (1982–2002)*. New York: Jewish Women's Resource Center, 2002.

(Sources: Cohen; http://www.miraspektor.com/)

Cynthia Cozette Lee (October 19, 1953, Pittsburgh–), who is also listed as Cynthia Cozette, received her masters of arts degree in music composition in 1977 from the University of Pennsylvania, the first African American woman to do so from that institution. She went on to study music copying at the Juilliard School of Music. Subsequently she earned her master's of public administration from Rutgers University in 2005 and her doctorate in education in 2009 from Rowan University. Her works continued to be recognized and to receive awards, but they were not published and were only rarely performed. In 2000 she decided to write poetry and fiction novels, as music composition tends not to be lucrative. She and her sister, Hazel Ann Lee, turned to songwriting, and cowrote *Magazine Watchtime*, a musical. In the early 1980s she hosted and produced a classical music radio interview program, which provided African American classical musicians in Philadelphia with a forum for discussing their works. She also was a consultant on classical music for a weekly radio show, again promoting African American classical musicians.

Works

1982 *Adea*, opera, excerpts
1982 *The Black Guitar*
(Sources: Cohen; Wikipedia)

Joyce Solomon Moorman (May 11, 1946, Tuskegee–) received her BA from Vassar College, her MAT from Rutgers University, an MFA from Sarah Lawrence College, and an EdD from the Teachers College, Columbia University. She received an NEA jazz study grant in 1976. She served for three years on the Advisory Music Panel for the New York State Council on the Arts and is on the faculty of Borough of Manhattan Community College. Her compositions include music for orchestra, chamber groups, piano, vocal music, and electronic music.

Works

Elegies for the Fallen, opera, commemorating the Soweto Massacre, based on the poetry of Rashidah Ismaili (female)
(Sources: Cohen; Vassar1968.com)

Noa (Susan) Ain (1941–) graduated from the Juilliard School of Music in 1965, then went on to earn a diploma from L'Ecole des Beaux-Artes at Fountainebleu, France. She continued her studies privately. Miriam Gideon (see entry) was one of her teachers.

Works
1982 *Bring On the Bears*, opera, Librettist: Ain
1984 *Trio*, jazz/gospel chamber opera, Librettist: Ain
1988 *The Outcast*, opera, after the story of Ruth and Naomi, Librettist: Ain

(Sources: Cohen; http://operadata.stanford.edu/; composers-classical-music.com)

Judith Lang Zaimont (November 8, 1945–) studied piano at the Juilliard School of Music from 1958 to 1964. She then earned a diploma at the Long Island Institute of Music in 1966. That same year she earned her BA at Queens College. After earning an MA from Columbia University she studied orchestration in France. From 1980 to 1988 she taught at Hunter College in New York; subsequently she taught at Adelphi University in Garden City, New York, for two years. She then was appointed senior professor of composition at the University of Minnesota in Minneapolis.

She has received numerous commissions and awards, including the Pauline Alderman Prize for new scholarship on women in music, a Guggenheim Foundation fellowship, MacDowell Colony fellowships, and a Woodrow Wilson National Foundation Fellowship. She was Featured Composer at the 1995 Society of Composers International Meeting and Honored Composer at the 11th International Van Cliburn Competition in 2001. Her music has won many prizes and awards and has been the focus of several doctoral dissertations. Her teaching was also widely recognized with numerous awards before she retired from full-time teaching in 2005. She was also creator and editor-in-chief of the book series The Musical Woman: An International Perspective, published by Greenwood Press.

Her compositions include orchestral works, music for chamber ensembles, works for piano, vocal and sacred music.

Works
1983 *The Thirteen Clocks*, chamber opera
1985 *Goldilocks and the Three Bears*, chamber opera, Librettist: Doris Kosloff

Books by or about Judith Lang Zaimont:

Zaimont, Judith. *The Musical Woman: An International Perspective.* With Catherine Overhauser and Catherine Gottlieb. Greenwood, 1984.

(Sources: Sadie and Samuel; http://www.jzaimont.com/biography.html; Cohen)

Shirl Jae Atwell (20th–21st century) received her bachelor's degree in music education from Kansas State Teachers College and a master of music in theory/composition from the University of Louisville. She then completed four years of postgraduate work in composition at the University of South Carolina. Throughout her career she has been involved with music education. Her opera *Sagegrass* opened in New York in 1984; that same year she was awarded the Clifford Shaw Memorial Award for Kentucky Composers in 1984. In 1993 six of her scores were placed in the permanent collection of the Paris Bibliotèque Internationale de Musique Cotemporaine at the invitation of the Contemporary Music International Informational Service. She has won numerous awards. Her compositions include music for the ballet *Lucy*, inspired by the discovery of the 3.2 million-year-old skeleton that became known as "Lucy."

Works

1984 *Sagegrass*, folk opera, Librettist: Delmas W. Abbott
1991 *Esta Hargis*
(Source: sjaea.home.mindspring.com)

Ann Loomis Silsbee (July 21, 1930, Cambridge, Massachusetts–2003) earned an AB at Radcliffe College in 1951. She participated in the Ferienkurs fuer neue Musik in Darmstadt in 1964. In 1969 she received an MMus from Syracuse University and a DMA from Cornell University in 1978. From 1973 to 1974 she studied in Paris. She received numerous fellowships, awards and grants, including the Burge-Eastman Prize. She also was active professionally and served as board member for several organizations. Her works include orchestral music, chamber music, vocal and choral works, incidental music and electronic music.

Works

1989 *The Nightingale's Apprentice*
(Source: Cohen)

Odaline de la Martinez (October 31, 1949, Matanzas, Cuba–) moved to the United States when she was twelve; in 1971 she became an American citizen. She graduated from Tulane University in New Orleans with a BFA in 1972; subsequently she was a scholarship student at the Royal Academy of Music in London from 1972 to 1976. In 1976 she helped found Lontano, a professional chamber ensemble to perform and record contemporary music, and is their principal conductor. She attended the University of Surrey and earned an MM in 1977 and a PhD in 1980. In 1984 she was the first woman to conduct at the *BBC Promenade Concerts* (the Proms). She also formed an all-woman orchestra for the first Chard Festival in Music in May 1990. Subsequently the group reformed as the European Women's Orchestra, for which Martinez remained as director. In 1991 she cofounded a recording company that would focus on contemporary Latin American and women's music. In 1987 she was awarded the Villa-Lobos medal from the Brazilian government for her championing of the music of Heitor Villa-Lobos and other Brazilian composers. Her compositions include orchestral music, works for chamber ensembles, vocal music and electronic music.

Works

1984 *Sister Aimée: An American Legend*, Librettist: John Whiting
2005–2008 *Imoinda*, about slavery and the beginning of the Afro-Caribbean culture, the first of the *Slavery Trilogy*, with libretto by Joan Anim-Addo
2012 *The Crossing*, Part II of the *Slavery Trilogy*
(Sources: Sadie and Samuel; operaamerica.org; Wikipedia)

Elaine Erickson (April 22, 1940, Des Moines–) received her MM in music composition from Drake University. She also studied composition at the University of Iowa and the Peabody Conservatory in Baltimore. Her honors include fellowships and awards from the Ford Foundation and the National League of American Pen Women. She is a published poet.

Works

1985 *The Upstairs Bedroom*, opera, Librettist: Elaine May Erickson
1987 *From Winter Darkness*, opera, Librettist: Elaine May Erickson
(Sources: http://www.iowacomposers.org/?p=85; http://operadata.stanford.edu/)

Mary Carol Warwick (October 28, 1939, Lumberton, North Carolina) earned her BA in 1961 and her BM in 1962 from Meredith College in Raleigh, North Carolina. Subsequently she received an MM in 1964 and a DMA from Florida State University. Her postdoctoral work was with Carlisle Floyd at the University of Houston. She has written nine operas for children that were commissioned by the Houston Grand Opera. She received an Opera New World Grant for *The Velveteen Rabbit* and *The Emperor's New Clothes*. Her opera *Texas!* received a National Endowment for the Arts Challenge Grant. *The Achilles Heel*, for which she was the librettist, won first prize in the National Opera Association's Chamber Opera Competition, in recognition of the collaboration as librettist with composer Craig Bohmler. Her compositions include orchestral and chamber music, and dance scores.

Works

1985 *The Twelve Months Brothers*, opera, Librettist: Mary Carol Warwick
1985 *Lealista*, Librettist: Mary Carol Warwick, after Hemingway: *The Fifth Column*
1985 *Sisters of Faith*, opera, Librettist: Mary Carol Warwick
1988 *The Last Leaf*, opera, Librettist: Mary Carol Warwick, after O. Henry
1989 *Twins*, opera, Librettist: Mary Carol Warwick
1990 *Drycop's Dilemma*, opera, Librettist: Mary Carol Warwick
Cinderella in Spain, bilingual opera, for children
Rapunzel, bilingual opera, for children
The Princess and the Pea, opera for children
Strega Nona, opera for children
The Velveteen Rabbit, opera for children
The King Stag, opera for children based on a folk tale
The Clever Wife, opera for children based on a folk tale
Texas!, historical opera for children

(Sources: Cohen; http://www.marycarolwarwick.com/)

Susan Hulsman Bingham (1944–) began her musical career as a concert pianist, but in 1974 she turned her focus to composing, specifically children's operas and liturgical operas. In 1979 the Chancel Opera Company of Connecticut, Inc., was formed, which eventually became the Chancel Opera Company. The operas first toured in northeastern United States and several have also been performed in Germany. In addition to her liturgical operas, Susan has written operas for children that often are based on traditional tales. She has also written at least one ballet.

Works

1984 *The Gift of the Magi*, children's opera, Librettist: Bingham, after O. Henry
1984 *The Last Leaf*, children's opera, Librettist: Bingham, after O. Henry
1984 *Makes the Whole World Kin*, children's opera, Librettist: Bingham
1988 *The Wild Swans*, children's opera, Librettist: Bingham
1988 *Alice Meets the Mock Turtle*, children's opera, Librettist: Bingham, after Lewis Carroll
1991 *The Fisherman and His Wife*, Librettist: Bingham, after Brothers Grimm
The Emperor and the Nightingale, children's opera
Eli W, children's opera
Tiny Operas, children's opera
The Little Match Girl, children's opera
Rabbi Nachman's Chair, children's opera
Old Befana, children's opera
The Musicians of Bremen, children's opera
The Twelve Dancing Princesses, children's opera
The Changeling, children's opera
Char Face, children's opera
The Legend of the Bluebonnet, children's opera

Anniversary Tales Daniel's Gift, children's opera
The Other Wise Man, children's opera
The Talking Stones of Machu Picchu, children's opera, based on Inca tales

(Sources: http://www.choristersguild.org/document//64/; http://operadata.stanford.edu/)

Judith Sainte Croix (20th–21st century) began performing professionally when she was in her teens. She earned her masters of music composition at Indiana University School of Music. Through the years she received numerous awards for her compositions and support from a number of Foundations. Her music has been widely performed.

Works

The Secret Circuit, children's opera
The Rainbow Mother Weaves Hummingbird Dream Bundles, children's opera
How Music Came into the World children's opera (bilingual English and Spanish), based on a poetic text from an ancient Mayan Indian Codex
The Vine of the Soul, children's opera

(Source: http://www.judithsaintecroix.com/jsc/bio.htm)

Sally Johnston Reid (January 30, 1948, Ohio–) plays the oboe and cor anglais. Her BME is from Abilene Christian University, 1971, and her MM from Hardin-Simmons University in Texas. She received her PhD in theory and composition from the University of Texas at Austin in 1980. She was on the faculty of Abilene Christian University and was also director of the music department and the electronic music studio. She maintained her performing career, playing with the Abilene Philharmonic and the San Angelo Symphony. Her compositions include music for symphonic band, for chamber ensembles, incidental music, electronic music, vocal music, and music for piano.

Works

1986 *Healing*, chamber opera, Librettist C. Willerton

(Sources: Sadie and Samuel; Cohen)

Mae Cohen (June 30, 1929, Chicago–November 2011) earned her bachelor of music in piano and composition at the University of Illinois, with high honors. Subsequently she did postgraduate study in piano with Leonard Shure. She received numerous grants and was designated composer-in-residence with the American Opera Group in 1999. In addition to her operas she composed for string quartets, choral works, instrumental works and an oratorio. She was also the author of at least eight plays and several books.

Works

1986 *Vaudeville Fantasy*, opera
1988 *Significant Lives*, opera
1989 *Variations on a Theme*, opera
1993 *No Place Like Home*, opera
1994 *Etude*, opera
1995 *The Rendezvous*, opera
1997 *The Overcoat*, opera
1999 *The Other Wife*, opera
2003 *A Modern Wife*, opera
2005 *The Competition*, opera
2006 *Annabel, My Dear*, opera
2007 *My Pretty One*, opera
2008 *The Day They Met*, opera
2010 *Exit*, opera

(Source: selected papers of Mae Cohen, privately held)

Sorrel (originally "Doris") Hays (August 6, 1941, Memphis, Tennessee–) earned a BM at the University of Tennessee in Chattanooga then studied at the Munich Hochschule für Musik, where she earned a piano and harpsichord diploma in 1966. In 1968 she received an MM from the University of Wisconsin. The next year she studied composition and electronic music at the University of Iowa. During the 1970s and 1980s she toured in Europe and the United States numerous times, always advocating new music. She often premiered music of other composers. She has been active professionally throughout her career, has received numerous awards and commissions, and has held many positions in a variety of organizations. In 1985 she took the name Sorrel in place of Doris. Her compositions include numerous pieces for chamber ensembles, music for piano, vocal music, and a significant amount of electronic music and music for multimedia. She is a prolific composer with numerous pieces for chamber ensembles,

Works

1986 *Love in Space*, radio opera
1989 *Touch of Touch*, video opera
1989–93 *The Glass Woman*, Librettists: Sorrel Hays, S. Ordway, and N. Rhodes
The Venus Project, radio opera, Librettist: J. Smith
1994 *The Everybodydom*, children's radio opera, Librettist: Sorrel Hays
1995 *Dream in Her Mind*, Literary source, Gertrude Stein

(Source: Sadie and Samuel)

Marjorie Merryman (June 9, 1951, Oakland, California–) taught at Macalester College, where she held an endowed chair, and at Harvard, MIT, and the New England Conservatory. She was chair of the theory and composition department at Boston University School of Music. Since 2007 she has been at the Manhattan School of Music as a faculty member in composition. She is also provost and dean of the college. Throughout her career she has received numerous commissions and has performed in the United States, Europe and Asia. She is the recipient of numerous awards and grants, has been composer-in-residence for several orchestras, and has served on many boards. Her compositions include music for orchestra, choral groups, chamber ensembles, two oratorios, and vocal music.

Works

1986 *Antigone*, opera

(Sources: Wikipedia; http://www.msmnyc.edu/FacultyBio/FID/1011047691)

Barbara Harbach (February 14, 1946, Pennsylvania–) earned her BA from Pennsylvania State and her MMA from Yale. Her doctorate in composition is from the Eastman School of Music. She also studied organ at the Musikhochchule in Frankfurt, Germany. From 1991 to 1997 she was professor of music at Washington State University. She moved to Wisconsin, where she was visiting professor of music at the University of Wisconsin–Oshkosh, then visiting professor of fine arts at the University of Wisconsin–Stevens Point. In 2004 she accepted a position as professor of music at the University of Missouri–St. Louis.

An organist and a harpsichordist, she has given recitals in North America, Asia, and Europe. Her compositions include orchestral works, music for organ, harpsichord, chamber ensembles and choir. She has composed several "musicals" for youth, precursors of opera. In 1959 she founded the music publishing company Vivace Press, which specializes in music by women and other composers who traditionally are underrepresented. She also produces performing editions of 18th century keyboard music. She and Jonathan Yordy founded the journal *Women of Note Quarterly* in 1993.

Works

1987 *The Littlest Angel*, opera, Librettist: Jonathan Yordy
1988 *Daniel and the Beastly Night*, opera, Librettist: Jonathan Yordy
1989 *A Page from the Christmas Story*, opera, Librettist: Jonathan Yordy
1990 *The Loneliest Angel*, opera, Librettist: Jonathan Yordy
2009 *O Pioneers!* opera, based on Willa Cather's novel

(Sources: http://www.umsl.edu/~harbachb/bio.htm; Wikipedia)

Victoria Bond (May 6, 1945, Los Angeles–) began composing when she was five. She was a student at the Mannes College of Music, studied composition and singing at the University of Southern California, earning her

BA, then continued her studies at the Juilliard School focusing on composition and conducting. She received her MMus in 1975 and her DMA in 1977, the first woman to receive the doctorate in conducting at Juilliard. She was an Exxon/Arts Endowment conductor with the Pittsburgh Symphony Orchestra and music director of the Pittsburgh Youth Orchestra and, from 1978 to 1980, the music director of both the Pittsburgh Youth Orchestra and the New Amsterdam Symphony Orchestra. In 1982 she made her European debut in Dublin, and in 1993 her Chinese debut with the Shanghai Symphony Orchestra. From 1983 to 1988 she was music director of the Bel Canto Opera in New York. Almost simultaneously, from 1984 to 1986, she was conductor and responsible for the programming of Albany Symphony Orchestra's youth concerts. She became director of the Roanoke Symphony Opera (Virginia) and artistic director of Opera Roanoke. While she is perhaps best known as a conductor, she also has an active career in composing. She has composed chamber music and ballets and works for narrator and orchestra, both significant interests of hers, as well as vocal music and film music. .

Works

1988 *Gulliver*, opera, after Swift's *Gulliver's Travels*, Louisville, withdrawn, revised as *Travels* c1994 with Librettist Ann Goette
Clara, opera, about Clara Schuman, Librettist: Barbara Zinn Kreiger
2012 *Mrs. President*, about Victoria Woodhull

(Sources: Cohen; Sadie and Samuel)

Kate Waring (April 22, 1953, Alexandria, Louisiana–) earned her BMus in flute and MMus in composition from the Louisiana State University in Baton Rouge. Her DMus is from the Sorbonne in Paris. She has composed orchestral works, music for chamber ensembles, vocal music and ballets.

Works

1988 *Rapunzel*, chamber opera, Librettist; Rudiger Gollnick, after Grimm, in German
Legacy of the Pioneers, chamber opera, Librettist: Karin E. Seifert
2005 *The Caravanserai*, opera, Librettist: Don Mowatt
Are Women People?
Porcelain and Pink

(Sources: Cohen; http://keyworksmusic.com/about/)

Joelle Wallach (June 29, 1946, New York–) spent several years in Morocco as a child. On her return to New York she attended the Juilliard Preparatory School. She received a BA in composition from Sarah Lawrence College in 1967, an MA in 1969 from Columbia University, and a DMA in 1984 from the Manhattan School of Music. She taught at the City University of New York for several years. Her works have been widely performed in the United States in Europe. Her compositions include orchestral works, music for chamber ensembles, vocal and sacred choral music, and music for piano. Some of her works incorporate Hebrew chant and North African dance traditions.

Works
1989 *The King's 12 Moons*, chamber opera
(Sources: Cohen; Sadie and Samuel)

Marjorie Maxine Rusche (November 18, 1949, Sturgeon Bay, Wisconsin–) received an MA in theory and composition in 1975 from the University of Minnesota. Her DM in music composition is from the Jacobs School of Music at Indiana University in Bloomington. She is a pianist and a conductor as well as a composer. She has received numerous awards and commissions. Her compositions include orchestral works, music for chamber ensembles, vocal and sacred music.

Works
1983 *The Scarlet Letter*, opera, Librettist: Rusche after N. Hawthorne
Dance of Death, opera, Librettist: Dan Pinkerton
She Stoops to Conquer, opera, from Oliver Goldsmith
(Sources: Cohen; operadata.Stanford.edu)

Ludmila Ulehla (May 20, 1923, Flushing, New York–2009) first wrote music when she was five. She received her BMus in 1946 and her MMus in 1947 from the Manhattan School of Music. That year she became a professor at the Manhattan School, and from 1970 to 1989 she was chairperson of the Composition Department. She also taught at the Hoff-Barthelson Music School in Scarsdale, New York (see entry for Barthelson). She was active professionally and held positions with several organizations including the American Society of University Composers and the National Association for American Composers and Conductors. She was named outstanding educator in *Who's Who of American Women*. Her book *Contemporary Harmony: Romanticism Through the 12-Tone Row*, was published by Advance Music.

Her compositions include orchestra works, music for chamber ensembles, piano music, and vocal music.

Works
1992 *Sybil of the Revolution*, chamber opera, Librettist: S. Schefflein
(Sources: Sadie and Samuel; Cohen; Wikipedia)

Gladys Mercedes Nordenstrom (May 23, 1924, Minnesota–) studied music and philosophy at Hamline University in St. Paul, Minnesota, then continued her studies at the University of Minnesota. Her husband was the Austrian composer Ernst Krenek (1900–1991); they married in 1950. Gladys was an elementary schoolteacher for several years until they moved to California. Krenek held visiting professorships in several locations, and Gladys accompanied him. Apparently they collaborated on some works. Krenek died in 1991; in 1998 Gladys founded the Ernst Krenek Institute, then in 2004 she founded Krems die Ernst Krenek, a private foundation in Vienna Austria. She was awarded the Decoration of Honour for services to the Republic of Austria in 2006. Her compositions include orchestral works, music for chamber ensembles, piano music, vocal music, and electronic music.

Works

1993 *The Neighbours*, chamber opera, Librettist: Krenek

(Sources: Sadie and Samuel; Wikipedia; women-in-music.com)

Tania Justina León (May 14, 1943, Havana–) is a Cuban-American composer. After earning a BA in music in 1963 and an MA in music education in 1964 from the Peyrellade's Conservatorio de Música in Havana, Cuba, she spent three years as a professional pianist. In 1967 she moved to the United States, where she studied at New York University, earning a BS in 1971 and an MS in 1975. While studying she was a pianist, conductor and composer with the Dance Theater of Harlem, an association she continued for many years. She also established a substantial career as a conductor, working with orchestras in the United States, Europe and South Africa. She became associate conductor of the Brooklyn Philharmonic Orchestra.

In 1985 she accepted a teaching position at Brooklyn College, where she also conducted. In 2000 she was named the Tow Distinguished Professor at the Conservatory of Music at Brooklyn College (one of the City Colleges of New York). She became adviser for new music with the New York Philharmonic Orchestra in 1993. She has received numerous commissions, including one from the New Music Theater for *Scourge of Hyacinths*. She has composed ballets and stage works, orchestral works, music for solo instruments and for chamber ensembles, and vocal music. Her awards include an ASCAP and a Meet the Composer Award. In 1975 she was a National Endowment for the Arts fellow.

Works

1994 *Scourge of Hyacinths*, opera, Librettist: León

(Source: Sadie and Samuel)

Judith Lane (20th–21st century) was born in Rochester, New York. She has a BA in music composition and creative writing from Bennington College, and she went on to earn an MFA from the Theatre Writing Program at New York University, where she received the Oscar Hammerstein II Scholarship and the Yip Harburg Fellowship. Her work in the Metropolitan Opera Guild's "Creating Original Opera" program led to her selection as ASCAP Composer-in-Residence. She also has received recognition from Yaddo Artist's Colony, Fundación Valparaíso in southern Spain, and the Julia and David White Artist's Colony in Costa Rica. Her two operas are for young performers and adults. Each focuses on young people in challenging situations: sheltering Jewish children in Nazi-occupied territory and a girl caught up in the struggle for shorter workdays in the clothing mills.

Works

The Secret Cave, opera, Librettist: Judith Lane, based on Claire Huchets Bishop's book *Twenty and Ten*
The Mill Girl, opera, Librettist: Judith Lane
(Source: http://www.judithclane.com/about.htm)

Susan C. Cohn Lackman (July 1, 1948, Tsing Tao, China–) is the daughter of a naval officer and traveled widely in her childhood. In 1970 she received her BMusEd from Temple University, where she took advanced courses in music theory and English. She then went to the American University, where she received her MA in composition and theory in 1971. While she was there she participated in the building of the new electronic music lab. Her PhD in theory is from Rutgers University. Her dissertation was *Lisa Stratos*, based on *Lysistrata*; she was composer and librettist. In 1981 she began teaching at Rollins College, where she taught a broad range of courses and held several positions on campus as well as teaching. She earned an MBA from Crummer Graduate School of Business. Throughout her career she has received many awards and honors. Her compositions include orchestral works, music for chamber ensembles, piano music, vocal music, and electronic music.

Works

Lisa Stratos, opera, Librettist: Susan Cohn Lackman, after Aristophanes: *Lysistrata*
(Sources: Cohen; Wikipedia)

Sheila Silver (October 3, 1946, Seattle–) earned her BA from the University of California-Berkeley in 1968. She was awarded the George Ladd Prix de Paris, which allowed her to study in Europe for two years. From 1972 to 1974 she held an Irving Fine Memorial fellowship from Brandeis University.

The following year she was awarded a prize for chamber music from GEDOK and a Rome Prize fellowship. She has also won a Koussevitzky Fellowship. In 2007 she received the Raymond and Beverly Sackler Prize in Music Composition in Opera for *The Wooden Sword*. More recently she was awarded a Guggenheim in 2013 for work on a new opera based on *A Thousand Splendid Suns*. She often uses classical Greek, Roman and Indian mythology, American jazz and Jewish chant in her compositions. Her cantata *The White Rooster* was commissioned by Smithsonian's Freer Sackler Gallery for their exhibit in 2010, "In the Realm of the Buddha."

Works

2010 *The Thief of Love*, opera, based on a 17th century Bengali tale, Librettist: Sheila Silver
The Wooden Sword, opera, Librettist: Stephen Kitsakos.
In progress "A Thousand Splendid Suns"
(Sources: Sadie and Samuel; http://www.sheilasilver.com/opera/)

USSR

Irina Arseyeva (September 21, 1941, Saratov–) graduated from the Saratov Conservatory in 1967. She went on to study composition at the Music Teachers' Institute in Rostov-on-the-Don, where she graduated in 1970. Subsequently she lectured at the Music Teachers' Institute. Her compositions include orchestral works, music for chamber ensembles and vocal music.

Works

1970 *Varshavskaya melodia*, opera, based on work by L. Zorin
(Source: Cohen)

Tamara Aleksandrovna Popatenko (b. ca. April 9, 1912, Moscow) graduated from the Moscow Conservatory. Her compositions include music for orchestra, for chamber ensembles, vocal music, music for theater and a ballet.

Works

1971 *Pryanich ni chelovechek*, operetta for children
Na lesnoi opushke, operetta for children
Zimhaya skazka, operetta for children
(Source: Cohen)

Yudif Grigorevna Rozhavkaya (November 12, 1923, Kiev–1983) graduated from the Kiev Conservatory in piano, with distinction, in 1946. She continued her studies privately. She received a medal for her actions on the war front during World War II.

Works

1971 *Skazka o poteryannom vremeni*, opera
1971 *Kazka pro zagublenii chas*, opera for children, Kiev
(Source: Cohen)

Olga Akimovna Golovina (May 26, 1924–) graduated from the Ural Conservatory in 1948. She then taught at the Sverdlovsk Music School. Her compositions include orchestral pieces, works for chamber ensembles, piano music, a ballet, and vocal music.

Works

Zolotoi lotos, opera
(Source: Cohen)

Zhanneta Lazarevna Metallidi (June 1, 1934, Leningrad–) studied at the music college that is attached to the Leningrad Conservatory, from 1952 to 1955, then at the conservatory until 1960. She was an accompanist and composer of incidental music at the Leningrad Drama Institute from 1959 to 1963. In 1960 she began teaching at a children's music school in Leningrad; as part of her work there she composed for performing ensembles. Her diverse repertory of children's music was used in Russian schools for years. In addition to her many compositions for children she composed for stage works, orchestras, chamber ensembles, and for choral groups.

Works

1992 *Tarakanische* [The Cockroach], opera, Librettist K. Chukovsky
(Source: Sadie and Samuel)

Children's Operas

"Children's operas" can refer to operas written for children or to operas using children's voices. In this context it refers to operas written for children. While there have always been performances of all types geared for children's entertainment through the ages, children's operas emerged in the nineteenth century.

Lines between "opera" and "musical" are more blurred in children's operas. *American Operas: A Checklist*, compiled by Edith Borroff, includes many children's operas and many noted as "musical." In her introduction Borroff comments that "musical" is often used in reference to works for children. She is convinced "that producers found the word 'musical' more enticing to a prospective young audience than the word 'opera' and advertised their productions accordingly" (xi). Not only does this makes sense, but it also reminds us not to rely too heavily on labels. Children operas have always been popular in Europe, and many are listed in the text. Some composers focused on children's operas. Other composers worked more or less equally in both children's and standard operas, while still others focused primarily on operas for adults but apparently couldn't resist the lure of a children's opera.

We're lucky to have all of them. Aren't they contributing toward the future of opera?

1850–1899

The emerging market for children's operas during this time is coincidental with the emerging markets for children's books. Of course there have "always" been entertainments and stories for children, but at this time the trend is clear and specific. Subjects for operas draw from nursery rhymes (*Little Bo Peep*), literature (*The Water Babies* after Charles Kingsley), and stories, some probably written specifically for the opera. Some are noted as "fairy operas." Composers include Marian Arkwright, Lucia Contini Anselmi, Jessie Love Gaynor, Luise Le Beau, Florence Marshall, Hendrika van Tussenbroek, Clementine Ward, and Marie Wurm.

1900–1939

The popularity of children's operas and operettas, as many are termed, grows. Fairy operas continue to be popular. There are more Christmas operettas. Hans Christian Andersen is a popular source for operas. Composers include Claude Arrieu, Dina Appeldoorn, Saar Bessem, Radie Britain, Rebecca Dunn, Mirrie Solomon Hill, Carrie Lewis, Frances McCollin, Margaret More, Johanna Mulder, Mae Wheeler Nightingale, Giulia Recli, Mildred Barnes Royse, Lyubov Lvovna Streicher, Else Streit, Phyllis Tate, and Anice Terhune.

1940–1970

Children's opera was well established and well liked. Popular subjects continued to include folk tales, fairy tales, Christmas, historic figures and historic settings, and some just plain fun. Composers include Anne Boyd, Tatyana Alexeyevna Chudova, Meri Shalvovna Davitashvili, Isobel Dunlop, Eusebia Simpson Hunkins, Lili Mikhailovna Iashvili, Zhivka Klinkova, Elizabeth Maconchy, Tera de Marez Owens, Thea Musgrave, Eda Rapoport, Lia Robitashvili, Alice Samter, Zlata Tkach, Tatiana Ivanovna Vasilieva, Berthe di Vito-Delvaux, Sláva Vorlová, and Maria Zavalishina.

1970 to Present

Children's operas continue to flourish. Hans Christian Andersen continues to be a popular source—and there's something to be said for introducing children to opera with a story that's familiar. There are more bilingual operas and a broader range of sources and subjects. Among titles that sound intriguing are *How Music Came into the World*, children's opera (bilingual English and Spanish), based on a poetic text from an ancient Mayan Indian Codex (Sainte Croix); *The Talking Stones of Machu Picchu* (Bingham), based on Inca tales; *A.B.C. (America Before Columbus)* (Waring), about ancient peoples. Composers include Isabelle Aboulker, Liana Alexandra, Betty Beath, Susan Bingham, Gillian Bibby, Victoria Bond, Royce Dembo, Violeta Dinescu, Barbara Harbach, Sorrel Hays, Elizabeth "Libby" Larsen, Nicola LeFanu, Else Pade, Tamara Aleksandrovna Popatenko, Yudif Grigorevna Rozhavkaya, Judith Sainte Croix, Carol Sams, Ruth Schonthal, Ann Silsbee, Kate Waring, Mary Carol Warwick, Judith Weir, Gillian Whitehead, Inger Wikström, and Judith Zaimont.

Librettists

The words of the opera come first, then the music. There are exceptions of course, but that generally is the process. The librettist is the dramatist of the opera, and the libretto is the bones of the story. Sometimes a text is involved and the librettist works with the text and format to arrive at a libretto that's a basis for an opera. Other times there is no text or the text isn't used directly. And then there's the case where the composer has an idea for a "story" and the librettist goes from there.

When a text is involved it's not always clear how the text is used. Is there significant rewriting? Is there substantial use of the original wording? Terms such as "after" and "based on" don't really tell us how much of the original was incorporated into the libretto. And what about this collaboration between

the librettist and the composer? Like any working relationship the collaboration can be extraordinarily tricky and sometimes highly problematic. It
can also be highly charged, and there are stories and legends of disputes and
quarrels between composer and librettist.

In the early days of opera the libretto was paramount. Librettos were
literary and poetic, and audiences, while they enjoyed the music, came
for the libretto and the play. Some librettists, like Metastasio, were in
enormous demand. A single libretto might be used by several dozen composers who had bought the libretto from Metastasio. Of course there could
be problems when composers changed the original wording—which they
often did. The libretto was, after all, an original work of the poet/libret-
tist.

This relationship, the libretto being primary, changed with Gluck, in
particular in *Iphigénie en Tauride* where Oreste is singing "calm re-enters my
heart." He may be singing "calm" but the music proclaims something else,
and the audience is being told by the music that he is deluding himself. Prior
to that the music was an accompaniment. Now the music had become an
"actor" in the opera (*The Tenth Muse* 148). And so it is today. It's not uncom-
mon for the music to be indicating something contrary to what the singer is
singing.

Audiences often disparage the libretto, but in many cases the problem
probably lies with the translation. At that point the music is set; there is no
working back and forth with the translation. Coming up with a translation
that conveys the story and fits the music can be very difficult, especially if
the two languages aren't related linguistically.

One of the sources I used when compiling the material on librettists
was Charles Parsons' *The Mellen Opera Reference Index*, which has several
volumes dealing with librettists. Many of the names are incomplete; only the
initial of the first name is given, which gives us no clue as to the gender of
the librettist. Undoubtedly many of them were women.

(Source: Patrick J. Smith. *The Tenth Muse: A Historical Study of the Opera Libretto.*
New York: Alfred A. Knopf, 1970. The history of librettists tells a fascinating story
of opera from a different perspective. *The Tenth Muse* is interesting, well written
and informative—and a good read.)

1500–1636

Little is known of the life of **Laura Guidiccioni** (October 29, 1550,
Lucca?–1597), and while it seems clear she was a librettist, few details of her
writing are certain. As a noblewoman with good family connections she spent
time at the court in Florence after 1588. She was a poet and playwright.
Sources seem to agree that she wrote at least one, and perhaps more, libretto

for Emilio de' Cavalieri. It is said that she wrote poetry for Cavalieri's preexisting music, which became the opera *Il ballo del granduca*.

Works

Il ballo del granduca, Composer: Emilio Cavalieri

The Wikipedia entry for Emilio Cavalieri also shows her as librettist for the following operas:

1590 *La disperazione di Fileno*. Composer: Emilio Cavalieri
1590 *Il satiro*. Composer: Emilio Cavalieri
1595 *I gioco della cieca*. Composer: Emilio Cavalieri

(Sources: http://oxfordindex.oup.com/view/10.1093/gmo/9781561592630.article. 41024; Wikipedia: Emilio Cavalieri. An article in Opera Baroque has a different listing of her librettos and operas: http://operabaroque.fr/CAVALIERI.htm. What is consistent is that she was a very early librettist and active in the cultural life in Italy at that time.)

1637–1700

Countess Maria Aurora von Königsmarck (August 28, 1662–February 16, 1728) was a Swedish and German noblewoman. She had a complicated family and childhood—and she kept to that "tradition" into adulthood. She spent her early childhood in Germany, but after her father died the family traveled, visiting family properties in Sweden and Germany. They spent much time at the royal court, where Maria and her sister Amalia often participated in the amateur theatrical performances. They participated in the Swedish premier of *Iphigénie*, which was the first play of French classicism—and had an all-female cast.

Maria and her sister left Sweden upon the death of their mother in 1691 and spent several years in Hamburg. Eventually Maria became the mistress of the Elector Frederick Augustus I. She spent much of the rest of her life trying to resolve various inheritance issues regarding the family properties. Her great-great-granddaughter, Aurore Dupin, who was named after her, was the French novelist George Sand. No mention is made of Maria's literary activities in her entry with Wikipedia. However, it isn't unlikely that she was a literary woman and wrote, as many women of her station in life did at that time.

Works

1680 *Die drey Töchter Cecrops*, Composer: Johann Wolfgang Franck
(Sources: Wikipedia; http://operadata.stanford.edu/)

Mme. Gillot de Saintonge (1650–1718) was highly acclaimed during her lifetime for her writing: poetry, theatrical works that included comedy, tragedy, and works with pastoral settings, entertainments for the courts of King Louis XIV and King Philip V of Spain. She was the first woman to write libretti for the Paris Opera.

Works

1693 *Didon*, Composer: Henri Desmarets
1694 *Circe*, Composer: Henri Desmarets
(Sources: Mellen; "Dramatizing Dido, Circe, and Griselda, by Louise-Geneviève Gillot de Saintonge" by Perry Gethner, Norris Professor of French, Oklahoma State University, http://crrs.ca/publications/ov05/)

1700s

Marie Anne Barbier (end of 16th century–1742, Paris) was a close friend of Simon-Joseph Pellegrin. Together they wrote at least three libretti; he may also have collaborated with her on the four tragedies and the comedy she wrote for the theater.

Works

1718 *Le Jugement de Pâris* with (librettist) Simon Joseph Pellegrin, Composer: Toussaint Bertin de la Doué
1719 *Les Plaisirs de la Campagne* with (librettist) Simon Joseph Pellegrin, Composer: Toussaint Bertin de la Doué
1736 *Les Caractères de l'amour* with (librettist) Simon Joseph Pellegrin, Composer: François Collin de Blamont
(Sources: http://operadata.stanford.edu/; Wikipedia)

Luisa Bergalli ("Irminda Partenide") (April 15, 1703, Venice–July 18. 1770, Venice) married the poet and writer Gasparo Gozzi in 1739. She wrote poems, a novel, and plays. She was also a translator, both on her own and working with Gozzi. In 1747 they took over the management of the theater of Sant'Angelo in Venice; in addition Gozzi provided dramas (usually translated from French) to be performed. This was a financial move on their part, but the theater wasn't successful and they soon had to give it up. However, Gozzi continued to work as a dramatist.

Works

1725 *Agide, re di Sparta*, Composer: Giovanni Porta
1730 *L'Elenia*, Composer: Tommaso Ablinoni
(Sources: Wikipedia; http://operadata.stanford.edu/)

Eliza Haywood

Works

1733 *The Opera of Operas*, Composer: Thomas Arne
(Source: http://operadata.stanford.edu/)

Maria Antonia Walpurgis, Electress of Saxony (see entry), was librettist for her operas.

Works

1754 *Il trionfo della fedeltà*
1760 *Talestri, Königin der Amazonen*
(Source: http://operadata.stanford.edu/)

Marie-Justine-Benoîte Favart (née **Marie Duronceray**) (15 June 1727–22 April 1772) was one of those enterprising people of changing times. In her time she was an actress, opera singer, and dancer. Her husband was the dramatist—and prolific librettist—Charles Favart. He was director of the Opéra Comique, and the combined efforts of the two of them made the theater a success. Serious problems arose when her husband's patron Maurice, Comte de Saxe and a Marshal of France, became all too interested in Madame Favart. Her husband fled to Strasbourg, and Madame Favart became mistress of the marshal. However, when the marshal discovered the extent of her fickleness, she had to flee to a convent. After his death she returned to the theater, the Comédie Italienne, playing to enthusiastic audiences for twenty years. Jacques Offenbach fictionalized her as the title character in his opera *Madame Favart*.

Works

1760 *La Fortune au village* with librettist Charles Favart, Composer: Paul-César Gilbert
1762 *Annette et Lubin* with librettist Charles Favart, Composer: Adolphe Benoît Blaise
Annette et Lubin with librettist Charles Favart, Composer: Jean-Benjamin La Borde
1769 *Nanetta e Lubino* with Carlo Francesco Badini, Composer: Gaetano Pugnani
1773 *La belle Arsène* with Charles Favart, Francois-Marie Arouet Voltaire
1777 *Die Bezauberten* with composer/librettist Johann André, Composer: Johann André
1778 *Die Bezauberten* with composer/librettist Charles Dibdin, Composer: Charles Dibdin
1779 *Die Bezauberten*, Composer: Anton Kunz
1788 *Les Amours de Bastien et Bastienne* with librettist Charles Favart, Composer: (Kajetan Majer) Gaetano

1789 *Annette et Lubin* with librettist Charles Favart, Composer: Johann Paul Martini

(Sources: http://operadata.stanford.edu/; Wikipedia)

Maria Theresa Agnesi (see entry) was librettist for her opera.

Works
1766 *L'insubria consolala*
1753 *Ciro in Armenia*
(Source: Sadie and Samuel)

Lady Dorothea Dubois (1728–1774) was born a year after her father became Lord Altham. Subsequently he succeeded to the earldom. He made provisions for her mother and their children, but in 1740 he repudiated his marriage with Lady Dorothea's mother, declaring that his children were illegitimate and evicting them from their home. As a result of an action brought by Dorothea's mother the earl was obliged to pay them four pounds a week, but he never did so and the family was in dire straits.

Dorothea secretly married Dubois, a French musician, with whom she had six children. In 1759 she heard of a will her father had made in which she was left five shillings, quit of all demands as his natural daughter. The following year, as soon as she recovered from the birth of her sixth child, she went to visit her father, who was then ill, to have him acknowledge his marriage to her mother. Her efforts were unsuccessful. Upon his death in 1761 she decided to tell the story of her father's perfidy and published *Poems by a Lady of Quality*, which she dedicated to the king. When her mother died five years later Dorothea published *The Case of Ann, Countess of Anglesey, Lately Deceased*, again detailing her father's wretched actions and stating her claims. She was persistent; a second novel on the same subject appeared in 1770.

The written word didn't seem to suffice, and a year later she published *The Divorce*, a musical entertainment. In *The Magnet* she broadened her scope to women who were victimized by unfair laws and had no recourse in justice. Sadly, her attempts all failed.

Works
1771 *The Magnet.* Composer: Samuel Arnold, who also used Elizabeth Craven and Frances Plowden as librettists for his operas.
(Source: Wikipedia)

Elizabeth Craven (see entry)

Works

1781 *The Silver Tankard*, Composer: Samuel Arnold (Craven is thought to have composed some of the music; Arnold also used Frances Plowden and Lady Dorothea Dubois as librettists for his operas.)

(Source: Sadie and Samuel)

Caroline Wuiet (see entry) was librettist for her opera.

Works

1786 *L'Heureuse erreur*
(Source: Sadie and Samuel)

Catherine II, Empress of Russia (May 2, 1729, Stettin–November 17, 1796, St. Petersburg), was known for her great interest in the arts including music, theater and opera. She commissioned music for her texts from well-known Russian and foreign composers.

Works

1786 *Fevey*, Composer: V. Pashkevich
1786 *Novogorodskoy Bogatir Boyeslavich*, Composer: E. I. Fomin
Gore Bogatyr Kosometovich, Composer: V. Martin
1790 *Nachalnoye Upreavlenie Olega*, Composer: C. Cannobbi et al.
1791 *Fedul s Detmi*, Composer: Vincent Martin y Soler and Pashkeysvich

(Sources: Mellen; Wikipedia)

Isabelle de Charrière (see entry) was librettist for her operas.

Works

1788 *Les Pheniciennes*
1788 *Penelope*
1790 *Polyphème ou le Cyclope*
1790 *Junon*
1790 *Les Femmes*
1790 *L'Olimpiade*
1791 *Zadig*
1792 Title unknown

(Source: Cohen, Letzer and Adelson)

Countess Maria Theresia Ahlefeldt (see entry) was librettist for her opera.

Works

1789 *La Folie, ou Quel conte!*
(Source: Sadie and Samuel)

Friederike Sophie Seyler (1737 or 1738, Dresden–November 22, 1789, Schleswig) was one of the greatest actresses in Germany in the 18th century. She first married Johann Gottlieb Hensel, an actor; later she married Abel Seyler, who already was a renowned theater director. She wrote plays, several of which were very popular in the 1770s. Her libretto for the Singspiel *Oberon* (originally titled *Huon und Amande*) is considered to be a major inspiration for Emanuel Schikaneder's libretto for the opera *The Magic Flute*.

Works

1789 *Hüon un Amande*, Composer: Karl Hanke
(Source: Wikipedia)

Ann Julia Hatton (April 29, 1764–December 26, 1838, Swansea) was born into a family of performers. Her father, Roger Kemble, was a strolling player, and Mrs. Sarah Siddons and John Philip Kemble were among her siblings. She married an actor, C. Curtis, when she was nineteen, not knowing he was already married. As a result she was left in a desperate position financially. Eventually she became a "model" in a brothel, a rackety place, where she was accidently shot in the face. Her next marriage, in 1792 to William Hatton, was more successful. They came to the United States in 1793, and a year later *Tammany: The Indian Chief* premiered in New York; it was very popular. This is likely the first libretto by a woman in the United States and the first significant opera libretto written in the United States with an American theme.

In the late 1790s Ann and her husband settled at Swansea. William died in 1806, at which point Ann left Swansea and began a dancing school in Kidwelly. Three years later she moved back to Swansea and embarked on a "career" as a writer. She wrote poetry, but her great success was her fourteen novels, which appealed to the public's taste for gothic fiction and social satire.

Works

1794 *Tammany; or, The Indian Chief*, Composer: James Hewitt
(Sources: http://operadata.stanford.edu/; Wikipedia)

Emilie (Amélie) Julie Candeille (see entry) was librettist for her operas.

Works

1792 *Catherine, ou La Belle fermière*
1793 *Bathilde, ou Le Duo*
1795 *La Bayadère, ou Le Français à surate*
1807 *Ida, ou L'Orpheline de Berlin*
(Source: Sadie and Samuel)

Comtesse de Salm-Dyck

Works

1794 *Sapho*, Composer: "Martini il Tedesco" a pseudonym for Jean-Paul-Égide
       Martini
(Source: http://operadata.stanford.edu/)

Marie-Émilie Mayon de Montanclos

Works

1799 *Les Habitans de Vaucluse*, Composer: Bernardo Mengozzi
1799 *Robert le Bossu, ou Les Trois soeurs*, Composer: Charles-Gabriel Foignet
1801 *La Famille Savoyarde*, Composer: Étienne de Fay
(Source: http://operadata.stanford.edu/)

1800–1849

Frances Plowden

Works

1800 *Virginia*, Composer: Samuel Arnold, who also used Elizabeth Craven and
       Lady Dorothea Dubois as librettists for his operas
(Source: WorldCat)

Joanna Baillie (sometimes listed as Miss Baillie)

Works

1817 *The Election* with librettist Samuel Arnold, Composer: Charles Horn
(Source: http://operadata.stanford.edu/)

Mme. Sophie de Bawr (Comtesse de Saint-Simon) (see entry) was librettist for her operas.

Works

1804 *Les Chevaliers du lion*
1811 *Léon, ou Le Château de Montaldi*
(Source: Sadie and Samuel)

Sophie Gay (July 1, 1776, Paris–March 5, 1852) was an author. As she was known for her writing and her attractive personality, her salon drew many writers. Her novels were very well received. In addition to libretti she wrote comedies. She composed many songs, writing both words and music.

Works

1808 *Les Deux portes*, Composer: Joseph Price Roger
1818 *La Serenade*, Composer: Sophie (née Edmée) Gail
1821 *Le Maître de chapelle*, Composer: Ferdinando Paer
Le Chevalier de Canolle, Composer: Hypolyte Fontmichel
(Source: Letzer and Adelson)

Mme. Lesparat

Works

1812 *Édouard, ou Le Frère par supercherie*, Composer: Camille Barni
(Source: http://operadata.stanford.edu/)

Madame Villiers

Works

1813 *Mademoiselle de Launay à la Bastille* with librettists Creuze de Lesser and R. Villiers, Composer: Sophie (née Edmée) Gail
(Source: Letzer and Adelson)

Mrs. Benjamin Dean Wyatt

Works

1823 *The Shepherd King, or the Conquest of Sidon*, Composer: Mary Fauche
(Source: http://operadata.stanford.edu/)

Helmina von Chézy (née Klencke) (1783–1856) was a journalist, poet and playwright. Her father was a Prussian officer, and her mother was a poet. Married when she was sixteen, Helmina divorced the next year. After the death of her mother she moved to Paris, where she not only edited her own journal commenting on political issues (which caused problems with the censors) but she was also a correspondent for several German papers. Her second husband was Antoine-Leonard de Chézy, a French orientalist. They divorced after several years. She then returned to Germany. During the Napoleonic Wars she was a military hospital nurse. Her criticisms of the field conditions brought an accusation of libel, but the Berlin court (under presiding judge E.T.A. Hoffmann of *Tales of Hoffmann* fame) acquitted her. She was living in Dresden when she wrote the libretto for *Euryanthe*. Weber is said to have thought her overly ambitious and difficult. Franz Schubert wrote incidental music for her play *Rosamunde*.

Works
1823 *Euryanthe*, Composer: Carl Maria von Weber
(Source: Wikipedia)

Louise Angélique Bertin (see entry) was librettist for her opera.

Works
1825 *Guy Mannering*
(Source: Sadie and Samuel)

Sarah Isdell

Works
1825 *The Cavern*, Composer: Sir John Andrews Stevenson
(Source: http://operadata.stanford.edu/)

Charlotte Birch-Pfeiffer (June 23, 1800, Stuttgart–August 24, 1868, Berlin) was an actress and writer. Her father was an estate agent; her early stage training was at the Munich court theater. By 1818 she was playing major tragic roles. After her marriage to the historian Christian Andreas Birch she continued her acting career. From 1837 to 1843 she managed the theater at Zurich while still touring and acting in Germany. In 1844 she began her affiliation with the royal theater in Berlin, which lasted until her death. She was a prolific writer of novels and tales throughout her life. Dramatization of popular novels was her specialty. She could draw on her knowledge of the technical necessities of the stage. Her plays, adapted and original, fill 23 volumes.

Works
1842 *Der Edelknecht*, Composer: K. Kreutzer
1848 *Toni der Wildschütz, oder Die Vergeltung*, Composer: Ernst II Herzog von Sachsen-Koburg-Gotha

1850 *Sophia Katharina*, Composer: Friedrich Flowtow
1854 *Santa Chiara*, Composer: Ernst II Herzog von Sachsen-Koburg-Gotha
1863 *La Réole*, Composer: Gustav Schmidt
(Sources: http://operadata.stanford.edu/; Wikipedia)

Carolina Uccelli (see entry) was librettist for her opera.

Works

1830 *Saul*
(Source: Sadie and Samuel)

Louise Beck

Works

1833 *Das Grubenlicht*, Composer: Peter Ritter
(Source: http://operadata.stanford.edu/)

Karoline (also spelled Caroline) **Pichler** (September 7, 1769, Vienna–July 9, 1843, Vienna) was an Austrian novelist. Karoline met Haydn as a young girl; Mozart (who taught her music) performed regularly in her parent's home. As an adult she became well known for her salon, which was considered the center of literary life in Vienna but also attracted Beethoven and Schubert. She began her publishing career in 1802 with an anonymous publication. The event that established her as a seasoned, able writer was the publication of her first mature novel, *Agathocles*, in 1808, which was an answer to Gibbon's attack on him in *The History of the Decline and Fall of the Roman Empire*. Her *Complete Works* are contained in 60 volumes.

Works

1826 *Mathilde*, Composer: Moritz Hauptmann
1831 *Die Karmeliterin*, Composer: Karl Friedrich Keller
1834 *Mathilde*, Composer: Louis Schindelmeisser
(Sources: http://operadata.stanford.edu/; Wikipedia)

Klara Grill was a Hungarian librettist.

Works

1835 *Die Liebeszauberin*, Composer: Johann Grill
(Source: http://operadata.stanford.edu/)

Mary Russell Mitford (December 16, 1787, Alresford, Hampshire–January 10, 1855, Swallowfield) was a very success English author and dramatist, probably best known for her book *Our Village*. Her books continue to be read. She was very successful during her lifetime, but her father had an extravagant streak and there were continual money problems. Matters improved in 1837 when she received a civil list pension. Five years later her father died, and money was raised to pay his debts. Whether she wrote *Sadak and Kalisrade; or, The Waters of Oblivion* as a libretto is not clear. It may have been used as the basis of the opera or libretto.

Works

1835 *Sadak and Kalasrade, or The Waters of Oblivion*, Composer: Charles S. Packer
(Sources: http://operadata.stanford.edu/; Wikipedia)

Amalie, Prinzessin von Sachsen (see entry) wrote librettos for the following operas, and perhaps others.

Works

1823 *Elisa ed Ernesto*, opera, Librettist: Amalie, Princesse von Sachsen
1826 *La fedelta alla prova*, opera, Librettist: Amalie, Princesse von Sachsen
1828 *Vecchiezza e gioventù*, opera, Librettist: Amalie, Princesse von Sachsen
1831 *Il figlio pentito,* or *Il figlio perduto*, opera, Librettist: Amalie, Princesse von Sachsen
1833 *Il marchesino*, opera, Librettist: Amalie, Princesse von Sachsen
1835 *La casa disabitata*, opera, Librettist: Amalie, Princesse von Sachsen
(Sources: Wikipedia; http://operadata.stanford.edu/)

Luisa Amalia Paladini

Works

1837 *Rosmonda di Ravenna*, Composer: Giuseppi Lillo
1838 *L'orfanella di Lanissa*, Composer Giuseppe Mazza
1855 *Gonzalvo di Cordova*, Composer: Alessandro Biaggi
(Source: http://operadata.stanford.edu/)

Irene Ricciardi Capecelatro (1802–1870)

Works

1837 *La soffitta degli artisti*, Composer: Vincenzo Capecelatro
1843 *Sara, ovvero La Pazza di Scozia*, Composer: Nicolo Gabrielli
1854 *Gastone di Chanley*, Composer: Vincenzo Capecelatro
(Source: http://operadata.stanford.edu/)

Adele Beckmann

Works

1838 *Die Entführung in Duplo*, Composer: Heinrich Rötsch
1840 *Das Auge des Teufels* with or literary source Eugène Scribe, Composer: Franz Gläser
1843 *Die Verhangnisvolle Omelette*, Composer: Hermann Schmidt
(Source: http://operadata.stanford.edu/)

Henriette Heinze-Berg

Works

1846 *Loreley*, Composer: Gustave Adolf Heinze
1847 *Die Ruinen von Tharand*, Composer: Gustave Adolf Heinze
(Source: http://operadata.stanford.edu/)

1850–1899

Caroline Berton

Works

1853 *La Clef du secrétaire*, with Henry Boisseaux, Composer: C.E. Poisot
(Source: http://operadata.stanford.edu/)

Madame Roger de Beauvoir

Works

1856 *À deux pas du Bonheur*, Composer: Dieudonné Joseph Guillaume Félix Godefroid
(Source: http://operadata.stanford.edu/)

Carlotta Ferrari (see entry) was librettist for her opera.

Works

1857 *Ugo*
1866 *Sofia*
1871 *Eleonora d'Arborea*
(Source: Sadie and Samuel)

Anna Löhn-Siegel (November 30, 1830, Naundorf–January 1, 1902, Dresden

Works

1881 *Der Flüchtling*, Composer: Edmund Kretschmer
(Source: http://operadata.stanford.edu/)

Éléonore Tenaille de Vaulabelle (1801–1859) often used the name Jules Cordier.

Works

1860 *Daphnis et Chloé*, Composer: Jacques Offenbach
(Source: http://operadata.stanford.edu/)

Adèle Laboureau

Works

1865 *Un Mariage per quiproquo*, Composer: Mme. Sabatier-Blot
(Source: http://operadata.stanford.edu/)

Agnes Grans

Works

1866 *Die Corsen*, Composer: Karl Gotze
(Source: http://operadata.stanford.edu/)

Ingeborg von Bronsart (see entry) was librettist for her opera.

Works

1909 *Die Sühne*
(Source: http://operadata.stanford.edu/)

Mme. Mélanie Waldor

Works

1868 *Le Double piège*, Composer: Georges Douay
(Source: http://operadata.stanford.edu/)

Mme. Lionel de Chabrillan (Élisabeth-Céleste Vénard) (December 27, 1824, Paris–February 17, 1909)

Works

1863 *Nédel*, Composer: Marius Boulard

1865 *Pierrot en cage*, Composer: Peret Kriesel
1868 *À la Bretonne*, Composer: André Mario Oray
(Source: http://operadata.stanford.edu/)

Mme. Hermance Lesguillon (1800, Paris–September 29, 1882) was a novelist and a poet, as was her husband, Jean-Pierre Lesguillon.

Works

1872 *Le Vieux maestro*, Composer: P. Edmund Hochmelle
1873 *Ninette et Ninon*, Composer: Jean Penavaire
(Source: http://operadata.stanford.edu/)

Louise Otto-Peters (March 26, 1819, Meissen–March 13, 1895, Leipzig) received a very good education, but her parents died when she was young and she had to earn her own living. Like many women she began writing and produced short stories, novels, poetry and political articles that she sold to journals. The industrial revolution that was taking place in Germany had a strong effect on her, and she became politically active, supporting political and social reform. It was 1848, a time of great change in Europe.

She founded a newspaper that year, *Frauen-Zeiting* (Women's News), which inspired women across Germany to organize. In 1852 the newspaper was suppressed, and she retired from political life, at least for the time being. Thirteen years later she and Auguste Schmidt, along with others, founded the General Union of German Women, of which one of the main tenets was "Women's Right to Work." By 1876 there were 11,000 members in the union. She and Schmidt were jointly president as long as Otto-Smith lived.

Works

1872 *Theodor Körner*, Composer: Wendelia Weissheimer
(Sources: Wikipedia; http://operadata.stanford.edu/)

Elisa Adam-Boisgontier

Works

Le farouche ennemi, Composer: Jean-François Pillevestre
Grande nouvelle, Composer: Leo Delibes
1859 *Clara Tempête*, Composer: Francesco Chiaromonte
(Source: http://operadata.stanford.edu/)

Elysée Bach

Works

1874 *Raphael* (with librettist Corny), Composer: Rouvier
(Source: http://operadata.stanford.edu/)

Margaret Williams

Works

Columbus
(Source: Cohen)

Augusta Holmés (see entry) was librettist for her operas.

Works

1875 *Héro et Leandre*
c1880 *Lancelot du Lac*
1895 *La Montagne noire*
Astarte
(Sources: Sadie and Samuel; opera.stanford.edu/composers)

Carmen Sylva (29 December 29, 1843–2 March 2, 1916) was the (29 December 1843–March 2, 1916) was the literary name of Elisabeth of Wied, Queen Consort of Romania. She was the wife of King Carol I of Romania. When she was sixteen she was considered as a possible bride for the son of Queen Victoria, the future Edward VII of the United Kingdom. Her future, however, was with Prince Karl of Hohenzollern-Sigmaringen, who would be Prince Carol I of Romania. In 1881 she was crowned Queen of Romania. She worked for higher education for women and established charitable societies. She was well educated, fluent in German, Romanian, French and English, and wrote prolifically in a variety of genres including poems, plays, novels, short stories, and essays.

Works

1885 *Neaga*, Composer: Ivar Christian Hallström
1903 *Ullranda*, Composer: Walter Dost
1906 *Editha*, Composer: Antonio Francesco Carbonieri

Note: various sources attribute other operas to her.
(Sources: http://operadata.stanford.edu/; Wikipedia)

Mathilde Wesendonck (December 23, 1828–August 31, 1902), a poet and author, is perhaps best known as the friend of Richard Wagner, who used her writing as the text for the *Wesendonck Lieder*. Her husband greatly admired Wagner and after meeting him designated a cottage on his estate for Wagner's use.

Works

1879 *Aschenbrödel* with composer Heinrich Schülz-Beuthen, Composer: Heinrich Schülz-Beuthen

(Sources: http://operadata.stanford.edu/; Wikipedia)

Marie Červinková-Riegrová (August 9, 1954, Prague–January 19, 1895, Prague)

Works

1879 *Zmarená svatba*, Composer: K. Sebor
1882 *Dimitrij*, Composer: Anton Dvorak
1889 *Jakobin*, Composer: Anton Dvorak

(Source: http://operadata.stanford.edu/)

Ethel R. Harraden (see entry) was librettist for her operas.

Works

1880s *All About a Bonnet*
1891 *His Last Chance*

(Source: Sadie and Samuel)

Alice Durand (October 23, 1842, Paris–1902) wrote under the name Henry Gréville. She spent a number of years in St. Petersburg with her father, some of that time studying science and languages. She had several novels published in St. Petersburg journals. While there she met and married Émile Durand, a French law professor. In 1872 they returned to France, where she continued to write novels, often depicting Russian society.

Works

1881 *L'Explication de Savelé*, Composer: Gabriel Sinsoilliez

(Sources: http://operadata.stanford.edu/; Wikipedia)

Maria Torelli-Viollier

Works

1878 *La Creole*, Composer: Gaetano Coronaro
1882 *Il violino di Cremona*, Composer: Giulio Litta

(Source: http://operadata.stanford.edu/)

Elise Henle (August 10, 1831, or 1832, Munich–August 18, 1892, Frankfurt am Main)

Works

1883 *Das Schloss de l'Orme*, Composer: Richard Kleinmichel
1887 *Murillo*, Composer: Ferdinand Langer
(Source: http://operadata.stanford.edu/)

Émilie Mathieu

Works

1883 *Une Heure de liberté*
(Source: Cohen)

Abbie Gerrish-Jones (see entry) was librettist for her operas.

Works

1885 *Priscilla*
1917 *The Snow Queen*, based on Hans Christian Andersen
Abou Hassan
The Milkmaid's Fair
Two Roses
The Aztec Princess
(Source: Sadie and Samuel)

Valentina Semenova Serova (see entry) was librettist for her operas.

Works

1885 *Uriel Acosta* with Pavel Ivanovich Blaramberg (who also was a composer), after Carl von Gutschow's novel
1880s *Marie d'Orval*
1899 *Il'ya Muromets*
1904–05 *Vstrepenulis* [They Roused Themselves Up]
(Source: Sadie and Samuel)

Mary Lafon

Works

1886 *Les Paques de la reine*, Composer: Paul Mériel
(Source: http://operadata.stanford.edu/)

Mme. Erminia Marzochi

Works

1889 *Occhi azzurri*, Composer: Ciro Cavalieri
(Source: http://operadata.stanford.edu/)

Hendrika van Tussenbroek (see entry) was librettist for her opera.

Works

Three Little Lute Players
(Source: *Women of Notes*)

Amélie Péronnet (see entry) was librettist for her opera.

Works

1890 *Je reviens de Compiègne*

She also was librettist for:

Gilles de Brétagne 1877, Composer: Henri Kowalski
La Cigale Madrilène 1889, Composer: J. Perronet
(Sources: Cohen; Mellen)

Madame Bellier-Klecker

Works

1890 *Le Chat botté*, Composer: Charles Haring
1899 *Peau d'âne*, Composer: Raoul Laparra
(Source: http://operadata.stanford.edu/)

Mme. la Marquise Teresa Venuti

Works

1891 *Ginevra* from Alfred Lord Tennyson, Composer: Giuseppi Vignoni
(Source: http://operadata.stanford.edu/)

Adelheid Wette (1858–1916)

Works

1893 *Hänsel und Gretel*, from Jakob and Wilhelm Grimm, Composer: Engelbert
   Humperdinck
1895 *Die sieben Geisslein*, Composer: Engelbert Humperdinck
1896 *Elsi, die seltsame Magd*, from Goethe, Composer: Arnold Mendelssohn

1900 *Der Barenhäuter*, Composer: Arnold Paul Mendelssohn
(Source: http://operadata.stanford.edu/)

Clara Schönborn

Works

1894 *Jone*, Composer: Rudolf Thoma
(Source: http://operadata.stanford.edu/)

Mary Carr Moore (see entry) was librettist for at least one of her operas.
(See also **Sarah Carr.**)

Works

1894 *The Oracle*, operetta, Librettist: Moore, San Francisco
(Source: Sadie and Samuel)

Mme. Simone Arnaud (1850, Limoges–July 10, 1901) wrote poems and
dramatic and comedic works, often in verse. Her husband, Paul-Joseph
Copin, or Paul Copin-Albancelli, was a journalist.

Works

1894 *L'Oiseau bleu*, Composer: Arthur Coquard
1895 *La Jacquerie* with librettist Édouard Blau, Composer: Edouard Lalo, com-
    pleted posthumously by Arthur Coquard
1900 *Jahel* with Louis Gallet, Composer: Arthur Coquard
1912 *Myrdhin*, Composer: Louis Albert Bourgault-Cucoudra

(Sources: Encyclopédie de l'art lyrique français; http://www.artlyriquefr.fr/person
nages/Arnaud%20Simone.html; http://operadata.stanford.edu/)

Annie Wilson Patterson (see entry) was librettist for her operas.

Works

The High-King's Daughter
Oisín, opera
Bard of Eire
(Source: Sadie and Samuel)

Gemma Bellincioni (August 18, 1864–April 23, 1950) was a well-known
opera singer in the late 1800s.

Works

1895 *Eros* with Enrico Golisciani, Composer: Nicolò Massa
(Source: http://operadata.stanford.edu/)

Marie Vernet

Works

1900 *Les Secrets de la baronne*, Composer: Charles Pourny
(Source: http://operadata.stanford.edu/ [Anne Copin-Albancelli])

Frau von Waltershausen

Works

1895 *Der letzte Ruf*, Composer: Joseph Erb
(Source: http://operadata.stanford.edu/)

Rosa Mayreder

Works

1896 *Der Corregidor*, Composer: Hugo Wolf
(Source: http://operadata.stanford.edu/)

Anezka Schulzová (March 24, 1868, Prague–1905) was a literary critic, essayist, and wrote theater reviews. She studied composition with Zdeněk Fibich.

Works

1896 *Hédy*, Composer: Zdeněk Fibich
1897 *Šárka*, Composer: Zdeněk Fibich
1900 *Pád Arkuna*, Composer: Zdeněk Fibich
(Sources: http://operadata.stanford.edu/; http://www.kapralova.org/WOMEN.htm)

Fanny Gröger

Works

1897 *Die fromme Helene*, Composer: Adalbert von Goldschmidt
(Source: http://operadata.stanford.edu/)

Martha Friedemann

Works

1896 *Ingo*, Composer: Philipp Rüfer
(Source: http://operadata.stanford.edu/)

Virginia Tedeschi Treves (1855–1816) used the pseudonym Cordelia at times.

Works

1890 *Gringoire* with Oreste Raffaelli, Composer: Antonio Scontrino
1903 *Un curioso accidente* with Carlo Goldoni, Composer: Gaetano Coronaro
(Source: http://operadata.stanford.edu/)

Mme. Lucy de Montgomery (see entry) was librettist for her opera.

Works

1894 *Aréthuse*
(Source: http://operadata.stanford.edu/)

Mme. Aline Fredin

Works

1897 *Blanc et noir*, Composer: Pietro Tirindelli
(Source: http://operadata.stanford.edu/)

Dame Ethel Mary Smyth (see entry) was librettist for her operas.

Works

1898 *Fantasio*, with H. Brewster, after Alfred de Musset
1902 *Der Wald*, with H. Brewster
1906 *The Wreckers* with H. Brewster
1913 *The Boatswain's Mate*, after W.W. Jacobs
1922 *Fête galante*, with E. Shanks
1925 *Entente cordiale*
(Source: Sadie and Samuel)

Dora Duncker (March 28, 1855, Berlin–October 9, 1916)

Works

1898 *Assarpai*, Composer: Ferdinand Hummel
1902 *Das Hexenlied*, Composer: Eugenio Pirani
1914 *De heilige Berg*, Composer: Christian Sinding
(Source: http://operadata.stanford.edu/)

Anna Boberg

Works

1898 *Tirfing*, Composer: William Stenhammer
(Source: http://operadata.stanford.edu/)

Selma Lagerlöf (November 20, 1858, Marbacka, Sweden–March 16, 1940, Marbacka) was awarded the Nobel Prize for Literature in 1909, the first Swedish writer and the first woman to be awarded the prize. She trained as a teacher and taught from 1885 to 1895. That year she was awarded a traveling scholarship. In 1899–1900 she was in Egypt and Palestine. From that experience she wrote *Jerusalem*, a two-volume work that had a significant impact on readers. She's perhaps best known for *Värmland Trilogy*.

Works

1899 *Frithiof's Saga*, unperformed, Librettist: Selma Lagerlöf, Composer: Elfrida Andrée (Her Scandinavian legend of Astrid was the basis for the opera *Astrid* by Charlotte Labey.)

(Sources: Sadie and Samuel; Encyclopedia Britannica; http://www.musimem.com/labey.htm)

Eleanor Farjeon (February 13, 1881–June 5, 1965) was a prolific author of plays, poetry, biography, history and satire; however her best known works were children's books. The Farjeons were a literary family; her father was a novelist and her two younger brothers were writers. Her older brother Harry Farjeon was a composer. She wrote the libretto for his opera. She also collaborated with her youngest brother, who was a Shakespearean scholar and dramatic critic. Her friends included D. Lawrence, Walter de la Mare, and Robert Frost. She never married. Her literary awards include the Carnegie Medal for British children's books and the first Hans Christian Andersen Medal.

Works

1899 *Floretta*, Composer: Harry Farjeon
1900 *The Registry Office*, Composer: Harry Farjeon
1902 *A Gentleman of the Road*, Composer: Harry Farjeon
1924 *The Eve of St. John*, Composer: Sir Alexander Mackenzie
1932 *Philomel* with Clifford Bax, Composer: Martin Shaw

(Sources: http://operadata.stanford.edu/; Wikipedia)

1900–1939

Berthe Gaston-Danville used the pseudonym Madame Rosenval.

Works

1902 *Margot la Rouge*, Composer: Frederick Delius
(Source: http://operadata.stanford.edu/)

Luise Adolpha Le Beau (see entry) was librettist for her opera.

Works
1901 *Der verzauberte Kalif* with L. Hitz
(Source: Sadie and Samuel)

Teresa Bedogni-Fulloni

Works
1901 *Elena*, Composer: Pietro Melloni
(Source: http://operadata.stanford.edu/)

Luisa Anzoletti

Works
1903 *La Montanina*, Composer: Elisabetta Oddone Sullie-Rao
(Source: http://operadata.stanford.edu/)

Madeleine Guitty

Works
1906 *Mominette*, Composer: S. Simon
(Source: http://operadata.stanford.edu/)

Emma Coccanari-Marconi

Works
1905 *Pergolese*, Composer: Fillippo Guglielmi
(Source: http://operadata.stanford.edu/)

Louisa Emily Lomax (see entry) was librettist for her operas.

Works
1905 *The House of Shadows*
1906 *The Wolf*
1907 *The Brownie and the Piano-Tuner*

She was likely the librettist for her opera *The Marsh of Vervais*. She was librettist for *The Demon's Bride*, Composer: Walton O'Donnell.
(Source: Sadie and Samuel)

Virginia Ghigi-Belisardi

Works

1906 *Zingarella*, Composer: Antonio Zoboli
(Source: http://operadata.stanford.edu/)

Mathilde Kralik von Meyrswalden (see entry) was librettist for her opera.

Works

1907 *Der heilige Gral*
(Source: Sadie and Samuel)

Therese Lehmann-Haupt

Works

1907 *Warum der Frühling kommen muss*, Composer: Liza Lehmann
(Source: http://operadata.stanford.edu/)

Lena Stein-Schneider (see entry) was librettist for her operettas.

Works

1909 *Der Luftikus*
1919 *Lustige Liebe*
1928 *Ein Hundert Küsse*
(Sources: Wikipedia; http://operadata.stanford.edu/)

Maddalena Meini-Zanotti (see entry) was librettist for her opera.

Works

1909 *La principessa Iris*
(Source: Cohen)

Sarah Carr

Works

1909 *Narcissa; or, The Cost of Empire*, Composer: Mary Carr Moore
1922 *The Flaming Arrow (The Shaft of Ku'pish-ta-ya)*, Composer: Mary Carr Moore
(Sources: Sadie and Samuel; http://operadata.stanford.edu/)

Florence Maud Ewart (see entry) was librettist for her operas.

Works

c1910 *Ekkehard*
1930 *The Courtship of Miles Standish*, after Longfellow
1933 *Mateo Falcone*, after Prosper Mérimée

She may also have been the librettist for her operas:

1933 *Nala's Wooing*, after the Mahabharata
c1945 *Pepita's Miracle*, after A. Bridge
1949 *A Game of Chess* after G. Giacosa
(Source: Sadie and Samuel)

Dora Estella Bright (see entry) was librettist for at least two of her opera.

Works

1911 *The Portait*
(Source: Sadie and Samuel)

Amalie Nikisch (see entry) was librettist for at least two of her operas.

Works

1907 *Prinz Adolar und das Tausendschoenchen*
1911 *Meine Tante, deine Tante*, with Ilse Friedlander
1914 *Aebolo*, composer Gustav Mraczeck
1915 *Immer der Andere*, opera with Ilse Friedlander
(Source: http://operadata.stanford.edu/)

Ilse Friedländer

Works

1911 *Meine Tante, deine Tante*, with Amalie Nikisch, Composer: Amalie Nikisch
1914 *Daniel in der Löwengrube*, Composer: Amalie Nikisch
1915 *Immer der Andere*, with Amalie Nikisch, Composer: Amalie Nikisch
(Source: http://operadata.stanford.edu/)

Frances Allitsen (see entry) was librettist for her opera.

Works

1912 *Bindra the Minstrel*
(Source: Sadie and Samuel)

Francesca Allores-Castellino

Works

1912 *Il rosignolo*, Composer Michele Mondo
(Source: http://operadata.stanford.edu/)

Bessie Marshall Whitely

Works

1913 *Hiawatha's Childhood*
(Source: Cohen)

Agnès Aube (1854?–) was the second wife of French composer Julien Aube.

Works

1914 *L'Ouvrière*, Composer: Lucien Aube
(Source: http://operadata.stanford.edu/)

Mary Fairweather

Works

1914 *Wa-Kin-Yon*, Composer: Frederick Zech
1916 *La Paloma*, Composer: Frederick Zech
(Source: http://operadata.stanford.edu/)

Eleni Lambiri (see entry) was librettist for her opera. The music is lost but there is said to be a recording of excerpts.

Works

1915 *Isolma*
(Source: Sadie and Samuel)

Celeste de Longpré Heckscher (see entry) was librettist for her opera.

Works

1918 *Rose of Destiny*
(Source: Sadie and Samuel)

Yuliya [Veysberg] Weissberg (see entry) was librettist for her operas.

Works

1923 *Rusalochka* [The Little Mermaid], with S. Parnok, after Hans Christian Andersen

1935 *Gyul'nara*, with S. Parnok
1937 *Gusi-lebedi* [Geese-Swans] with S. Marchak
(Source: Sadie and Samuel)

Elia W. Peattie

Works

1925 *Massimilliano, the Court Jester; or, the Love of Caliban,* Composer: Eleanor
        Everest Freer
(Source: Sadie and Samuel)

Adeline Appleton (see entry) was librettist for her opera.

Works

1926 *The Witches' Well*, with Percy Davis
(Source: Cohen)

Anna Schuller

Works

1927 *Die Pfingstkrone*, Composer: Berta Bock
(Source: http://operadata.stanford.edu/)

Eleanor Everest Freer (see entry) was librettist for her operas.

Works

1928 *The Masque of Pandora*, after H.W. Longfellow
1928 *Preciosa; or, The Spanish Student*, after Longfellow
1929 *Frithiof*, after C. Shaw's translation of E. Tegner *Frithiof's Saga*
1929 *Joan of Arc*
1931 *A Legend of Spain*, after Irving's *Tales of the Alhambra*
1934 *Little Women*, after L.M. Alcott
(Source: Sadie and Samuel)

Clara Anna Korn (see entry) was librettist for her opera.

Works

1932 *Their Last War*
(Source: Sadie and Samuel)

Laura Sweeney Moore

Works

1932 *Flutes of Jade Happiness*, Composer: Mary Carr Moore
(Source: Sadie and Samuel)

Edith Emilie Ohlson

Works

1932 *The Rose and the Ring*, Composer: Ethel Leginska
(Source: http://operadata.stanford.edu/)

Peggy Glanville-Hicks (see entry) was librettist for her operas.

Works

1933 *Caedmon*
1954 *The Transposed Heads*, after Thomas Mann: *Die vertauschten Köpfe*
1959 *The Glittering Gate*, after Lord Dunsany
(Source: Sadie and Samuel)

Mae Wheeler Nightingale (see entry) was librettist for her opera.

Works

Queen of the Sawdust
(Source: Cohen)

Saar Bessem (see entry) was librettist for her operas and operettas.

Works

Floris en Blancefloer
Assepoester
Doornroosje
De nieuwe kleren van de keizer
De pirinses op de erwt
Reinaard
De varkenshoeder
Zwaan kleef aan
(Source: Cohen)

Catherine Amy Dawson-Scott

Works

1935 *Gale*, Composer: Ethel Leginski
(Source: http://operadata.stanford.edu/, one-act)

Varvara Andrianovna Gaigerova (see entry) was librettist for her opera.

Works

1937–40 *Krepost u kamennogo broda*, based on Lermontov and Caucasian poets
(Source: Cohen)

Adelina Jacobs Marais

Works

The Bride of the Cango Caves
(Source: Cohen)

Gerda Wismer Hoffman

Works

Sakura-San, Composer: Abbie Gerrish-Jones
(Source: Sadie and Samuel)

María Grever (see entry) was librettist for her opera.

Works

1939 *El cantarito*
(Source: Sadie and Samuel)

1940–1970

Josephine Royle

Works

1946 *The Gooseherd and the Goblin*, Composer: Julia Frances Smith
(Source: Sadie and Samuel)

Constance D'Arcy Mackay

Works

1953 *Cockcrow*, Composer: Julia Frances Smith
The Shepherdess and the Chimneysweep, Composer: Julia Frances Smith

Helen Schuyler

Works

1948 *Against the River*, Composer: Evelyn LaRue Pittman
(Source: Cohen)

Dorothy Livesay (October 12, 1909–December 29, 1996) was a noted Canadian poet. A graduate of Trinity College in the University of Toronto, she was active in political movements, social work, teaching, and publishing; much of which is reflected in her poetry.

Works

1952 *The Lake*, Composer: Barbara Pentland
(Sources: Sadie and Samuel; http://operadata.stanford.edu/)

Julia Amanda Perry (see entry) was librettist for her opera.

Works

1953 *The Bottle*, after Poe's *The Cask of Amontillado*
(Source: Sadie and Samuel)

Evelyn LaRue Pittman (see entry) was librettist for her opera.

Works

1954 *Cousin Esther*
(Source: Cohen)

Joan Simon

Works

1956–58 *Bell Witch of Tennessee*, from an American folktale, Composer: Netty Simons
(Source: Sadie and Samuel)

Marcia Hamilton

Works

1957 *To Please Mr. Plumjoy*
(Source: Cohen)

Elizabeth Maconchy (see entry) was librettist for her operas.

Works

1957/58 *The Three Strangers*, after Thomas Hardy
1968 *The Birds*, after Aristophanes
1969 *Johnny and the Mohawks*
1975 *The King of the Golden River*, after John Ruskin
(Source: Sadie and Samuel)

Edna Baxter

Works

The Return of the Native, Composer: Jean Coulthard (she may have worked with
Edna Baxter on the libretto)
(Sources: Sadie and Samuel; http://operadata.stanford.edu/)

Miriam Gideon (see entry) was librettist for her opera.

Works

1958 *Fortunato*
(Source: Sadie and Samuel)

Freda Swain (see entry) was librettist for her operas.

Works

1959 *Second Chance*, with M. Rodd
The Shadowy Waters, based on Yeats
(Source: Sadie and Samuel)

Adrienne Clostre (see entry) was librettist for her opera.

Works

1960 *Le Chant du cygne*, after Chekhov
(Source: Sadie and Samuel)

Grace Mary Williams (see entry) was librettist for her opera.

Works

1961 *The Parlour*, after Guy de Maupassant's *En famille*
(Source: Sadie and Samuel)

Gloria Coates (see entry) was librettist for her opera.

Works

1962 *Fall of the House of Usher*, after Poe

(Source: Sadie and Samuel)

Bertita Harding (November 11, 1902, Nuremberg–December 31, 1971) was a popular author who specialized in biographies. When she was two her family moved to Mexico City, where she grew up. She made frequent trips to Europe and the United States with her family, and in addition to Spanish and German she learned English, Hungarian and French. Her family determined she would be a concert pianist. While she was attending the University of Wisconsin she met her future husband, Jack Harding. They settled in Indianapolis. In 1927 Bertita became a naturalized American citizen and embarked on her career as a concert pianist, with some success.

Then she wrote *The Phantom Crown: The Story of Maximilian and Carlota of Mexico*, and her writing career was launched. She published more biographies with continued success. Most of her subjects were royalty, but she also wrote a biography of Clara Schumann and one of Richard Wagner. She also had a successful career as a lecturer. After her husband died she moved back to Mexico City and continued to write.

Works

1963 *Daisy*, opera about Juliette Gordon Low, founder of the Girl Scouts, Composer: Julia Frances Smith

(Sources: Sadie and Samuel; Wikipedia)

Thea Musgrave (see entry) was librettist for her operas.

Works

1963 *Marko the Miser*, with F. Samson, after A.N. Afanas'yev
1977 *Mary Queen of Scots*, after Elguera's *Moray*
1979 *A Christmas Carol*, after Charles Dickens
1981 *An Occurrence at Owl Creek Bridge*, after Ambrose Bierce
1984 *Harriet, the Woman Called Moses*
1992 *Simón Bolívar*

(Source: Sadie and Samuel)

Wen-Ying Hsu

Works

1964 *Cowherd and Weaving Maiden*

(Source: Cohen)

Elisabeth Lutyens (see entry) was librettist for her operas.

Works

1964 *Infidelio*
1973 *The Waiting Game*
1975 *The Goldfish Bowl*
(Source: Sadie and Samuel)

Judith Dvorkin (see entry) was librettist for her operas.

Works

1964 *Cyrano*
1983 *Blue Star*
1988 *Humpty Dumpty and Alice*
1993 *The Frog Prince*
(Source: Sadie and Samuel)

Yvonne Desportes (see entry) was librettist for her opera.

Works

1965 *Le Forgeur de merveilles*, after J. O'Brien
(Source: Sadie and Samuel)

Tatyana Alexeyevna Chudova (see entry) was librettist for her opera.

Works

1966–67 *O myorvoy tsaverne i semi bojatiryakh* [The Dead Princess and the Seven Heroes] after Pushkin
(Source: Sadie and Samuel)

Joyce Barthelson (see entry) was librettist for her operas.

Works

1969 *Greenwich Village, 1910*
1973 *The King's Breakfast*
1977 *Devil's Disciple*
1981 *Lysistrata*
(Sources: Cohen; http://operadata.stanford.edu)

Bernadetta Matuszczak (see entry) was librettist for her operas.

Works

1967 *Julia i Romeo*, after William Shakespeare

1978 *Pamiętnik wariata* [The Diary of a Madman], after Nikolay Gogol
1979 *Apocalypsis*

(Sources: Sadie and Samuel; http://operadata.stanford.edu)

Melanie Ruth Daiken (see entry) was librettist for her opera.

Works

1968 *Eusebius*

(Source: Sadie and Samuel)

Alice Ferree Shields (see entry) was librettist for her operas.

Works

1968 *The Odyssey of Ulysses the Palmiped* (*Odyssey 1* based on *The Egyptian Book of the Dead* and Gilbert-LeConte's *The Odyssey of Ulysses the Palmiped*
1970 *Odyssey 2*, based on *The Egyptian Book of the Dead* and Roger Gilbert-LeConte's Dada play *The Odyssey of Ulysses the Palmiped*
1975 *Odyssey*, based on the Homer's *The Odyssey*
1978 *Shaman*, with Edward Barrett
1989 *Wraecca*, utilizing Anglo-Saxon poems and Gregorian chant
1992 *Mass for the Dead*, using text from Bharata Natyam dance-drama
1993 *Shivatanz*, based on a traditional South Indian poem and dance
1994 *Apocalypse*
2000/2011 *Komachi at Sekidera*, based on a Noh play
2010 *Criseyde*, using Chaucer's *Troilus and Criseyde*
2013 *Zhaojun: A Woman of Peace*

(Sources: Cohen; aliceshields.com)

1970 to Present

Teresa Procaccini (see entry) was librettist for her opera.

Works

1970 *La vendetta di Luzbel*, after F. Lopé de Vega

(Source: Sadie and Samuel)

Dawn Constance Crawford (see entry) was librettist for her opera.

Works

1971 *The Pearl*, after John Steinbeck

(Source: Cohen)

Elena Firsova (see entry) was librettist for her opera.

Works
1972 *Pir vo vremya chumï* [Feast in Plague Time]
(Source: Sadie and Samuel)

Alicia Urreta (see entry) was librettist for her opera.

Works
1972 *Romance de Doña Balada*
(Source: Sadie and Samuel)

Verna Arvey (February 16, 1910, Los Angeles–November 22, 1987) was a concert pianist and author in addition to being a composer. She studied music and journalism in Manual Arts High School in Los Angeles. After graduation she gave "lecture-recitals" and was an accompanist for dancers. She was interested in Latin American and black composers, and her programs always included their music. She toured widely in North America and South America. In 1934 she met William Grant Still, who had come to Los Angeles as a result of a Guggenheim Award, and they began collaborating on their music. In 1939 they married. Her book *In One Lifetime* (University of Arkansas Press, 1984) is her personal story of Still. The William Grant Still and Verna Arvey papers are at the University of Arkansas in Fayetteville. Her compositions include vocal music, and a ballet. She wrote the librettos for almost all of the operas of William Grant Still including:

Works
A Bayou Legend
Costaso
From the Furnace of the Sun
Highway 1, U.S.A.
Minette Fontaine
Mota
The Pillar
A Southern Interlude
(Sources: Cohen; http://libinfo.uark.edu/specialcollections/findingaids/still/still1 aid.html#arvey)

Violet Archer (see entry) was librettist for her opera.

Works
1973 *Sganarelle*, after Molière
(Source: Sadie and Samuel)

Margaret Garwood (see entry) was librettist for her operas.

Works

1973 *The Nightingale and the Rose*, based on Oscar Wilde
1980 *Rappaccini's Daughter*, after Nathaniel Hawthorne
(Source: Cohen)

Elizabeth "Libby" Larsen (see entry) was librettist for her operas.

Works

1973 *Some Pig*, from E.B. White
1977 *The Words Upon the Windowpane*, after Yeats
1982 *Psyche and the Pskyskraper*, chamber opera
1985 *Holy Ghosts*, opera, after Linney
1989 *Beauty and the Beast*, opera
1990 *Frankenstein; or, the Modern Prometheus*, after Shelley
(Source: Sadie and Samuel)

Anna Egyud

Works

1974 *Yehu*, Composer: Jeno Zador
(Source: http://operadata.stanford.edu/)

Alice Parker (see entry) was librettist for her operas.

Works

1975 *The Family Reunion*
1982 *The Ponder Heart*, after Eudora Welty
(Source: Sadie and Samuel)

Fleur Adcock

Works

1984 *The King of the Other Country*, Composer: Gillian Whitehead
(Sources: Sadie and Samuel; http://operadata.stanford.edu/)

Anna Maria Dell'oso

Works

1986 *The Pirate Moon*, chamber opera, Composer: Gillian Whitehead

1988 *Bride of Fortune*, chamber opera, Composer: Gillian Whitehead
1995 *The Art of Pizza*, opera, Composer: Gillian Whitehead
(Sources: Sadie and Samuel; http://operadata.stanford.edu/)

Joan Aiken

Works

1979 *The Tinker's Curse*, children's opera, Composer: Gillian Whitehead
(Source: Sadie and Samuel)

Louise Talma (see entry) was librettist for her opera.

Works

1976 *Have You Heard? Do You Know?*
(Sources: Sadie and Samuel; American National Biography online)

Janice Giteck (see entry) was librettist for her opera.

Works

1976 *A'agita*, after Pima and Papgo texts
(Source: Sadie and Samuel)

Nicola Frances LeFanu (see entry) was librettist for her opera.

Works

1977 *Dawnpath*
(Source: Sadie and Samuel)

Edith Borroff (see entry) was librettist for her opera.

Works

1977 *The Sun and the Wind*
(Source: Sadie and Samuel)

Vivian Fine (see entry) was librettist for her opera.

Works

1978 *The Women in the Garden*
(Source: Sadie and Samuel)

Bonnie Grice has won numerous awards as a producer, host, and broadcaster. She is the author of *From Z to A*, a guide to the great composers from Zappa to John Adams.

Works
1993 *Mrs. Dalloway*, Composer: Libby Larsen
(Source: Borroff)

Julia Marie Morrison
Works
1979 *Rübezahl*
(Source: Cohen)

Jean Eichelberger Ivey (see entry) was librettist for her opera.

Works
1980–82 *The Birthmark*, after Nathaniel Hawthorne
(Source: Sadie and Samuel)

Zhivka Klinkova (see entry) was librettist for her operas.

Works
1980 *The Most Improbable*
1992 *Vassil Levski*
(Source: Sadie and Samuel)

Gertrude Stein (February 3, 1874–July 27, 1946) received a BA from Harvard in 1897. From 1897 to 1901 she attended Johns Hopkins Medical School. Two years later she moved to Paris, joining her two brothers who already lived there. Increasingly she became involved with the visual arts. Her first book, *Three Lives*, was published in 1909. She was very sociable and formed friendships with many people in the arts, her most notable friendship being with Alice B. Toklas. The period between World War I and World War II was her most productive; she was very influential on literary matters, and seemingly knew "everyone." Her friendship with Virgil Thomson led to her writing the libretto for *Four Saints in Three Acts*.

Works
1927–1928 *Four Saints in Three Acts*, Composer: Virgil Thomson
1971 *The Three Sisters Who Are Not Sisters*, Composer: Ned Rorem

Additionally, various works of Gertrude Stein have been the literary source for other operas, including:

1981 *Ladies Voices: A Short Opera,* Composer: Kay Gardner
1995 *Dream in Her Mind,* Composer: Sorrel Hays
(Source: DLB)

Elizabeth Raum (see entry) was librettist for her operas.

Works

1981 *The Final Bid*
1985 *The Garden of Alice,* after Lewis Carroll's *Alice in Wonderland*
1991 *Eos: The Dream of Nicholas Flood Davin*
(Source: Sadie and Samuel)

Judith Shatin (see entry) was librettist for her opera.

Works

1981–82 *Follies and Fancies* with Gloria Russo, after Molière: *Les Précieuses ridicules*
(Source: Sadie and Samuel)

Susan Cohn Lackman (see entry) was librettist for her opera.

Works

Lisa Stratos, after Aristophanes: *Lysistrata*
(Sources: Cohen; http://www.sai-national.org/home/ComposersBureau/Lackman SusanCohn/tabid/345/Default.aspx)

Noa (Susan) Ain (see entry) was librettist for her operas.

Works

1982 *Bring on the Bears*
1984 *Trio*
1988 *The Outcast,* after the story of Ruth and Naomi
(Source: Cohen)

Mira Spektor (see entry) was librettist for her opera.

Works

1982 *Lady of the Castle* with Andrea Balis, after Lea Goldberg
(Source: Cohen)

Elena Petrová (see entry) was librettist for her opera.

Works

1982/83 *As If the Sun Were Never to Return*, after C.F. Ramuz
(Source: Sadie and Samuel)

Kazuko Hara (see entry) was librettist for her operas.

Works

1982/1983 *On the Merry Night*, after I. Kikumura
1985 *Sute-hime*, after S. Muro
1987 *Beyond Brain Death*, after S. Fujimura
1988 *The History of Yosakoi-bushi*, after F. Tosa
1991 *Pedro Kibe*, after G. Matsunaga
(Source: Sadie and Samuel)

Carol Sams (see entry) was librettist for her opera.

Works

1983 *The Beauty and the Beast*
(Source: Wikipedia)

Judith Weir (see entry) was librettist for her operas.

Works

1979 *King Harald's Saga*
1984 *The Black Spider*, after J. Gotthelf
1985 *The Consolations of Scholarship*
1987 *A Night at the Chinese Opera*
1989 *Heaven Ablaze in His Breast*, after E.T.A. Hoffmann
1990 *The Vanishing Bridegroom*, after *Popular Tales of the West Highlands*
1994 *Blond Eckbert*, after J.L. Tieck
2011 *Miss Fortune*
(Source: Sadie and Samuel)

Patricia Hampl (March 12, 1946–) received her BA from the University of Minnesota in 1968 and her MFA in 1970 from the University of Iowa. She worked for several years as a freelance writer and editor before joining the faculty of the University of Minnesota. She writes in a variety of genres but is best known for her writing of memoirs. Her numerous awards include a Guggenheim Foundation Fellowship, a National Endowment for the Arts grant, and a Fulbright Fellowship.

Works

1984 *Clair de Lune*, Composer: Elizabeth "Libby" Larsen
(Sources: Sadie and Samuel; Wikipedia)

Mary Carol Warwick (see entry) was librettist for her operas.

Works

1985 *The Twelve Months Brothers*
1985 *Lealista*, after Hemingway, *The Fifth Column*
1985 *Sisters of Faith*
1988 *The Last Leaf*, after O. Henry
1990 *Drycop's Dilemma*, opera, Librettist: Mary Carol Warwick
(Sources: Cohen; operadatastanford.edu)

Elaine May Erickson (see entry) was librettist for her operas.

Works

1985 *The Upstairs Bedroom*
1987 *From Winter Darkness*
(Source: Cohen)

Sheila Silver (see entry) was librettist for her opera.

Works

1986 *The Thief of Love*, based on a 17th century Bengali tale
2013 *Beauty Intolerable*, from Edna St. Vincent Millay
(Source: Sadie and Samuel)

Natela Damianovna Svanidze (see entry) was librettist for her opera.

Works

1987 *Gaul-Gavkhe*, after T. Maglaperidze
(Source: Sadie and Samuel)

Kate Pogue is the librettist for numerous children's operas.

Works

1994 *Texas!*, Composer: Mary Carol Warwick
2001 *The Emperor's New Clothes*, Composer: Mary Carol Warwick
2004 *The Velveteen Rabbit*, Composer: Mary Carol Warwick
(Source: operadatastanford.edu)

Ruth Schonthal (see entry) was librettist for her opera.

Works

1988 *Princess Maleen*, after Grimm
(Source: Sadie and Samuel)

Marielli Sfakianaki (see entry) was librettist for her operas.

Works

1988 *The Pagic Muper*
1988–93 *Minos*
(Source: Sadie and Samuel)

Ann Loomis Silsbee (see entry) was librettist for her opera.

Works

1989 *The Nightingale's Apprentice*
(Source: Cohen)

Fay Weldon (September 22, 1931, Worcestershire, England–) lived in New Zealand until she was ten, when her family went to the UK. She studied economics and psychology at the University of St. Andrews, Scotland. Subsequently she worked for the Foreign Office in London, was a journalist, then embarked on a career as an advertising copywriter. Her first novel, *The Fat Woman's Joke*, in 1967 received great acclaim, and her writing career was well launched. She has written plays for television and radio, numerous books, stage plays and dramatizations. In 1990 she received an Honorary Doctorate from St. Andrews. She was awarded the CBE in 2001.

Works

1989 *A Small Green Space*, Composer: Ilona Sekacz
(Sources: Museum of Broadcast Communication, Chicago, Illinois; *Encyclopedia Britannica*)

Susan McCully received her BA in Theater and Dance from DeSales University, her MFA in playwriting from Catholic University of America, and her PhD in theater history, theory, and criticism from the University of Wisconsin. She is on the faculty in the theater department at the University of Maryland, Baltimore County, Maryland.

Works

1989 *Faustina*, after *Faust*, Composer: Linda Dusman
(Sources: Borroff; http://theatre.umbc.edu/faculty/susan-mccully/)

Sorrel Hays (see entry) was librettist for her operas.

Works

1989–93 *The Glass Woman*, with S. Ordway, and N. Rhodes
1994 *The Everybodydom*
(Source: Sadie and Samuel)

Tania Justina León (see entry) was librettist for her opera.

Works

1994 *Scourge of Hyacinths*, after W. Soyinka
(Source: Sadie and Samuel)

Ann Goette

Works

c1994 *Travels*, revision of an earlier opera by Victoria Bond, *Gulliver's Travels*, for which Moses Goldberg wrote the libretto, Composer: Victoria Bond
(Sources: Sadie and Samuel; http://www.newyorkwomencomposers.org/profiles.php4?zdm_id=BON01)

Judith Lane (see entry) was librettist for her operas.

Works

The Secret Cave, based on Claire Huchets Bishop's book *Twenty and Ten*
The Mill Girl
(Source: www.judithclane.com)

Barbara Zinn Krieger is the founder of Making Books Sing, which began as a family theater and education program at the Vineyard School. In 2001 it was established as a not-for-profit dedicated to promoting children's literacy and social development through arts-in-education programs and professional theater productions. The program has grown substantially and works with over 400 urban schools, providing subsidized tickets for thousands of students. Barbara has a BFA in theater from Columbia University School of the Arts, and an MA in speech and theater from Teachers College, Columbia University. She has written books and lyrics for a wide variety of musical presentations. She received the Opera America Distinguished Service Award.

Works

Clara, about Clara Schuman, Composer: Victoria Bond
(Source: http://www.yelp.com/biz/making-books-sing-inc-new-york)

Diana Burrell (see entry) was librettist for her opera.

Works

1997 *The Albatross*, after Susan Hill
(Source: Sadie and Samuel)

Johanna Doderer (see entry) was librettist for her operas.

Works

2000/01 *Die Fremde*, after Euripides' *Medea*
2002–06 *Strom*, after Euripides' *The Bacchae*
(Source: operadatastanford.com)

Janice Galloway (December 2, 1955, Saltcoats, Scotland–) studied music and English at Glasgow University. After working as a teacher and waitress for ten years she began her writing career. In addition to libretti she's written novels, short stories, nonfiction and prose-poetry. She has also written and presented radio series for BBC Scotland and has received numerous awards for her writing.

Works

2002 *Monster*, Composer: Sally Beamish
(Source: Wikipedia)

Joan Anim-Addo holds a BEd with honors, an MA and a PhD. She is professor of Caribbean Literature and Culture, and director of the Centre for Caribbean Studies at Goldsmiths, University of London.

Works

2005–2008 *Imoinda*, the first of the *Slavery Trilogy*, Composer: Odaline Martinez
(Sources: Sadie and Samuel; http://www.gold.ac.uk/ecl/staff/j-anim-addo/)

Toni Morrison (February 19, 1931, Lorain, Ohio–) received a BA from Howard University in 1953 and an MA in English in 1955 from Cornell

University. From 1957 to 1964 she was on the faculty of Howard University. She worked with Random House, primarily as a fiction editor, for several years, and also taught at Yale and Bard College. She is professor emeritus at Princeton University. Perhaps the best known of her books are *Song of Solomon, Tar Baby* and *Beloved*. Among the various awards she has received are (1988) the Pulitzer Prize and the American Book Award for *Beloved*; (1993) the Nobel Prize in Literature; (2012) the Presidential Medal of Freedom.

Works

2005 *Margaret Garner*, Composer: Richard Danielpour

(Sources: http://en.wikipedia.org/wiki/Margaret_Garner_(opera); *Encyclopedia Britannica*; DLB)

Bibliography

Abbate, Carolyn, and Roger Parker. *A History of Opera.* New York: W.W. Norton, 2012.

Blom, Eric, ed. *Grove's Dictionary of Music and Musicians.* 5th ed. London: Macmillan, 1954.

Borroff, Edith. *American Operas: A Checklist.* Edited by J. Bunker Clark. *Detroit Studies in Music Bibliography.* no. 69. Warren, MI: Harmonie Park, 1992.

Bowers, Jane, and Judith Tick, eds. *Women Making Music: The Western Art Tradition, 1150–1950.* Urbana: University of Illinois Press, 1987.

Cohen, Aaron I., ed. *International Encyclopedia of Women Composers.* 2nd ed. New York: Books & Music USA, 1987.

Elson, Arthur. *Woman's Work in Music: Being an Account of Her Influence on the Art, in Ancient as Well as Modern Times; a Summary of Her Musical Compositions, in the Different Countries of the Civilized World; an Estimate of Their Rank in Comparison with Those of Men.* Boston: L.C. Page, 1903.

Fuller, Sophie. *Women Composers During the British Musical Renaissance.* London: University of London, 1998.

Giroud, Vincent. *French Opera: A Short History.* New Haven: Yale University Press, 2010.

Glickman, Sylvia, and Martha Furman Schleifer, ed. *From Convent to Concert Hall: A Guide to Women Composers.* Westport, CT: Greenwood, 2003.

Grove, George (Sir), ed. *Dictionary of Music and Musicians [Grove's Dictionary of Music and Musicians].* 1927 edition. New York: Macmillan, 1927–1928.

Laurence, Anya. *Women of Notes: 1000 Women Composers Born Before 1900.* Richards Rosen. New York, 1978.

Letzer, Jacqueline, and Robert Adelson. *Women Writing Opera: Creativity and Controversy in the Age of the French Revolution.* Berkeley: University of California Press, 2001.

Mattfeld, Julius. *A Handbook of American Operatic Premieres, 1731–1962. Detroit Studies in Music Bibliography.* no. 5. Detroit: Information Service, 1963.

Matthew, H.C.G, and Brian Harrison, ed. *Oxford Dictionary of National Biography.* Oxford: Oxford University Press, 2004.

Parsons, Charles H. *The Mellen Opera Reference Index.* Lewiston, NY; Queenston, ON: Edwin Mellen Press, 1986.

Sadie, Julie Anne, and Rhian Samuel. *The Norton/Grove Dictionary of Women Composers.* New York: W.W. Norton, 1994.

Sadie, Stanley, and John Tyrrell, ed. *The New Grove Dictionary of Music and Musicians.* 2nd ed. London: Macmillan, 2001.

Solenière, Eugène de. *La Femme Compositeur, par Eugène Solenière, Avec Quatre Portraits Hors Texte par E. Couturier, Désiré Fortoul, Léon Lebègue, Marc Mouclier.* Critiques d'art series. Paris: La Critique, 1895.

Index